Censored Sentiments

Censored Sentiments

Letters and Censorship
in Epistolary Novels
and Conduct Material

Barbara Maria Zaczek

Newark: University of Delaware Press
London: Associated University Presses

© 1997 by Associated University Presses, Inc.

All rights reserved. Authorization to photocopy items for internal or personal use, or the internal or personal use of specific clients, is granted by the copyright owner, provided that a base fee of $10.00, plus eight cents per page, per copy is paid directly to the Copyright Clearance Center, 222 Rosewood Drive, Danvers, Massachusetts 01923. [0-87413-608-3/97 $10.00 + 8¢ pp, pc.]

Associated University Presses
440 Forsgate Drive
Cranbury, NJ 08512

Associated University Presses
16 Barter Street
London WC1A 2AH, England

Associated University Presses
P.O. Box 338, Port Credit
Mississauga, Ontario
Canada L5G 4L8

The paper used in this publication meets the requirements of the American National Standard for Permanence of Paper for Printed Library Materials Z39.48–1984.

Library of Congress Cataloging-in-Publication Data

Zaczek, Barbara Maria, 1949–
   Censored sentiments : letters and censorship in epistolary novels and conduct material / Barbara Maria Zaczek.
   p. cm.
   Includes bibliographical references and index.
   ISBN 0-87413-608-3 (alk. paper)
   1. Epistolary fiction, English—History and criticism. 2. English fiction—18th century—History and criticism. 3. Epistolary fiction, Italian—History and criticism. 4. Didactic literature—History and criticism. 5. Fern, Fanny, 1811–1872. Ruth Hall. 6. Conduct of life in literature. 7. Letter-writing in literature. 8. Letters in literature. 9. Women and literature. 10. Censorship. I. Title.
PR858.E65Z33   1997
813'.509—dc20   96-43046
                                                                                 CIP

PRINTED IN THE UNITED STATES OF AMERICA

Contents

Acknowledgments

Introduction	11
1. Female Letters in Conduct Material	21
2. Letters as a Means of Liberation for Female Correspondents	52
3. *Clarissa*—Woman Writer and Reader in an Epistolary Web	75
4. Female Epistolary Strategies in *Evelina, Lady Susan,* and *Lettere di una novizia:* The Tactics of Caution, Convention, and Cliché	103
5. Deconstructing the Definition of Female Letters as Sentimental, Nonliterary, and Private	138
Conclusion	175
Notes	178
Bibliography	198
Index	206

Acknowledgments

I WOULD LIKE TO BEGIN THE ACKNOWLEDGMENTS BY RECALLING AN absence, vividly present in my memory—the absence of my benefactor, mentor, colleague, and a most wonderful friend, the late Professor Emmanuel Hatzantonis. It had been his belief in my abilities to deal with the pressures of an American graduate school and a professional life in two foreign languages, his constant support and encouragment that gave me motivation and stamina to gather materials and organize ideas for this manuscript. He died after he had read and commented on the first two chapters, so I can only hope that he would have approved of the rest.

Special thanks and recognition are due to Professor Steven Rendall, an ideal reader and censor of the first draft, textually meticulous, intellectually demanding, and infinitely patient, whose friendship and sense of humor saw me through struggles against the vicissitudes of definite and indefinite articles, split infinitives, and other, user-hostile peculiarities of the English language. Professors Barbara Pope, Regina Psaki, and Mary Wood proved to be not only excellent editors and critics during the early stages of this manuscript but also wonderful friends who encouraged and supported me in every aspect of my professional life. I am thankful to Professor Joseph Hynes who advised me on the final version of this manuscript and assisted me in tedious textual revisions, offering useful suggestions for improving both the contents and the stylistic form of this book. I thank my friend and colleague from Clemson University, Professor Joni Hurley, for reading substantial parts of my work and for helping me to clarify my thoughts and ideas.

My research received assistance from the University of Oregon Center for the Study of Women in Society, and the Oregon Humanities Center. Special thanks are due to Diana Sheridan and Robin M. Cochrane for their help in the first and last stages of this manuscript.

I am grateful to all my American, Italian, and Polish friends who encouraged and stimulated me to continue working on this manuscript despite setbacks. Beyond all others, however, I am grateful to my husband, Jerzy, and to my son, Leszek, whose unconditional love and support of every imaginable kind helped me survive the tough mo-

CENSORED SENTIMENTS

ments of daily struggles to combine a professional career with that of a wife and a mother. Their willingness to share in every domestic chore and openness to novel solutions to family problems could provide guidelines for a conduct book.

* * *

Copyright permission has been granted from the following sources:

Oriana Fallaci and the Rizzoli Publishing House (Casa Editrice Rizzoli) for quotations from Oriana Fallaci's novel *Lettera a un bambino mai nato*.

Dacia Maraini for quotations from her novel *Lettere a Marina*.

The heirs of Guido Piovene and the Bompiani Publishing House (Casa Editrice Bompiani) for quotations from Guido Piovene's novel *Lettere di una novizia*.

Introduction

MARTIAL LAW, DECLARED IN POLAND IN DECEMBER OF 1981, GAVE official sanction to the censure of private correspondence. Of course, all Poles knew that letters were already being picked at random and read by censors, but the government had never admitted it openly. Now it was a new rule. Shortly after the official announcement, I got a letter from a friend of mine in England. The envelope had been torn open and covered with black inscriptions that read: censored by No. so and so, Warsaw, date. I still remember vividly the moment of absolute terror: what did my friend write in that letter, had the censor crossed out in black ink the offensive phrases or words (as I heard people say was a common practice)? Will there be any repercussions? But the most important question was: "Will I be able to write letters at all with a faceless censor peeping over my shoulder?" Then I heard a supposedly true story (all those stories are always true) that gave a different dimension to the letter writer/censor relationship and provided a certain solution to my dilemma.

According to the story, a man addressed an envelope to himself, and enclosed a letter to the censor with the following request. During World War II, in Nazi-occupied Poland, he collected envelopes with all kinds of official stamps, marks, censor's comments, etc. and he would like to add another specimen to that collection, could the censor stamp the letter with all the possible marks, seals, inscriptions, etc? He got back his letter with "OK" scribbled on it and the envelope covered with official stamps. By displacing the censor into the position of an addressee, the anonymous man undercut the very core of censorship—how could a censor censure a letter addressed to himself? His gesture then, a letter written to the censor and the ultimate erasure of the addressee, is one possible strategy that precludes control, and renders the act of letter writing devoid of any manipulative potential—no one can use such a letter as a compromising document against the letter writer.

A similar story occurs in Fanny Burney's *Evelina,* an eighteenth-century epistolary novel in which the heroine, during the process of "entering the world," learns a painful lesson about the risks and dangers involved in letter writing. Thus when Evelina's fiancé, Lord Orville, asks her permission to correspond with her, Evelina answers: "No, indeed, my Lord! Can you indeed desire, my Lord, that I should, a second time, expose myself, by an unguarded readiness, to write to you?"[1] Like the anonymous man in Poland, Evelina decides to dispose of Orville as an addressee and replace him with Villard, her guardian/censor. The Pole's gesture is an obvious act of protest against the government's invasion of privacy and a mock solution to the oppression of censorship. What kind of rebellion, one might ask, stands behind Evelina's vehement refusal to correspond with a young man?

The aim of the present study is to trace the censoring practices that prompted Evelina's decision. I use the plural term "censoring practices" to emphasize the multiple ways in which a female letter in the eighteenth century came to be watched with the "eyes of a lynx" and turned into an object of relentless scrutiny and analysis in a body of writings.[2] Among writings "for, about, and by women" for which "at the inception of modern culture the literate classes in England suddenly developed an unprecedented taste," the letter, hailed as an attribute of femininity, commanded an unprecedented attention.[3] And yet despite, or maybe because of, this attention, letter narratives by and for women experienced a turbulent history, "a history of restrictions or failed interactions."[4] To assemble the jigsaw puzzle of this history, we must reread epistolary fiction in conjunction with texts on female letters, namely, contemporary conduct books and reflections on literature. It will allow us to trace each new development in all three areas and pinpoint the ways in which they participated in producing the rules that governed the category of female letters both inside and outside epistolary fiction. The correspondents in the literary and social exchange I propose to examine will be not only the letter writers and their addressees but also censors who, from various vantage points, watched, read, intercepted, suppressed, praised, criticized, corrected, altered, forged, falsified, censored, misdirected, and rewrote female letters in an effort to achieve a perfect specimen of female epistolary writing.

The host of verbs that describe what can actually be done to, and with, a letter points to the ways in which the letter can be manipulated and controlled. Unlike speech, writing leaves an indelible trace. It turns ephemeral words into a script whose permanence precludes any possibility of taking back or altering the message. A letter, more than any other kind of writing, is rooted in a tangible reality, since it normally contains a date, an address, and a signature. All these elements locate it in time and space. Moreover, the writer's signature and handwriting establish the letter's authorship. Once written, a letter never loses its value as a document, always locatable and traceable to its author. The undeniable mark of authorship makes the writer vulnerable to being exposed and held accountable for the letter's existence. According to Terry Eagleton,

> It is the iterability of script—the fact that its materiality allows it to be reproduced in changed conditions—which makes it such an efficient instrument of oppression. The free utterances of the heart, once taken down in writing, may always be used later in evidence against the speaker.[5]

The act of writing a letter, however, involves not only its writer but also its receiver, whose participation in the epistolary exchange makes him/her equally susceptible to the claims made on the sender. In passing between the sender and the recipient, the letter is prone to all sorts of mishap: it can be intercepted, misdirected, or misplaced, and thus fall into the hands of a third party who may take advantage of its existence. Its holder may also exploit the letter's potential for such manipulative schemes as forgery, citing out of context, misinterpretation, and misreading. Thus the possession of a letter gives its holder the power to manipulate and control both the letter writer and the addressee.[6]

A letter could thus be considered an almost ideal object of social control; almost, because its potential for transgression offers grounds for resistance. A letter as a mere slip of paper may reach its destination even despite the utmost vigilance on the part of those who want to censure or exploit it. It is also easy to hide from prying eyes. In Poe's story "The Purloined Letter," the narrator ponders various possibilities that render the search for a letter a tedious and virtually futile task:

> But you could not have removed—you could not have taken to pieces *all* articles of furniture in which it would have been possible to make a deposit in the manner you mention. A letter may be compressed into a thin spiral roll, not differing much in shape or bulk from a large knitting-needle, and in this form it might be inserted into the rung of a chair, for example.[7]

Besides its small size, which facilitates concealment, a letter can also escape detection in other ways, such as, using "a different seal on a stamp of another color, the mark of a different handwriting in the superscription."[8] These properties make a letter an effective means of illicit communication, a crucial element in promoting transgressive schemes, and a perfect means of crossing various borderlines.[9]

Delicately poised at the intersection of private and public, literary and nonliterary, true and false, lawful and illicit, a letter is liable to the laws which guard these territories, with "both Care and Skill."[10]

As a censor of the communication flow, the law of decorum focuses on the content and direction of letters, determining "who can write what to whom under which circumstances." The law of genre establishes the rules on "how" to write letters, by prescribing the appropriate form and style. The manipulative and transgressive aspects of letters play a significant role in these control systems, since they provide the writers, the readers, and the censors of letters with the reasons and the means to justify, or to oppose, the existence of censorship.

In *Revolution and the Form of the British Novel 1790–1825*, Nicola Watson discusses "the relation between sentimental fiction and radical politics that took an unprecedented intensity in the imagination of the British reading public during the years of the French Revolution, the Napoleonic wars, and their aftermath of social unrest."[11] Using Rousseau's *La Nouvelle Héloïse* as a model plot which legitimates revolutionary desires, Watson examines a series of fictions by women novelists between 1790–1825 to define the strategies used to "discipline the errancy of the letter by intercepting, readdressing, and redelivering it to multiple and repeatable rereading" (19). Watson proposes to examine "the fate of the letter within the novel as a pointer to the changing concerns of literary-political discourse over the period, thereby offering a coherent account of one neglected and especially pertinent subgenre at a crucial moment of its evolution" (3).

My study could be read as a sequel to Watson's book, but it is a sequel in reverse, not only because I focus on the epistolary fiction from an earlier period, but also because I trace the fate of the female letter in conduct books and literary theories—representatives of the law of decorum and the law of genre—as "a pointer" to the changes in the narrative patterns within the epistolary novel. The censoring practices regarding letters by women, developed in conduct material and literary theories, I argue, affect the ways in which plotlines in epistolary fiction are allowed to progress, leading to a fairly rigid and uniform narrative pattern in mid-eighteenth century. The censorship-plot relation is not, however, a straight line but rather a circular and a reciprocal movement—the role letters play within the epistolary novel affects in turn the modes of control, and accounts for adaptation and application of new censoring strategies.

My point of departure will not be the novel in letters but the sudden interest that literary critics lavished on letters by women, and the motives that stood behind it. In seventeenth- and eighteenth-century France and England, these critics set out to prove that there existed a natural affinity between women and letters. According to La Bruyère, the Abbé Cotin, and others who defined the models of female epistolarity, women's letters, as opposed to those written by men, belonged to the category of the sentimental, nonliterary, and private. In other words, women had a natural knack for expressing sentiments, and as a consequence their writing would focus on the thematics of love. It was nature not art that informed their writing so they did not need to study the rules of rhetoric or grammar. Reiterating views that had already been circulating for over a century in Europe, Thomas Gisborne wrote in 1799 that:

> Women are ambitious to be distinguished for writing, as the phrase is, good letters. Not that a lady ought not to write a good letter. But a lady who makes it her study to write a good letter, commonly produces a composition to which a very different epithet ought to be applied. Those letters are only good, which contain the natural effusions of the heart, expressed in an unaffected language. Tinsel and glitter, and laboured phrases dismiss the friend and introduce the authoress.[12]

It was precisely that fear of the authoress that conceded women the territory of letters, in the hope of excluding them from other genres such as tragedy, epic, poetry—genres that belonged to the category of the public and literary. But this concession proved to be a blessing in disguise mainly due to two crucial elements that formed the basis for excluding women—spontaneity and passion. Love letters or familiar letters, whose hallmarks were spontaneity and passionate outbursts, opened for women writers the publishing markets and became passports to fame and money (to mention only Aphra Behn, Mary Hearne, and Eliza Haywood in England, or Mme de Sévigné and Françoise Graffigny in France). In addition to epistolary novels, women writers, disguised as aunts, mothers, elderly friends, used the letter form for conduct books offering friendly advice "in unadorned phrases."[13]

Spontaneity and passion also became the force that prompted the heroines of early epistolary novels to take full advantage of the letter's transgressive potential and to use it as a means of illicit communication. Typical situations presented heroines in convents, harems, locked rooms (enclosed spaces) from which they managed to smuggle out slips of paper that promoted clandestine affairs and defied the authority of parents and husbands (*Lettres portugaises*, Mary Hearne's *The Lovers' Week*, Aphra Behn's *Letters between a Noble-man and his Sister*). In fact, as I will show later, the heroines often taught their female readers lessons in deceptive practices, providing detailed descriptions of how to elude the vigilant eyes of their guardians.

Letters as necessary attributes and accomplices in every clandestine love affair began to pose a serious threat to the stability of the family and the social order (daughters eloping with undesirable suitors, wives deceiving husbands, nuns breaking the convent rules). Women's letters went from being considered an innocent outpouring of emotions to a position of danger, a position that required careful scrutiny. Turned into objects of familial surveillance and censorship, they were added to the list of what Michel Foucault calls "disciplinary practices." Born in the eighteenth century, the disciplines mark a shift in the mechanisms of social control resulting in a new "political anatomy"—the economy of detail: "A meticulous observation of detail, and at the same time a political awareness of these small things, for the control and use of men, emerge through the classical age bearing with them a whole set of techniques, a whole corpus of methods and knowledge, descriptions, plans and data."[14] Letter writing, as one of those "small things," fitted perfectly into the newly formulated "machinery of control" and became one of the factors involved in the production of "docile" female bodies (139).

The threat posed by uncontrolled correspondence to the smooth operation of the disciplines provoked a prompt response from the authors both of conduct books and of epistolary fiction, and brought on stage the figure of a family censor, a figure either virtually nonexistent in early epistolary fiction or easily duped by the heroine. The role of this guardian-censor was not only to intercept and read all correspondence (as happens in Montesquieu's *Persian Letters*) but also to keep track of supplies of paper and ink (cf. the scenes in *Clarissa* and *Les Liaisons dangereuses* where rooms and drawers are being searched for paper, ink, letters; Clarissa has to keep all the letters she gets as well as make copies of all the letters she sends). The power of these domestic censors resided in their visibility and in their easy physical access to letters, which allowed them at any point to intercept and to stop the correspondence.

Their visibility and the predictability of the strategies they employed, however, left room for deception. Despite vigilant eyes, the letter, a mere slip of paper, somehow managed to find its way out of the house, wreaking havoc in the family order. The physical control of letters, a control based on coercion, that is, on searches, interception, and confiscation of paper and ink, proved inefficient. Clarissa, in spite of all the precautions taken by her relatives, carried on a clandestine correspondence with Lovelace, and eventually eloped with him, just as Usbek's most cherished wife, Roxana, corresponded freely with her lover. Thus the inefficacy of one controlling mode called for a change in strategy.

The new strategy discarded force and coercion as elements of control, and replaced them with persuasion. The censor who existed outside the text now hid in the text itself, assuming a double identity:

that of an epistolary seducer and that of a guardian/editor. The epistolary seducer exploited the art of letter writing to achieve his goal: to make an advantageous match, or to seduce the object of his vile desires. The guardian/editor provided reading and writing guidelines to help innocent girls deal with these rakes and avoid "ruin." In *Familiar Letters on Important Occasions* (a book with model letters that also provided readers with models of conduct), Samuel Richardson used both figures; on the one hand, to illustrate the danger of uncensored correspondence; on the other, to devise a system of censoring practices through reading.[15] A sample letter from an epistolary rake together with a detailed explanation of his motives and plans, was followed by a step-by-step procedure that would keep such rakes at bay. The letters/texts of epistolary seducers were better left unread but if they had to be read, the guardian text would provide a model for reading and response. So instead of having a guardian who would intercept a letter, read it, and decide if it complied with the law of decorum before sending it off, Richardson suggested the shift of responsibility onto the letter writer and the conduct book text which would offer ready-made advice and solutions.

Richardson's *Clarissa*, a novel that seeks to improve and further explore the modes of controlling female correspondence, is a crucial text in my interpretation of the female epistolary tradition, for three reasons. Firstly, because it silences a woman who embarks on an independent venture in letter writing, thus initiating a series of spectacular deaths of epistolary heroines, against which Fanny Burney's Evelina reacts with a refusal to write letters to a young man.[16] Secondly, because it discards spontaneity as the hallmark of female letters and replaces it with caution. Over a hundred years and dozens of conduct books later, the issue of caution in writing letters is still a burning one: in *A New Letter Writer for the Use of Ladies*, published around 1860 in Philadelphia, an anonymous writer instructs young ladies:

> And finally, remember that whatever you write is written evidence either of your good sense or your folly, your industry or your carelessness, your self-control or your impatience. What you have once put in the letter-box, may cost you lasting regret or be equally important to your whole future welfare. And for such grave reasons, think before you write, and think while you are writing.[17]

The insistence on premeditation and caution versus spontaneity and passionate outbursts shows how profound and painstaking were the changes in the definition of female epistolarity in the two hundred years that separated the publication of *Lettres portugaises* and *A New Letter Writer for the Use of Ladies*.

Another reason for *Clarissa*'s significance in the female epistolary tradition is its demonstration of the mechanisms operating behind the two censoring systems—the coercive mode of early epistolary fiction and conduct material, and the disciplinary mode. It marks a shift from the strategy of terror to the strategy of protection, from a censoring person to a censoring text.[18] Richardson's editor in *Clarissa* does not want to scare his female readers, as does Richard Allestree in *The Ladies Calling* (1696); he wants only to protect them and to show his concern for their well-being.[19] The conduct books and epistolary novels that come after *Clarissa* rework and revise the censoring strategies and mechanisms in order to come up with the most effective and least apparent system of control. In Foucault's words "Describing them [disciplines] will require great attention to detail: beneath every set of figures, we must seek not a meaning, but a precaution; we must situate them not only in their inextricability of a functioning, but in a coherence of a tactic" (139). In the first part of my book I use Foucault's suggestion to trace the journey of a letter within the system of disciplines. That journey by no means proceeds in a smooth, linear motion. Rather, its course, like a course of a letter lost in the mail, encounters unpredictable obstacles, changes direction, reaches the wrong destination, somehow never quite making it to the right mail box.

If the first part of my study discusses epistolary fiction from the viewpoint of a censor, the second part focuses on the viewpoint of the writers caught in the web of various censoring practices. According to a comment made by a Polish censor in an interview conducted in 1981, censorship is like a game of chess in which each movement is a reaction to and an anticipation of the adversary's behavior.[20] In order to avoid censoring the history of epistolary fiction by following only the motions of the censor, it is necessary to consider those of the other player, the writer. One of the most famous and conscientious prisoners of our times, Antonio Gramsci, tried to define and analyze what he called "prison psychology."[21] The central issue in his discussion is censorship of letters and the prisoner's encounter with the very visible figure of the prison censor. To be able to maintain contact with the outside world through letters, Gramsci resorts to writing in what he calls an "epistolografia convenzionalmente carceraria," "modo di scrivere carcerario," "la carcerite," a writing style that follows a set of rules devised to appease the censor. I argue that, like Gramsci, women writing letters in the eighteenth century had to develop strategies which would take into account the demands of their censors and would include careful selection of addressees, appropriate content and style.

Gramsci admits to putting on "a skin that is half-ass, half-sheep" (L 84, 181) as a tactics of survival. Gramsci's metaphor may, I think, help to read at least some epistolary works by women, not necessarily as fictions of compliance (a view shared by a number of critics, including feminist ones) but rather as fictions of survival, a site of struggle for literary expression along an extremely narrow path, closely guarded by letter writing laws.[22] Thus, Fanny Burney's writing strategy in *Evelina* cannot be fully understood or appreciated unless it is read against a desperate attempt on the part of Eliza Haywood to retain her position as a writer of epistolary fiction, and at the same time to appease the outrage of conduct books at the violation of the law of decorum. The death of a certain kind of epistolary fiction—the tale of seduction and betrayal—at the end of the eighteenth century marks, I think, a conscious reaction on the part of women writers who rejected it as a form that fostered the image of a female victim. It is a sign of rebellion against an ever-tightening grip of social control over women exercised through the means of letters, a rebellion that at the end of the eighteenth century results in abandoning a genre that "has specialized in narrowing the possible inflections for feminine expression."[23]

In the last part I discuss a nineteenth-century American novel (*Ruth Hall* by Fanny Fern) and two contemporary epistolary novels by Italian women writers (Dacia Maraini and Oriana Fallaci). I have selected these novels because they can be read as an uncensored response to eighteenth-century correspondence. They unmask clichés and stereotypes that pervade our perception of the association of women and letters and affect our interpretation of that association. They deconstruct the censoring practices that both defined and confined women's letters, and strip them of legislative authority. They defy the laws of exclusion, and practice a strategy of conscious transgression, blending previously strictly separated categories, disregarding generic rules, and challenging precepts of decorum. By openly admitting to transgression, they move out from the shadowy area of concealment and secrets with a Lacanian "odor di femina" to a well-lit spot on the literary stage. They reclaim the female epistolary tradition as a part of their literary heritage, and restore it to the modern reader through the process of revision and rewriting.[24]

Although Michel Foucault's insights into the discursive practices and his notion of discipline provide the main theoretical framework for my study, I also draw on a number of theoretical concepts developed in feminist and reader response theory. Joan Kelly-Gadol's concept of "the double vision" is particularly useful because it considers the position of women both from inside and outside of the conventions that inscribed them, and so "it should account for the voices that are silent as well as those that are heard: it should gauge the way in which social and discursive practices both exclude and empower."[25] Like communication by letters, the critical practice of double vision consists in a constant shifting back and forth between texts in order to "relocate the site in which analysis takes place" and thus displace the censoring conventions and discourses.

Since an epistolary exchange relies on the acts of writing and reading, the issue of "correct" and "incorrect" interpretation of letters is a crucial one. In her article "On the Superficiality of Women," Susan Noakes uses the notion of a "semiotically informed feminist hermeneutics" to explore "the ways in which gender differences have been employed in accounts of sign production and of interpretation in order to make manifest the traditional exclusion of women from the hermeneutic process."[26] Noakes discusses the topos of women as superficial readers in Western culture, the most prominent example being Flaubert's Emma Bovary. I relate that stereotype to the images of women writers and readers created in the epistolary fiction and I show how the clichés that grew out of it have affected their perception in contemporary fiction (a case in point is Guido Piovene's novel *Letters of a Novice*).

In *Special Delivery: Epistolary Modes in Modern Fiction*, Linda Kaufman wonders if it is not "a quixotic" venture "to study epistolarity (defined as the theory and practice of writing letter fiction) when letter-writing has practically become a lost art, supplanted by telephones, fax machines, computers, camrecorders."[27] One could ask the same question about a study of censoring practices in the eighteenth century. But the application of new technology does not remove possibilities of controlling individuals through the access to their signature, their voice, their image; it only marks a shift in the controlling mechanisms—an E-mail message can be as easily intercepted and altered as Clarissa's letters, although in order to do it one needs computer skills, not the ability to imitate other people's writing. The word "to censor" means "to register," "to write down," "to assess," "to give an opinion." Any act of communication which involves two people and results in a material document, whether it is a piece of writing, a tape, or a computer disc, lends itself to assessement or opinion of a third party—a jealous husband, an envious colleague, a political opponent. A study of the censoring practices in the eighteenth century will not provide a guide of preventive measures, but will rather offer a reflection on the complexity and ubiquity of censorship.

1
Female Letters in Conduct Material

IN *BEHAVIOR BOOK*, PUBLISHED IN 1859, ELIZA LESLIE PROVIDES THE FOLlowing epistolary guidelines for her young women readers:

> No young lady ever engages in a correspondence with a gentleman that is neither her relative nor her betrothed, without lessening herself in his eyes. Of this she may rest assured. With some men it is even dangerous for a lady to write a note on the commonest subject. He may show the superscription or the signature, or both to his idle companions and make insinuations much to her disadvantage, which his comrades will be sure to circulate and exaggerate. Above all, let no lady correspond with a married man, unless she is obliged to consult him on business, and from that plain straight path let her not diverge.[1]

In Leslie's view the territory of letters is a minefield ready to explode if not treaded with the utmost caution and prudence. Women who enter that territory are particularly vulnerable to the subterfuges and assaults that may cost them the loss of virtue and reputation, and thus, irrevocably harm their social status.

Leslie obviously pays no attention to the formal and stylistic aspects of letter writing, that is, how to write a letter. Instead, she focuses on the content and address of letters by women and she places letter writing in the category of conduct rather than in the category of stylistic guidelines. The section on letters in her book defines the permissible boundaries of who can write what to whom, thus emphasizing the role letters play within a social structure. Leslie's text acts then as a censor who establishes the rules of propriety through and in correspondence. Her admonitions provide a censoring grid which is the end result of a long process during which the rules of decorum with regard to female correspondence were being formulated, corrected, and changed in order to establish the most efficient mode of social control.

That process took place mainly in the eighteenth century, a key historical moment in the transition from the aristocratic to the bourgeois society, a period of profound socio-economic changes that touched every level and every aspect of the social structure.² Two elements of that transition affected significantly the image of a female letter writer. The first one involved redefinition of femininity and, in consequence, of the role women played within a family. An aristocratic ideal ceased to dominate the social scene and was replaced by a bourgeois model founded on a new set of values. If an aristocratic woman was viewed as desirable in terms of physical attractiveness, noble origin, wit and sensuality—attributes necessary for a perfect companion of a courtier—a bourgeois woman (a domestic woman) represented spiritual rather than physical beauty, professed rigid moral standards, and displayed tireless concern for the well-being of others.³ The Enlightenment produced or promised to produce a woman "who, in contrast with her aristocratic counterpart, possessed the virtues of frugality and self-restraint," in other words, a perfect mistress of a perfect household.⁴ Texts aimed at the female reading public, mainly novels and conduct books, participated vigorously in that construction and accounted greatly for its successful completion and its long-lasting consequences. As Janet Todd points out "the domestic woman of Halifax or Steele was a forerunner of 'the angel of the house,' still living in the twentieth century when Virginia Woolf tried to murder her."⁵

The second element crucial in the transition from the aristocratic to the bourgeois society was the change of attitude towards the modes of social control. In Michel Foucault's view that shift occurred through the development of "the disciplines." The monarch's power, made visible through the spectacle of the scaffold, was replaced by disciplinary practices in "an effort to adjust the mechanisms of power that frame the everyday lives of individuals; an adaptation and a refinement of the machinery that assumes responsibility for and places under surveillance their everyday behavior, their identity, their activity, their apparently unimportant gestures."⁶ The disciplines which entered the social scene through the back door of such institutions as schools, prisons, and hospitals made possible the shift from what Jacques Donzelot calls "a government of families" into "a government through the family."⁷ Under their unwavering gaze every moment of an individual's life assumed importance in unassuming ways.

In this chapter I will use the double lenses of conduct material and the disciplines to look at letters by women. Tracing the itinerary of the female letter in conduct material I will show how the changing modes of control influenced and shaped the strategies of censoring women's letters, reaching its culmination point in Eliza Leslie's words of prudence and caution. A letter proves a particularly sensitive indicator for spotting and evaluating these shifts because of its delicate position on the boundary of the private and the public. Its value as an object of control stems not only from its manipulative potential as material evidence, but also from an easy access to private thought that, however, can always be rendered public and thus accorded careful scrutiny by an appropriate censoring system. If a private letter reproduces the innermost, true sentiments and convictions of its writer, it provides its censors with a wealth of knowledge that permits the isolation of potentially dangerous areas and the selection of the best tactics to deal with rebellious or subversive elements. "The disruptive potential of female sexuality and its associated epistolarity" turned a female letter in the eighteenth century into a gauge which conduct books in conjunction with the disciplines used to probe and measure the sentiments that could hamper the construction of the new feminine ideal.[8]

It is difficult to situate conduct books on the socioliterary scene since their hybrid nature eludes any attempts at classification. Considered neither pure historical documents nor completely fictional works, a sort of document tainted by literary elements, conduct material (until very recently) has rarely been considered a source of precious information for either historical or literary research. Whereas a number of conduct manuals for men, despite the odds, have managed to secure a reputable position of both historical and literary value—to mention only Castiglione's *Il Cortigiano,* or Lord Chesterfield's *Letters to My Son*—conduct books for women have occupied a position in a no-man's-land. "Despite remarkable parallels between literature of conduct and the conduct of literature," observes Nancy Armstrong, "literary histories rarely, if ever, contain references to the literature of female conduct, and even more rarely are conduct books for women allowed to contribute to our notion of cultural history" (IC, 3).

The reluctance to include conduct material in the study of the literary representations stems partly from the ambivalent relationship between them. Carol Flynn and Rosalind Jones "understand this relationship as one of difference, in which conduct books present the more conservative, and literature the more liberal attitude towards women" (IC, 19). Yet another difference would consist of regarding literature as entertainment and conduct books as instruction. Such views suggest, however, that there exists a rigid line dividing pure literature from conduct material. A more cautious way of perceiving that relationship would be to regard it as one of symbiosis—in which conduct material and literary fiction complement and interact with each other, mixing conservative and liberal elements, and instruction with entertainment. Thus, conduct material supplies fiction with norms of social acceptance and literary representations provide a palatable form to couch these prescriptions.

A case in point is the literary career of Samuel Richardson, a major eighteenth-century figure in both camps. In 1755, Samuel Richardson published A *Collection of the Moral and Instructive Sentiments;* the collection was to be "a kind of rebuke" to those who read his novels "for a story."[9] Innumerable revisions of *Pamela* and *Clarissa* did not satisfy his craving for a perfect reader's response to his novels. Frustrated by what he considered misreadings, misinterpretations, and misunderstandings of his novels, he embarked on a plan that would remedy that situation. The aim of *Pamela* and *Clarissa* was to "properly mingle Instruction with Entertainment, so as to make the latter seemingly the View, while the former is really the End" (ix). The aim of *A Collection . . .* was to dispense with entertainment and focus on instruction. Richardson selected what to him seemed his most precious observations from *Pamela, Clarissa,* and *Sir Charles Grandison,* and arranged them under alphabetical headings to provide the reader with an easily accessible guide to life; e.g., under A we find the following topics:"Adversity," "Affliction," "Advice and Caution to Women," "Air and Manners," "Address," "Anger," etc.

Richardson undertook the task of compiling this collection rather than writing a new novel, which he was fully aware would have been eagerly snatched up by his avid readers and would have brought him ample financial rewards. Richardson, however, was not prepared to yield to the tempting prospects of fame and money. As he notes in a letter to Lady Echlin,

> Your Ladyship's kind opinion of my last book is an encouragement to me which was wanted; because some of my best friends wished that I had bestowed the time the collection cost me, in writing another story; and declared they would not read it; yet, regarded the three pieces I have published more for the sake of instruction, than the story. So they said. However, I can faithfully assure them, that this collection was set about and carried through (and a very painful and laborious task it was) more with a view to do good, than to profit. I could not expect a great sale of it, though it is the pith and marrow of nineteen volumes, not unkindly received. (xiii)

In the Preface to *A Collection,* Dr Benjamin Kennicott, a contemporary of Richardson and a Fellow of Exeter College in Oxford, explains why the act of reading a novel does not fully guarantee the reader's absorption of its "pith and marrow,"

> Such is the great plan, such the benevolent scheme, of these collections of *Familiar Letters* (meaning *Pamela, Clarissa,* and *Grandison*), which have been already translated into several foreign languages, and received in our country with uncommon favours. But as the *narrative* part of those Letters was only meant as a vehicle for the *instructive,* no wonder that many readers, who are desirous of fixing in their minds those maxims which deserve notice distinct from the story that first introduced them, should have often wished and pressed to see them separate from the chain of engaging incidents that will sometimes steal the most fixed attention from its pursuit of serious truth. (ix, Kennicott's emphasis)

With the story discarded as superfluous, and the readers' attention fixed wholly on the moral instruction, *A Collection* could be equally valuable to those who have and those who have not read the novels. As Richardson himself observes in the letter to his Dutch translator: "What I am employing myself about, is, to collect the sentiments of all three Pieces . . . and to print all in one Pocket Volume, to serve as a kind of Vade Mecum to such as either have read, or having not read can dispense with stories, for the Sake of the Instruction aimed to be given in them" (ix). The author of the recent Introduction to *A Collection,* James Evans, points out that,

> the suggestion that this volume would be useful to those who had not read the novels, as well as to those who had, probably reflected more frustration on Richardson's part in getting his audience to read him as he wished and some final shifting of the balance of instruction and entertainment even further toward the former. (xi)

In a way, then, Richardson's career came full circle—he started out as a writer of conduct books with *The Apprentice's Vade Mecum* and *Familiar Letters on Important Occasions,* and concluded his literary career by compressing his three novels into the format of another conduct book. Richardson's last literary gesture points to his preoccupation with giving the readers prescriptions for life rather than descriptions of it. The mistrust of readers' abilities to draw instructive elements from life descriptions prompted him to construct a frame of moral and social values that would contain these descriptions. Kennicott stresses the importance of such a frame in his preface:

> Sententious Maxims and Moral Aphorisms, collecting into a point and concisely but strongly expressing elevated thoughts, beautiful sentiments, or instructive lessons have always been well received by the public, they have been considered as the first strokes of a picture, in which are seen the justness and beauty of the painter's design, though it has not the coloring. (vii)

Literary fiction is thus regarded as an embellishment, a mere supplement to the moral framework. The mutual dependence of fiction and conduct material exposed by Kennicott's comment makes it impossible to draw a clear-cut distinction between the two and suggests that reading them side-by-side would offer a vantage point.

Richardson's case not only attests to the popularity of conduct material in the eighteenth century but also illustrates the dilemmas and struggles of its writers and the uneasy tasks they had to face. The emphasis on the text as a censoring mechanism and the preoccupation with finding the most appropriate, yet least visible method of controlling the reader through the text recalls Foucault's analysis of the disciplines. A brief reflection on the way they operated may help us explain Richardson's drive toward achieving a perfect reader's response and his frustration at not being quite able to do it. Foucault distinguishes four main characteristics of the disciplinary mode of control. The first is attention to detail (Foucault refers to it as "utilitarian rationalization of detail in moral accountability and political control," DP, 139)—nothing is insignificant, and nothing is arbitrary; it is the little things that count since "fidelity to them may, by an imperceptible progress, raise us to the most eminent sanctity" (DP, 140). The second characteristic involves invisibility of control—"the policing power is either invisible or disguised under cover of other, nobler or simply blander intentionalities (to educate, to defend, to cure, to protect)."[10] The third element is adaptation of methods in response to particular needs, and the fourth, scrupulous concern with surveillance. The application of these factors allowed a machinery of control to function like "a microscope of conduct which formed around men an apparatus of observation, recording and training."[11]

Although Foucault examines these practices in disciplinary institutions such as prisons, hospitals, and schools, the principles on which they relied apply also to the conduct material. Like the disciplines, the conduct material was aimed at control of the body through the control of the mind. And like the disciplines, it needed to adhere to strict guidelines to achieve that control. The first textual sign of this adherence is the scrupulous attention to minutiae, reflected by the size of content tables which sometimes run for several pages. Each moment of a woman's life had to be accounted for in the smallest detail; nothing could escape the probing eyes of the writer/supervisor.[12] It is also evident in the rhetoric employed by the conduct book writers. They viewed themselves as "creators" of perfect women and it is only their own dedication and skill that would result in full success.[13] An anonymous contributor to the magazine *Il Caffè*, published in Italy between 1764 and 1775, writes that

Questo sesso è fatto per esser la delizia della società, e se noi ci prendessimo la pena di istruigli la mente, e presentargli le idee più belle, di dirigergli il cuore, ed elevarlo al di sopra dell'umile rango in cui giace, corrisponderebbe egli perfettamente ai nostri desideri e perverrebbe a quella nobile meta, alla quale fosse indirizzato.[14]

[The female sex is made for the delight of the society and if we took pains to cultivate their minds and feed them with the loftiest ideas, to direct their hearts and elevate them above the base rank which they occupy now, women would perfectly fulfill our desires and would aspire to that noble end for which they have been destined.]

Hubbard Winslow in *Woman as She Should Be* (1838) professes a similar view and observes that "our daughters are to be corner-stones polished, and polished after the similitude of a palace."[15] In his vision of the world, Christ is to be the master of the palace, i.e., the society, in which women serve as cornerstones. The stability and endurance of the structure depends on the material used for the cornerstones and the mechanical processes that would make them fit for the palace's needs. In *Noble Womanhood,* published in 1900, Charles Dole advocates spiritual rather than factual knowledge for women:

We see women, and men also, whose education is like the grand plan of some godly building. The foundation has been laid in costly material, but the walls have not been reared; the roof has never been put on the building. We would rather have a smaller and less ambitious house, which nevertheless sheltered its inmates from the weather, than this pretentious beginning of a palace in which no human being can live.[16]

Praising the superiority of inward beauty over outward prettiness, he notes that "the instrument, the piano, the violin ought to have a case that fits it. But what is the use of the most finished case if the instrument itself is mean or out of tune?" (13) Winslow and Dole, like the anonymous Italian writer before them, view the process of reeducating, reforming, or reshaping women as analogical to the mechanical processes of polishing cornerstones, constructing a building, or making a perfect case for an instrument. That analogy suggests that the risks involved in any constructional work may also occur in the act of creating a perfect woman and have to be avoided at all costs. The creator/maker has to have excellent skills, reliable equipment, and raw material of first quality. If one or more of these fail, the whole structure will collapse. Thus, each element, even the one that seems least important, has its role to play in creating a faultless product.

"Disciplinary power constitutively mobilizes a tactic of tact," observes D. A. Miller in *The Novel and the Police* (17). It tends to become invisible or pose under carefully chosen disguises. The shift from the obvious forms of coercion, apparent in the display of power in the spectacle of the scaffold, to the power descending and operating in the "underground," can be noted when we compare the methods of persuasion advocated by Richard Allestree in *The Ladies Calling* (published in 1696) and those recommended by Reverend Wise and Charles Dole nearly two hundred years later. How to make women listen attentively to the prescriptive rules that should guide them into the right path in life? Richard Allestree believes in the efficiency of the spectacle of fear: "Women are generally timorous, and apt to start at the apprehension of danger; let them but see a serpent though at a great distance, and they will need no Homilies or Lectures to be persuaded to fly from it."[17] Reverend Wise and Francis Dole turn away in disgust from such measures. Their way of persuasion sounds much more benevolent and humanitarian; woman—the enemy, woman—the adversary of man, is replaced by a meek creature who "naturally" aspires to the ideal of obedience and submission.

The open attacks on women (such as presented in Castiglione and Tasso or in seventeenth century treatises against women) give way to praise and admiration of womanhood.[18] Francis Dole contrasts the old conception of womanhood with the new one: "The old world thought of woman as a creature provided for man, a being only of finite worth. The poets and prophets are teaching the new world to think of woman as divine and infinite being" (10). This magnificent ideal of womanhood is easy to achieve. Women have only to follow the guidance of men and submit to it without reservations: "Let every woman *pray* to be that which Wordsworth and Lowell saw in their visions, let every man *expect* this noble type of woman, and *the demand shall produce the supply.*"[19] But the last remark, which (probably inadvertently) uses crude economic terms, reveals that the "poet's vision" of an ideal woman is not rooted in some abstract "divine" world but in a society whose laws it strictly obeys.[20] The rhetoric of female idealization, which so expertly disguised the economic and social objectives, preempted the means of self-defence and condemned women to passive acceptance of praise. "The overt misogyny of Gould or Rochester is distasteful," notes Janet Todd, "but it could at least be countered with some of the crude language that would later be unusable by women."[21] Thus, by replacing the rhetoric of abuse with the rhetoric of female virtue the "producers" of ideal women dampened the spirit of bold resistance and did away with any urge to fight.

The aim of disciplinary techniques was also to respond promptly to any factor that could improve the scope or mode of their operation.

This required constant alertness to the changing social needs and continual readjustment to those needs. In the conduct material that elasticity of attitude relies on a mechanism which I propose to call "the imperfect model of perfection." On the most general level conduct books attempt to solve the conflict between a real life and an ideal. The maxims, instructions, and moral lessons are designed to replace the existing set of values with a new one and turn the reality into the desired model, thereby obliterating the conflict. The title of James Cochrane's book *Woman as She Is and as She Should Be* reflects the gap between "a live woman" and "a model woman" required by the society for which he speaks. Charles Dole's *Noble Womanhood* portrays the discrepancy between existing womanhood and "a noble womanhood" which he advocates. Thus, both Cochrane and Dole prescribe means that would transform "what is" into "what should be."

Seemingly the clash between the reality and the ideal is solved by the prescriptive measures that, if obeyed, will eventually lead to the realization of that ideal. However, a glance in retrospect at the finished model will always reveal some cracks, fissures, inadequacies that necessitate further revisions and improvements of what was once considered "a perfect model." Thus, each supposedly perfect model carries within it a possibility of further perfection; in consequence, even the most detailed instruction can always be expanded, ensuring a more prompt and less risky way of achieving the desired goal. Every perfect model, then, is always vulnerable and open to debate. Like Richardson, who struggled to obtain perfect reader's response to his novels and eliminate any possibility of a misreading, authors of conduct books attempted to create a grid that would hold in place the unruly elements in life. Richardson's frustration with the "imperfect model of reading" forced him to continue revising and rewriting his novels. The similar frustration of the conduct book writers made them keep on adding new versions to the already existing bulk of models for imitation.

But providing a model for imitation was not sufficient—one had to make sure that its traits would actually be copied in real life, bringing forth the required "supply" of replicas. Hence the preoccupation with the fourth element, which distinguishes the society of spectacle from the society of discipline—surveillance. Foucault perceives surveillance as a "decisive economic operator both as an internal part of the production machinery and a specific mechanism in the disciplinary power."[22] Although the functioning of surveillance mechanisms is best reflected by the architectural designs and supervisory arrangements in public institutions, such as prisons, hospitals, schools, and factories, it also played an important part, perhaps less discernible "structurally," in intrafamilial relations. *Advice to Young Ladies,* a collection of illustrations taken from "The London Journal" of 1855 and 1862, contains a number of graphic representations of familial vigilance—a mother eavesdropping on a conversation between her daughter and a young man, a father watching a daughter dance.[23] The great majority of these representations, however, refer to the watchful gazes directed at pieces of writing, among which letters become the prime target.

A stern gaze is a reminder that surveillance constitutes an integral part of censoring female correspondence. But the disciplines equipped conduct book writers with a whole arsenal of deathly strategies that helped adjust and tailor censoring practices to the current social needs. In the subsequent part of this chapter I will discuss the representation of women's letters in conduct books and the ingenious ways the censors of decorum developed to control them.[24] In John Dunton's *The Challenge, Sent by a Young Lady to Sir Thomas & C., or the Female War,* published in 1697, Sir Thomas Godfrey, who acts as a spokesman for men, regards letters as the only form of writing women should be allowed to practice:

> And for your Writing, 'tis yet more intolerable: Haven't we Paper-spoilers enough of our own Sex, that you must come in to help us? A Wise Man doubtless he was, that first taught you to Write, when your Mark it self had been too much. But if you must scribble now and then, that you mayn't quite forget it, one wou'd think a Billet-doux would suffice you, or at least a passionate Love-letter.[25]

Any other kind of writing, claims Sir Thomas, is "meddling beyond your Province" (104). That province is the private sphere; any departure from it constitutes for a woman such a grave offence that Sir Thomas contemplates drastic measures that would prevent it from happening:

> I cou'd heartily wish there were a Law to ty'em [three writing fingers] up a little, both for our sakes and yours; or to pin 'em down by your sides, as they do childrens, never to be let loose, till you had found sufficient Sureties for their Good Behaviour. (105)

A love letter becomes then, according to the male viewpoint represented by Sir Thomas, the only safe repository of female writing—safe because it limits that writing to the expression of the most intimate sentiments meant to be seen by one person only, therefore preventing it from being exposed to "Publick view" and from invading the public sphere reserved for men.

WHITE VIOLET—If not exactly improper, it is indiscreet to correspond with a young man, as a friend, while engaged to another, and without his knowledge. Clandestine friendships, like clandestine courtships, are always suspicious affairs. Besides, it is not allowed by strict propriety for young ladies to indulge in such correspondence. Drawing reproduced from "The London Journal" of 1855 and 1862, selected by R. D. for *Advice to Young Ladies* (London: Methuen, 1933, 27).

Rose must consult her mother. Clandestine courtships are the bane of families. They make fathers ill-tempered, brothers horse-whippish inclined, mothers nervous and ill, and the girls themselves generally the dupes of fortune-hunters. Drawing reproduced from "The London Journal" of 1855 and 1862 selected by R. D. for *Advice to Young Ladies* (London: Methuen, 1933, 39).

The reference to female letters in Dunton's book crops up in the course of a more general discussion devoted to "women's province" and the questions of female education. There are no specific guidelines regarding letter writing. Such guidelines, however, may be found in a work attributed to Hannah Wooley—*The Gentlewoman's Companion*, published in 1673.[26] Wooley's book has a separate section on letters, entitled "Some general and choice Rules for writing of Letters." After a few general remarks regarding the rules of grammar, punctuation, and composition, Wooley rather unexpectedly makes the following observation: "for sometimes it is not convenient to trust that in a sheet of paper, which if lost or miscarried may be the great detriment, if not the utter ruin of a person."[27] Wooley's remark contains a warning concerned with the content of a letter. A letter, she cautions, is a signed document, and as such may be prone to all sorts of mishap. If it happens to fall into unwanted hands, it may be used to incriminate the writer or the addressee.

To protect them, and to avoid such risks, she suggests under various rubrics a number of "safe topics" whose disclosure would not cause any harm. Those topics are: "Of intelligence of good advice," "How elegantly to complain of injuries done," "Of requesting a kindness," "Of consolation," etc. Although Wooley does not specify which topics are "unsafe" and what kind of "ruin" she alludes to, these rather oblique terms are partially clarified in a model letter included in the section "Letters upon all occasions," containing letters that are to be regarded not only as models of style, composition, etc., but also as models of behavior. These letters teach not only how to write, but also what to write and to whom. After the usual opening remarks, H. G., a schoolgirl at a Boarding School in Hackney, writes to "her quondam schoolfellow" in London:

> Our governess is as active and watchful as ever, down with the sun and up with the lark . . . She aims not only at the benefit, but the eternal welfare of our Souls, in the performance of our Duties to God and our Parents. She continues her former jealousie, not suffering a *Letter* to come into the House without her knowledge thereof; and herein her prudence is highly commended, for by her strict examination of these *Paper-messengers,* she shuts the doors against many which might be the Bawds that might betray the Obedience of some and the Chastity of others. Neither are there *any Answers returned to any Letters but what she is privy to;* by which means there is nothing we write we need be ashamed of, were it legibly written on our Foreheads as well as Papers. (234, my emphasis)

The girls living at a boarding school, deprived of parental vigilance, need a surrogate parent, a governess, to monitor closely their every move. Since the only way of communicating with the outside world is by means of letters, these innocuous yet potent "paper-messengers," the girls' correspondence, must be strictly censored to rule out any possibility of an unwanted connection. As the girls explain, such measures guard their chastity and prevent any act of filial disobedience. What Wooley fears, although she does not make it explicit, is the possibility that a clandestine correspondence between a young girl and a man may eventually lead either to seduction out of wedlock (assault on "chastity") or to a marriage against her parents' wishes ("betray the Obedience"). The family law is at stake here since both cases constitute a threat to the proper order of transmission of blood and property. That is why the most important law devised by the family code is the law of filial obedience. Its breach, contends Wooley, is unthinkable:

> The duties of a child (Male or Female) to Parents, may be branch'd out into these particulars; Reverence, Love, Obedience (especially in Marriage). But of all the acts of Disobedience, that of Marrying without the consent of Parents is the highest. We see under the Law, the Maid that hath made any Vow, was not suffer'd to perform it without the consent of the Parent. (23–24)

Needless to say, every act of disobedience, but especially the gravest—choosing a husband against the parents' wishes, is bound to bring about disastrous consequences.[28]

Bernard Mandeville in *The Virgin Unmask'd; or Female Dialogues betwixt an Elderly Maiden Lady and her Niece, on Several Diverting Discourses on Love, Marriage, Memoirs and Morals, & c. of the Times*, published in 1724, provides an illustration of these consequences. Lucinda, an elderly maiden lady, tells Antonia, her young niece, a story, which she assures her is true, about Amelia and Dorante. Amelia was a beautiful girl, an only daughter of very rich parents. She had just returned from a boarding school, when

> One Day coming from Hide-Park, Amelia fell in love with a Gentleman she saw on Horseback; Dorante happen'd to turn his Eyes that way and meeting with hers, found so much Disorder in her Countenance, that having a good Opinion of himself, he presently suspected the Cause; he sent a Porter to follow the Coach, and being informed of her Name, and Circumstance, *writ* to her very passionately the next Day; she *answered* presently and *thus a Love Intrigue began.*[29]

Amelia's father intercepted one of their letters, discovered Amelia's love for Dorante, and, being aware of Dorante's pecuniary interests, forbade his daughter to correspond with him. Amelia, despite her father's orders, continued the clandestine correspondence, and finally managed to elope with and marry him. Having learned of the marriage, her father disinherited Amelia, condemning her to a miserable life with a selfish brute (the author stresses the fact that Dorante was Irish). Eventually Dorante's untimely death freed Amelia from her wretched fate, and she managed, with some help from an honorable Englishman, to bring up her daughter in decent conditions, and instill in her from the very beginning the virtue of filial obedience and the abhorrence of clandestine correspondence.

For Wooley and Mandeville, then, the transgressive potential of letters justifies the parents' right, even duty, to control their daughters' correspondence. The recourse to "paper-messengers" could prove injurious to parental authority, and shatter the model of filial obedience so carefully created and fostered by society. Letters leaving the household therefore required careful scrutiny; every letter was to be intercepted and checked for content and address. The figures of familial censors, acting as guardians of family forts, exuded power by their sheer visibility and the authority to stop and monitor women's correspondence. But, as numerous examples proved, for instance the often quoted story of Lady Wortley Montagu, who, carrying on a clandestine correspondence with Wortley, managed to deceive her parents, elope, and marry him, physical control of letters might not always be successful. After all, no system of censorship imposed from the outside is perfect.[30]

The possibility of such failure called for a new way of dealing with the question of female letters. Samuel Richardson's *Familiar Letters on Important Occasions,* published in 1741, marks a shift from the transgressive to the manipulative potential of letters. This is a crucial moment in the operation of the law of decorum since it moves away from visible, coercive measures and leans towards benevolent persuasion. The preoccupation with physical control of letters, interception and close monitoring of the content, gives way to a more subtle mode of supervising female correspondence. The familial censor abandons his post of high visibility and disappears into a text. Introducing a new strategy of control, Richardson focuses on the danger residing in the letters entering the household from the outside. To magnify that danger, he devises a figure of an epistolary seducer (a prototype of Lovelace) who exploits the art of writing letters to achieve his goal—to make an advantageous match, or to seduce the object of his vile desires. That libertine would not hesitate to resort to any tricks at his disposal to initiate an epistolary love-intrigue. Richardson carefully delineates the steps to be taken in order to ward off such men:

> In the first place, she [a young orphan lady] ought to mistrust all those who shall seek to set her against her guardians; or those relations to whom her person or fortune is intrusted ... These industrious go-betweens, who hope to make a market of a young lady's affections, *generally by letter*, or word of mouth, if they have opportunity, set forth to the young lady that there is a certain young man who has fallen deeply in love with her.[31]

A young woman should be immediately aware that any attempt to approach her behind her guardian's back implies dishonest intentions; therefore, she "would not countenance any interview with a person capable of acting in such a manner, nor receive any letter from him" (127).

What, however, if she has already received such a letter and needs to reply to it to stop further correspondence? Richardson provides a model letter to be sent to "the clandestine Proposer of the Match." Her reply should be addressed to the go-between, not to the admirer, and should begin as follows:

> Mrs Pratt, I inclose the letter you put in my hands, and hope it will be the last I shall ever receive from you, or from any body else, on the like occasion. I am intirely satisfied in the care and kindness of my guardian, and shall encourage no proposal of this sort, but what comes recommended to me by his approbation. (128)

Just in case the model letter was insufficient as a preventive measure, Richardson elaborates on further precautions to be taken. If there is no go-between, and the man manages somehow to deliver the letter himself, the young woman should first keep a "contemptuous silence." If that has no effect on him, she should return his letters "*unopened, or in a blank cover* after she happens to have read them (129, Richardson's emphasis). If he still keeps pestering her with further protestations of love, she should ask a friend to write the reply for her. Do not ever write the reply yourself, cautions Richardson, because "even a denial, if given in writing *under your own hand*, will encourage some presumptuous men; or at least they may make some use of it to the lady's disadvantage" (Richardson's emphasis, 129). The friend's letter should bear no name on it, and should be signed "Yours unknown" (130).

A letter written by a woman and signed with her name becomes in male hands a powerful weapon to be used against her. If only women would realize this, they would never enter into a forbidden correspondence. Richardson thus casts himself in the role of a benevolent guardian whose instructions have the sole purpose of protecting naive women from male artfulness and cunning. He implies that if his instructions were obeyed there would be no need for physical control of letters on the part of parents or guardians. The text could take the place of the family censor in order to monitor and guide every movement of a woman's life. But the balance of power would, of course, remain intact—the control from without would be replaced by the control from within allowing a household to function smoothly according to the demands and needs of society. The apparent concern for the welfare of young women disguises the move to tighten invisibly the grip on the controlling handle.

Oddly enough, the risks involved in female correspondence are not mentioned either in Richardson's *A Collection of Moral and Instructive Sentiments,* or in any other conduct book published between 1750–1806. A possible explanation of this fact may be found in literary fiction rather than in conduct material. There is no further need to spell out the admonitions against illicit correspondence since, beginning with Richardson's Clarissa, each heroine of epistolary fiction in that period will be a living, or rather a dying, proof of the tragic results of writing uncensored letters to men. As the example of Evelina shows, a woman cannot even write a note without its being immediately abused by male hands.[32] It seems, then, that the combined effort on the part of the writers of conduct material and the writers of fiction produced the expected results and warded off the danger of uncontrolled correspondence.

Jane Aston's *The Young Woman's Guide and Instructor,* published in 1806, contains a section on letter writing which begins with the description of pleasures "derived from the power of holding an epistolary discourse with absent friends. It enables us to pour out our feelings upon paper; to convey sentiments of love and friendship."[33] These sentiments, however, are under the full control of the editor, who, by including sample letters which "are not mere samples of letter-writing but are to instruct their reader," thus feels she "has done something towards forming the characters of good daughters—amiable wives—and venerable mothers" (37). The sample letters suppress the anxieties expressed by Wooley or Richardson; there are no allusions to improper correspondence; the letters reflect the feminine ideal of modesty, prudence, and obedience. The table of contents reads: "A letter from a dutiful daughter to her mother," "A sister to another," "Refusal of marriage," "A letter to a fiancé" (approved by parents), "A mother to a married daughter," etc. The sample letters are used here to reinforce that ideal and present it as a monolithic structure where no doubts or apprehensions appear to mar its surface.[34]

Published two years later, Hannah More's essay "On the Danger of Sentimental or Romantic Connections" returns to the problem of female letters but presents it in a new light. Contrary to her predecessors, More thinks that the threat of unwanted liaisons is still very much alive. In her view sentimental fiction is a prime suspect in perpetrating the crime. She blames it for exaggerating the importance of letters in a young woman's life. It is sentimental fiction, asserts More, that proclaimed a letter to be "the fuel which principally feeds and supplies the dangerous flame of sentiment" and turned it into an indispensable attribute of any romantic liaison.[35] As More observes,

> sentiment in the present age is the varnish of virtue to conceal the deformity of vice; and it is not uncommon for the same persons to make a jest of religion, to break through the most solemn ties and engagements, to practice every act of latent fraud and open seduction, and yet to value themselves on speaking and writing sentimentally. But this refined jargon, which has infested letters and tainted morals, is chiefly admired and adopted by young Ladies of a certain turn, who read *sentimental* books, write *sentimental* letters, and contract *sentimental* friendships. (365, More's emphasis)

What made More so concerned about the popularity of sentimental fiction? After all, it worked hand in glove with the conduct material. The fate of a sentimental heroine was to illustrate the tragic consequences of female rebelliousness and ignorance of the wicked ways of men. As in the accounts of the lives of notorious criminals where "the last words of a condemned man" served as an example and an exhortation, the last words of a dying heroine (cf., Richardson's Clarissa or Rowson's Charlotte Temple) were to function as propaganda.[36] But like criminal literature, sentimental fiction in letters was equivocal both in its use and its effects. The heroine, a rebel in a domestic teapot, could turn into a hero who could undermine, if not damage completely, the tyranny of a familial structure. The epistolary fiction supplied the female readers with a whole stock of tricks and subterfuges to elude the vigilant eyes and allowed a tiny margin of hope that an escape was possible. The heroine of Mary Hearne's novel *A Lover's Week* quotes Aphra Behn's novel *Love-Letters between a Noble-Man and his Sister* as the source of useful tips in carrying on a clandestine correspondence. Lady Mary Wortley Montagu admitted that her escape from her father's house to marry Wortley against her father's wishes was staged according to the tenets of an epistolary novel.

Hannah More, then, sees the danger of female correspondence in the same light as Wooley, Mandeville, and Richardson, i.e., as a means of eluding parental control and defying authority. But while Richardson, Mandeville, and Wooley related the origin of that correspondence to the latent "natural wishes" and the desire for independence, More perceives it as a direct outcome of reading improper books.[37] It is life, she contends, that imitates fiction; if that fiction provides false models, those models will in turn contaminate life and unleash its disruptive forces. Her attack on sentimental fiction echoes, to a certain extent, Allestree's observation that reading romances is dangerous because they may leave "ill impressions. These amorous passions which 'tis their design to paint to the utmost Life, are apt to insinuate themselves, and by an unhappy inversion a Copy shall produce an Original."[38] Both Allestree and More perceive the power of fiction as a means of producing rather than imitating reality.

To avoid "the unhappy inversion," More's fictionalized conduct book, *Coelebs in Search of a Wife*, provides its readers with a perfect man, a perfect woman, and a perfect correspondence.[39] Coelebs, the ideal hero, after a long and tedious search, eventually manages to find his ideal mate, and when the marriage is approved by her parents, Coelebs is allowed to "maintain with Lucilla a regular and animated correspondence."[40] Lucilla, who is a paragon of filial duty and obedience, cheerfully accepts every restriction imposed on her by her parents (mainly her father). Coelebs admires the methods employed by Lucilla's father to "produce in his daughter such complete satisfaction in his sober and correct habits of life; her conformity was so cheerful that it did not look so much like *acquiescence as choice*" (325, my emphasis).

More aspires to a model of perfection that is self-regulated, or appears to be so, since the controlling threads that keep it in place are made invisible. This kind of model, which shifts the focus entirely from the exterior forms of control (parental supervision or governess's vigilance) to interior control (appeals to the "natural" feminine virtues, enhanced by proper upbringing), dominates the conduct books of the early nineteenth century. Thus, long passages, devoted to the resources of feminine goodness as a means of control from within, replace detailed directions regulating conduct imposed from without. More's "conduct novel" also marks a preference for positive models to imitate, rather than negative examples to avoid. A conduct book, in her view, should act as a filter that isolates any unruly aspects of life to prevent them from contaminating the perfect product.

So far the risks posed by female correspondence revolved around letters addressed to men. What about correspondence between women? Apart from a few model letters to friends (usually written on specific occasions, such as a birthday or a wedding) eighteenth-century conduct books do not include them as a separate category. The first time they are defined as such is in Hannah More's essay "On the Danger of Sentimental or Romantic Connections." Since in More's view they are as risky as letters addressed to men, she wants to warn parents to take the necessary steps to limit such correspondence. When a young woman and her confidante engage in an epistolary exchange, they usually conduct it in secret, and encourage "each other in the falsest notions imaginable" (359). And what do they write about?

> The favourite topic of these epistles is the grovelling spirit and the sordid temper of the parents, who will be sure to find no quarter at the hands of their daughters, should they presume to be so unreasonable as to direct their course of reading, interfere in their choice of friends, or interrupt their very important correspondence. (359)

Such letters ignite the flame of disobedience, defy the parents' authority, and encourage the practice of deceit. Writing in secret adds excitement, and creates the illusion that the young letter writers have been transported into the realm of romantic adventures. For, as More asserts, "a prohibited correspondence is one of the great incidents of a sentimental life, and a letter clandestinely received, the supreme felicity of a sentimental lady" (360).

The anonymous author of *The Young Lady's Friend* (1839), published twenty years after More, accepts the epistolary exchange with female friends as permissible:

> An extensive correspondence among girls of your own age is not desirable, it consumes too much time, but a few correspondents are useful as furnishing inducements for you to practice the art of letter-writing . . . Always notice the contents of your friend's letter and endeavor to write of those things which will most interest her.[41]

In her opinion, there are two positive aspects of this exchange. First, she notes its usefulness as an exercise in writing, like other "feminine" forms, such as the diary or journal.[42] But contrary to a diary or a journal kept in one's drawer, a letter had to be sent, thus violating the privacy in which it originated. The letter writer must carefully inspect the letter's content, remembering that a letter is meant to please the addressee rather than the writer, so the former's interests and concerns are to be given priority over those of the writer. The second positive point stresses the virtues letter writing promotes—it makes one considerate of others, teaches self-restraint, and fosters altruism. Even the danger of public exposure is perceived here from the viewpoint of the addressee rather than the writer: "Remember the liability of a letter to miscarry, to be opened by the wrong person, to be seen by other eyes than those for whom it is meant, and be very careful what you write to the disadvantage of anyone" (219). To ensure that the least harm will be done if a letter falls into the wrong hands, the author suggests that letters should discuss "safe" i.e., impersonal topics: "the more rational and elevated the topics are on which you write, the less will you care for your letters being seen, or for paragraphs being read out of them" (281).

The shift from spontaneity to cautious planning of every sentence contradicts the earlier characterization of feminine correspondence as the flowing from the heart. As Jane Aston noted, "an epistolary discourse enables us to pour out our feelings on paper; to convey sentiments of love and friendship."[43] The author of *The Young Lady's Friend* obviously disapproves of this opinion, and although she respects the right to privacy, she recommends parental supervision as an additional safeguard against any impropriety:

> If your correspondent requires that her letters be kept private from all friends, make it a point of honor to comply with her wishes; only make an exception in favor of your mother; in case she should desire to see the correspondence, for young ladies under age should gracefully acknowledge their parents' right of inspection. (281).

Like a love letter, a letter of friendship appears to be a site of contradictory forces—although intended primarily as a repository of private sentiments, it has to dispense with these sentiments to avoid becoming an object of manipulation. Its right to secrecy (it is meant for only one person, the addressee), has to be infringed upon by parental inspection for the same reason.

The next question which arises regards the importance of correspondence in a young woman's life. More thought that it was grossly exaggerated by sentimental fiction, and she attacked its escapist qualities. The flights of imagination that transported young girls to the realm of sick romances, encouraged by that correspondence, could only bring harm and disillusionment in real life. The anonymous author of *The Young Lady's Friend* is aware of young women's needs for an outlet of emotions, for a niche where one can trade one's own secrets for someone else's.[44] Worried about the potential dangers of intimate correspondence to the girls' reputation, she suggests:

> The letters of the past years should either be destroyed, or carefully locked up, with directions on the box, that in case of your death they are to be returned, unread, to the writers, or if that cannot be done, they should be burnt, unread. This disposal of letters after death is often *the only important part of a young girl's will, and yet this is rarely provided for. It*

is best to be always prepared, by making the necessary arrangements whilst in health. (282, my emphasis)⁴⁵

A few lines further on we find the following passage, regarding the same problem:

> The letters of young persons rarely have any interest beyond the period in which they are written; they are seldom read after they are a year old, and the idea of keeping them for future perusal, is altogether chimerical. Life is too short, and too much crowded with novel interests, to allow time for reading over quires of paper, filled with the chat of young girls, however good it may have been in its day, and therefore the wisest plan is, to agree with your correspondent, to make each a bon-fire of the other's letters when they shall be more than a year old. A year's letters are enough for a memorial of your friend, if she be taken from you; and, by keeping the latest, you will have her most mature compositions. (282)

This morbid interest in the fate of letters after the correspondents' death, rather strange in view of their tender age, and the urging to wipe out all the traces of correspondence, emphasize the ephemeral character of letter writing. Letters, like their writers, should not be allowed to leave a mark of their presence on the literary or social scene—they should quietly disappear into oblivion.

The fear of even a remote possibility of letters crossing the private/public line stands behind these measures of caution. Assigning a bourgeois woman to the hearth of domesticity, conduct material had to guard closely any crack which might provide a way of abandoning the home and entering the public sphere. An ideal woman was the one who was "never known to fame. She did nothing in public. She was one of the myriad of voices and mothers whom the world never thanked or praised."⁴⁶ "Woman thy name is anonymity," stated Rev. Wise, explaining the "natural" reasons for it:

> Women must abide in the peaceful sanctuaries of home, and walk *in the noiseless vales of private life*. Woman is formed for the calm of home. She may venture, like the land-bird, to *invade the sphere of men, but she will encounter storms which she is utterly unfit to meet.*⁴⁷

The letter, as a possible culprit in keeping women away of from the "noiseless vales" of domesticity, warranted the unprecedented attention of domestic censors.⁴⁸ The subversive potential of letters and the risks they posed to the production of female "docile" bodies (eluding parental vigilance, expressing rebellious sentiments, entering the public, literary territory) pushed the conduct material into creating an ideal woman letter writer. That creation came into being through a series of restrictions imposed on female correspondence. The pattern of these restrictions, supported by the disciplines, followed the imperfect model of perfection. Each restriction proceeded from a "crack" spotted on the earlier version of the model of perfection. The motivating forces were fear and hope—fear that the slightest omission or neglect on the part of the model creator might result in disastrous consequences; hope that if enough thought and care were dedicated to constructing that model, "a perfect model of perfection" would eventually materialize. Apparently it was no easy task, and its creator, like the watchman in George Weaver's vision, had to take into account even the smallest detail:

> He who stands upon the watch-tower of virtue should be faithful to give the alarm of danger when it is near. It should be sounded when the engulfing pool is yet in the distance, and the danger easily avoided. He who is upon the present watch beholds a perilous scene before him. It is a maelstrom, dark, whirling, yawning. It is roaring with wrecks, groans, and horrid ruin of fortunes and lives. It is named *Intemperance,* and is situated in the very center of the great sea of pleasure. The waters which form this ruinous pool come in from every direction. The descent to it is so gentle as to be scarcely perceptible without the closest observation ... Thus, without being aware of danger he glides at first slowly down, and then faster and faster and still faster down, till the waters break into foam, and envelop him in a cloud of darkness, in the midst of which he is hurried on, and still on to ruin. Thus is this fascinating sea of pleasure spread around the engulfing pool of intemperance, sloping in from every direction, inviting and still inviting its voyagers to sail down its danger-strewn declivities. Not one path alone leads to this sullen gulf of woe, not only one current, as too many have supposed, hurries down this dark abyss; but all around, on every side, the waters tend downward. There are a thousand currents leading in. Some, it is true, are more rapid than others. Some rush in quickly, and bear down all who ride upon their waters to quick and certain ruin. Others glide more slowly, but none the less surely, to the same end.[49]

Weaver's grim picture illustrates the significance of streamlets in forming the ruinous pool. In the same way "lesser lines," such as control of female correspondence, acquired importance in "the policing of families."

My reading of the conduct material exposes the hidden meaning of what many have taken to be an emerging bourgeois ideology and set of ideals by showing how the device of the letter was used to both enforce and subvert societal prescriptions. This is a novel way of getting at larger social changes, namely, the increasing definition and dominance of the bourgeois view of women and their place, which was taking place throughout Europe and America in the eighteenth century. One of the issues crucial to the transformation of a feudal to the capitalist society was the creation of rigid private and public spheres, with gender at the core of that separation. Let me outline briefly how that separation affected the role of women in the bourgeois society and what was at stake in redefining the concept of femininity in the eighteenth century.

In *Family Fortunes: Men and Women of the English Middle Class, 1780–1850*, Leonore Davidoff and Catherine Hall seek to answer these questions, providing a scrupulous study of the family life in England over a period of about a hundred years. They focus on the families from the middle and upper middle class and base their analysis on a vast range of facts from archival and literary sources (both fiction and conduct material). Their aim is to show how "the sexual division of labour within families" became central "for the development of capitalist enterprise" and to delineate the main factors that contributed to that division.[50] At its roots lay the ideal of domesticity that limited woman's sphere to her home and family. It extended in various directions, causing far-reaching consequences with regard to the conduct and social position of women.

In the first place, the ideal of domesticity contained female sexuality within a tightly guarded familial structure. Davidoff and Hall compare woman's virtuosity to "a plant in the pot, limited and domesticated, sexually controlled, not spilling out into spheres in which she did not belong nor being overpowered by 'weeds' of social disorder" (192). In order to keep that "plant" within its pot, "most writers on educational subjects preferred home education for girls," its main advantage being the possibility of supervising their moral and physical development as well as instilling in them the values of domestic life and the importance of well-fulfilled duties as future wives and mothers.[51] "Weeds of social disorder," such as seduction out of wedlock and adultery, perceived as the remnants of libertine practices of aristocracy, became targets of severe attacks and censure. "Sexuality regarded as one of the most irrational forces, was relegated to the inner core of marriage, suppressing male desire and denying women any sexual feelings."[52] The concern for eliminating that part of a woman's life affected women's access to literature, art, and language. Reading and writing, in the light of their transgressive potential, became activities that demanded close scrutiny and censorship. Numerous conduct book writers, Hannah More and Jane West among them, stressed that

> no knowledge should be given without the context and function of morality, and any works of science should be scrutinized for tinctures of immo-

rality or deism before being given to girls. Women should be morally rather than intellectually educated, they thought, for they required the constraints of Christianity more than men.[53]

Language itself needed to be carefully monitored and purified of unsuitable expressions. The first expurgated version of Shakespeare's plays appeared in 1818, under the title *Family Shakespeare*. The representations of a bawdy and sexually voracious woman, still very much alive in the seventeenth and early eighteenth century, faded from the social scene and gave place to an innocent and passive Victorian maiden whose language, dress, and manners reflected "gentle femininity."[54]

The containment of women in the private/domestic sphere meant also withdrawal of women from business life. The studies performed by "Alice Clark for the seventeenth and Ivy Pinchbeck for the eighteenth and early nineteenth centuries have outlined the slow shift from women's active participation in commerce, farming and other business pursuits."[55] Such occupations as "gaoler, whitesmith, plumber, butcher, farmer, seedsman, tailor, saddler" (312), as well as jobs in public breweries, still available to women in the seventeenth and early eighteenth centuries, became all-male domains. Even such a "female" profession as midwifery "became professionalized into a career for men" by the end of the eighteenth century" (*The Sign of Angellica*, 20). The change in meaning of the term "spinster" from the woman who spins to a pejorative expression for an unmarried woman, and the extinction of such species as "fishwife, alewife, oysterwife, applewife," attest to the gradual shrinking of women's economic function to that of a housewife.[56]

The growth in scale of manufacturing enterprises, and change in the profile of agriculture due to the use of steam-powered machinery and chemistry, further contributed to the exclusion of women from the economic domain. That exclusion operated on several levels. Since girls' education consisted in acquiring accomplishments (the arts, drawing, piano playing, dancing), rather than concrete knowledge, women lacked scientific and technical preparation, necessary for performing highly specialized jobs. Furthermore, they lacked capital for investment, and skills to maintain authority "over a larger, more distanced workforce."[57] Women were encourged to choose those occupations that copied family roles and were considered "extensions of child-rearing" (293) or housekeeping; that is, teachers, governesses, innkeepers, nurses, and writers of children's and conduct books—categories of utilitarian literature as opposed to high art practiced by men.

The separation of occupations into male and female ran along the line dividing the indoor and outdoor activities, constraining women to the existence within the walls of a home.[58] The definition of indoors that is home as a proper space for women hampered their mobility. Certain modes of transportation relatively cheap, such as horseback riding, were banned as inappropriate.[59] Moreover, the presence of a woman alone in a public place threatened loss of status and respect. Thus, any business requiring access to transport or interaction with people, for instance selling or buying goods, automatically excluded women. The process of banishing women from the public economy, initiated in the eighteenth century, was crowned with full success in the nineteenth century, when in 1851 the Registrar General officially "introduced a new fifth class" that

> comprises large numbers of population that have hitherto been held to have no occupation; but it requires no argument to prove that the *wife*, the *mother*, the *mistress* of an English *family*—fills offices and discharges duties of no ordinary importance; or that children are or should be occupied in filial or household duties, and in tasks of education either at home or school.[60]

The model of a perfect mistress of a household implied "a special form of femininity which ran directly counter to acting as a visibly independent economic agent" (315).

That invisibility on the economic scene accounted for women's financial dependence on men. Despite the shift from land as the main form of property, the new bourgeois class based their laws of property on patrilineality and patriarchy. The financial position of women "if anything had deteriorated from the seventeenth century" (276). Fathers, brothers, and husbands continued to control legally the property of their female relatives. Thus, even rich orphaned heiresses depended largely on a host of male well-wishers whose incompetence or negligence could turn them penniless overnight, as happened in the case of Fanny Burney's heroine in *Camille*. Even if women could profit from a capital they were not allowed to control it. Susan Staves points to a poignant distinction made "between the interest of the 'family' understood as economic interests, and the interests of women, who seem to be individuals competing against the 'family' interests rather than integral and necessary parts of the family" (203). Such a distinction relegated women to the category of burdensome dependents whose needs could significantly diminish the goods accumulated over the generations by industrious men.

Thus the question of a daughter's marriage involved a careful calculation of what it meant in terms of financial gain or loss for the family. As we will see, wealth is a decisive factor in the choice of Clarissa's husband. Susan Staves disagrees with Lawrence Stone and Randolph Trumbach's claim that daughters of aristocratic and middle class families enjoyed freedom in their choices of husbands after 1660, when "the law of 'strict settlement' deprived the father of his power to give or withhold, by stipulating the provision allocated to each unborn child at the time of the parents' marriage" (214). In fact, argues Staves,

> other settlements provided that a daughter who married without the permission of a named relative was not to have a portion, and the Marriage Act of 1753 required parental consent for the marriage of a minor. Well-known upper class women who were coerced into marriages with men they did not like for financial reasons that made sense to their relatives are easy enough to bring to mind . . . Of greater practical importance than explicit denials of portions or clear coercion, daughters in the classes that married with settlements had little opportunity to meet and form relationship with men of whom their parents would not have approved, and in this way the socialization of daughters itself effectively and severely limited misalliances. (214–215)

If the actual situation of women did not change despite the legal changes in women's favor, what did change, maintains Staves, was the voice of authority—the church and state that determined religious and moral obligations of women were no longer the only sources of power. Female conduct became the subject and object of interest in conduct books, domestic novels, newspapers, and magazines. "In these more secular places," notes Staves, "indeed more private sources we see new ideological formulation that also legitimizes the subordination of women, but on new, more sentimental grounds" (222). Thus the rhetoric of the heart that emphasized the importance of feelings in the choice of a husband "added sense of personal responsibility for the consequences" and made woman "more psychologically dependent on her relationship with her husband" (224). That rhetoric masked successfully the state's interest in controlling the family and covered up the significance of women's "domestication," intent on banishing women from virtually every spot of a public sphere: economic, educational, literary, political.

Despite essential differences in historical and economic developments between England and France, the process of domesticating women in France evolved along similar lines and applied identical means to complete it.[61] In *Le Paradis des Femmes*, Carolyn Lougee discusses the controversy over the rights and the social position of aristocratic and middle-class women in France in the late seventeenth and early eighteenth centuries. Her study includes a wide variety of writings (treatises, conduct books, fiction, legal documents) that concern women and their social status. Lougee presents the views of two groups in opposition; the feminists—a shorthand term she uses to denote "the positive response to the question whether women should play a public role in French society," and anti-feminists—critics of women's participation in the salons.[62]

The impact of "précieuses" (women who frequented salons) on the social, cultural, and literary life of the Parisian élite rekindled interest in redefining and reevaluating women's vocation and intellectual capacities. The feminists encouraged the education of women, understood, however, as a necessary attribute of social grace: "they urged women to acquire the knowledge that would prepare them to lead salons, specifically moral philosophy" (27). Knowledge had to be combined with refinement ("savant") to enable women to perform successfully the duties of society ladies. Madame de Scudéry advocated the ideal of a women who "had an enlightened mind, good judgement, and knew how to speak and write well" (29). Being aware of educating women primarily for social functions, she stressed, however, the importance of caring for the mind in equal measure with the care of the body:

> It must not, however, be thought that I wish a woman not to be socially correct, and that she know not how to dance or sing, for on the contrary I wish her to know everything entertaining; but to tell the truth, I would like to see as much attention paid to the embellishing her mind as her body.[63]

The positive view towards women's education contributed to a redefining of the concept of marriage. Marriage was viewed as a yoke that repressed women's intellectual pursuits, burdening them with household chores and obligations:

> Du Bosc lamented the assignment of household tasks to women; it was 'a tyranny and a custom no less unjust than it is old to eject them from public and private governance as if they were capable only of spinning their distaffs. Their mind is suited to more exalted deeds.' It was a personal tragedy to stifle a good mind with boring little household tasks even though they contributed to the family fortune. But it was also a national calamity, a waste of national resources to send to the needle those capable of rendering great services to the state. (22)

The critique of marriage went even further than that. Some feminists postulated free love "on the grounds that it satisfied both the demands of women and the goals of increasing the population" (23). Others "advocated marriages that presupposed divorce" or proposed "term marriages" (24). All these proposals virtually sanctioned adultery and proclaimed sexual freedom for women. Moreover, in the name of love, the feminists accepted and justified misalliances. Thus, they encouraged the mixing of classes, emphasizing personal merits and accomplishments and regarding "esprit" and "civilité" as a passport to the category of "belles gens," independently of birth.

If, for feminists, woman was a human being with a mind to cultivate and sexual desires to fulfill, for the antifeminists she was only a mute body enclosed within the four walls of a home. They opposed fiercely the access of women to the public sphere, and disparaged the role the salons played in French social structure. Madame de Scudéry's ideal of an educated woman was attacked and criticized. Instead, a new educational system was proposed in which girls' education should "omit the arts of conversation and letter-writing" (191).

The attack on the salons and the prominent roles women played in them brought a renewed interest in woman's household role. The housewife disdained by the feminists and described in derogatory terms stepped again onto the pedestal.[64] In the newly celebrated view of marriage adultery was, of course, banned; instead "marriage and family life were glorified for the woman to make them attractive to her, and the role of love within marriage was magnified to engulf all a woman's affections" (65). Chastity acquired particular importance, and female virtue tended to be "defined in terms of chastity alone as in the case of Grenaille's definition of the *honnête femme* as the woman who stays at home and does not get seduced" (92). Sexuality was "to be channelled into the service of reason through marriage" (66). Consequently, women became isolated from society; they were allotted a place only within the family structure, performing the duties of obliging daughters, wives, or mothers.[65] Perrault (1694) envisioned the ideal of a domestic woman in the following way : "Enter into the lodgings of honest families / And see the mothers and daughters working there, / Thinking only of their task and receiving well / Their father or their husband when he returns in the evening."[66]

The views professed by anti-feminists reflected the conviction that women's access to the public sphere would cause irreparable disruptions in the social structure. Marriage and the domestic sphere were offered as an antidote to the "reign of women" in which "the love of pleasure and money succeeds that of virtues" (84). The aftermath of the revolution made "aristocratic women scapegoats," blaming them "for all the intrigues that blocked reform."[67] The resolution of the controversy between feminists and antifeminists was a full victory for the anti-feminists, on legal, cultural, literary, educational, economic, and social grounds. "Au début du XIX siècle," observes Pierre Darmon,

> le territoire de la femme est circonscrit, codifié et normalisé selon des principes rigoureux enfin consacrés par la Code civil . . . L'insertion de la femme dans l'ordre nouveau s'opère alors selon des modalités strictement conformes au schéma bourgeois.[68]

> [At the beginning of the nineteenth century women's territory was circumscribed, codified, and normalized according to the strict rules of the civil code. The process of transplanting women into the new order followed closely the methods characteristic of the bourgeois scheme.]

The royal mistresses, the précieuses, those ambivalent and highly subversive figures appeared only on the pages of romances. The model of female perfection found its personification in Queen Victoria and her exemplary dedication to her husband and children. Thus, concludes Darmon, marriage and maternity became the only viable options for women.

The historical studies quoted above document the significance of the changes in the perception of women's role that occurred mainly in the eighteenth century. They show the centrality of the distinction between the public and private spheres to the development of the bourgeois society and consider gender the key to that distinction. Thus the husband/father, responsible for supporting his family, "became anchored in the occupational sphere outside the family," whereas the wife/mother "was anchored in the family," assuming "major responsibility for housework, child care, and making a happy home."[69] While women, forced by physical, psychological, and social barriers, remained within their small private worlds, men had the privileged position of being able to move freely between both spheres. When tired of the tumult and pace of their busy public lives, they could always retire to the niche of their homes. The poem "My Husband" (1825) paints a picture of marital bliss and eulogizes the figure of a devoted husband who shares with his wife the joys and sorrows of a daily life:

> Who first inspired my virgin breast,
> With tumults not to be expressed,
> And gave to life unwonted zest?
>   My husband.
>
> Who told me that his gains were small,
> But that whatever might befall,

> To me he'd gladly yield them all?
>   My husband.
>
> Who shun'd the giddy town's turmoil,
> To share with me the garden's toil,
> And joy with labour reconcile?
>   My husband.
>
> Whose arduous struggles long maintain'd
> Adversity's cold hand restrain'd
> And competence at length attain'd
>   My husband.[70]

Contrary to our expectations, the author of the poem, was not the wife, but the husband, James Luckcock, whose grave illness prompted him to write it. So complete was the woman's confinement to the private sphere, that the husband felt entitled to appropriate her voice in order to produce his own public eulogy. Thus the wife became a mute, faceless, and nameless presence, necessary to reflect and magnify his exceptional qualities.

2
Letters as a Means of Liberation for Female Correspondents

THE GOAL OF THE CENSORING MECHANISMS OPERATING IN CONDUCT material was to define a model of female correspondence that would reduce epistolary contacts to the minimum and thus limit the risks of jeopardizing the stability and the smooth functioning of a household. Detailed guidelines and instructions were aimed at keeping under strict control the content and direction of female letters in real life. The image of a perfect female writer (predominant in the conduct books published at the end of the eighteenth and at the beginning of the nineteenth centuries) was that of a meek, self-effacing creature whose letters—innocent compositions, a mixture of prudence and filial obedience—were destined for a "bonfire." That model should not, of course, have been limited to conduct books. The epistolary fiction of that period, working hand in glove with the censors of decorum, was also bound to raise the questions of how, of what, and to whom women could write letters. And yet the epistolary heroines in the novels of Aphra Behn, Mary Hearne, and Eliza Haywood were a far cry from the model letter writer promoted in conduct material. The discrepancy between these heroines writing transgressive letters and the model letter writer from conduct material provoked staunch attacks launched by Hannah More and other writers at the sentimental novel and called for refinement of censoring practices.

The puzzling question, however, is, how did these heroines and their adventures in, and through, letters, manage to enter and dominate the novel in the eighteenth century in the first place? Who sanctioned their presence? Which censoring mechanism failed to see the letter's potential for unruliness? Conduct material definitely fulfilled its obligation of closing any venue that could threaten the stability of the family and the separation of the private and public spheres. But the rule of conduct was not the only censor of letters. The other censor guarded the law of genre, which defined the appropriate form with regard to style and content of correspondence, seen as a literary

2: Letters as a Means of Liberation for Female Correspondents 53

activity, not as a mere act of communication. As I will argue, the law of genre is the main culprit in the abuse of decorum caused by women's letters.

Similarly to the law of decorum, the law of genre operated within the gender division into male and female domains. And similarly to the law of decorum, it was bent on keeping women within the private, domestic sphere, thus restricting women's access to the public literary scene reserved for men. In practice, it enlisted literary censors operating through book prefaces, reviews, treatises, and conduct books to search for a "genre niche" designed for women (cf. Dunton's or Gisborne's reflections on the literary genres suitable for women).[1] However, it was not enough to merely assign such a niche. Like the law of decorum with its persuasive rhetoric of feminine domestic virtue supported by religion and nature, the law of genre needed a backup of reasons that would correlate the feminine gender with a specific genre and account for that correlation in a rational, or rather a "natural," way.

The claim made by the French literary theoreticians in the seventeenth and eighteenth centuries that there existed a natural affinity between women and letters supplied a perfect tool to help create that feminine genre niche. As early as in 1635, Charles Du Boscq, the editor of *Nouveau Recueil des lettres des dames de ce temps avec leurs réponses* declared that "les lettres ne sont pas seulement l'héritage de notre sexe" [letters do not belong solely to our sex].[2] In 1663, the Abbé Cotin claimed that not only did women match men as letter writers but that they proved to be superior to men, at least in two categories of the epistolary domain: "les letters de compliment et de galanterie" (995) [letters of compliments and gallantry].

In the chapter "Des Ouverages de l'esprit" in his book *Les Caractères* (1687), La Bruyère voiced his own opinions on authors, works, and genres, providing "universal" criteria for establishing a literary canon. In the course of his discussion on letters "he granted status to the epistolary genre while, at the same time, encoding it as a sort of writing at which female practitioners excelled."[3] Analyzing the style of two famous letter writers, Balzac and Voiture, La Bruyère concludes that,

> Je ne sais si l'on pourra jamais mettre dans des lettres plus d'esprit, plus de tours, plus d'agrément et plus de style que l'on en voit dans celles de Balzac et de Voiture; elles sont vides de sentiments qui n'ont régné que depuis leur temps, et qui doivent aux femmes leur naissance. Ce sexe va plus loin que le nôtre dans ce genre d'écrire. Elles trouvent sous leur plume des tours et des expressions qui souvent en nous ne sont l'effet que d'un

long travail et d'une pénible recherche: elles sont heureuses dans le choix des termes, qu'elles placent si juste, que tous connus qu'ils sont, ils ont le charme de la nouveauté, et semblent être faits seulement pour usage où elles mettent; il n'appartient qu'à elles de faire lire dans un seul mot tout un sentiment, et de rendre délicatement une pensée qui est délicate; elles ont un enchaînement de discours inimitable, qui se suit naturellement, et qui n'est lié que par le sens. Si les femmes étaient toujours correctes, j'oserais dire que les lettres de quelques-unes d'entre elles seraient peut-être ce que nous avons dans notre langue de mieux écrit.[4]

[I do not know if one will ever be able to put into letters more wit, more turns, more pleasure and more style than what one sees in Balzac and Voiture; theirs are void of sentiments that have reigned only since their time, and which owe their birth to women. This sex goes further than ours in this sort of writing. They find beneath their pen turns of phrase and expressions which often in us are only the effect of long work and tiresome research; they are fortunate in their choice of terms, which they place so well that, as familiar as they are, they have the charm of novelty, and seem to be made exclusively for the purpose to which they are put; only they have the ability to render an entire feeling through one word, and to express delicately a thought that is delicate; they have an inimitable mode of association, which follows naturally, and which is linked only by meaning. If women were always correct, I dare say that the letters of some of them would perhaps be what is best written in our language.][5]

La Bruyère's comment on women and letters touches on a number of issues that concern the admission of women to the literary sphere. Firstly, La Bruyère makes a clear distinction between male and female modes of writing. Like Du Boscq, he divides the literary world into "notre sexe" and "notre langue" (us = men) and "ce sexe" and "les femmes" (they = women), himself adopting the position of authority as the spokesman for "notre langue" and "notre sex."[6] Secondly, his apparent praise for the superiority of women over men in the domain of letter writing consists in finding flaws and turning them into assets. If women write better letters than men, it is not because they have wit, or know the rules of grammar or rhetoric. Rather their writing is a result of a "natural" propensity to "charm," combined with luck in choosing the right word or expression. The area where they excel most is the domain of feeling ("sentiment") and delicate thoughts ("une pensée qui est délicate").

La Bruyère's comment implies a series of restrictions aimed at containing women's writing not only within a specific genre but within a specific form of that genre. By assigning women to the epistolary domain as the genre most suited to their talents, he implicitly excludes them from other genres, such as epic, tragedy, and complex forms of poetry where the knowledge of rhetoric, grammar, and rules of composition play an essential part. In John Dunton's *The Female War* (1697) Madam Godfrey, defending women from the attacks of Sir Thomas, who accuses them of invading the literary, that is male, sphere, says,

> A few Airy Songs, or a Copy of whineing Love-Verses to our Faithless unconscionable Bajazets, it is for the most part what we pretend to do. If by a Miracle we write a New Play now and then, or vamp up an old one, you know that is our Top ... But for High and Mighty Epic, for the most perfect Work of Human Nature, we leave that entirely to you, none of us having ever invaded that Province.[7]

Her reply attests to the importance of keeping women away from "high" genres and reflects men's fear of women's ventures into the forbidden territory.

Moreover, La Bruyère's remarks on style and content of female letters assign them to a specific category within the broad epistolary area. The particular propensity for the expression of sentiments affects how and what they write. Female epistolary writing is regarded as a spontaneous flow of emotion—women write as naturally as they breathe. Their writing resembles automatic writing; the female hand transcribes the dictates of the heart while the mind keeps silent. As Louis XIV himself noted, the letters of Mme de Coligny "étaient toutes de feu; le coeur y avait subtilisé l'esprit, qui fait bien de se taire quand le coeur parle" [were all fire; the heart replaced the mind, which would better keep silent when the heart speaks].[8] Since women's writing comes from the heart, the logical consequence is that it will be limited to the matters of sentiment. The female epistolary creation is then narrowed down to only one type—a love letter *sensu stricto,* or a letter expressing familiar sentiments, those of a mother, a daughter, a wife.[9]

The fact that the act of letter writing presupposes the existence of an addressee provides an additional safeguard against granting women too much independence. A letter writer is always inscribed in an epistolary relationship in which the bond between the writer and his/her partner shapes their correspondence and determines its content. The writer of a love letter or a familiar letter, situated vis-à-vis the addressee, participates in a dialogue in which the absent interlocutor occupies as much space and requires as much attention as the letter writer. Thus the "I" of a letter does not have a life of its own—it is dependent on the "you" of the addressee.

Granting women access to the epistolary domain allows their voices to speak only from within a relationship, confining them to their societal and familial roles. And this is the only proper place for women to be. James Cochrane envisions the ideal woman defined only in her relationship with a man: "the empire of love and sense is appropriate to Woman: the ascendent to genius belongs to Man: to acquire his love and esteem is the highest aim at which female ambition ought to soar."[10] Moreover, according to the anonymous author of *A Lady's Friend* (1837), letter writing promotes altruism since it requires the letter writer to take into account the concerns and interests of the addressee.

La Bruyère's comment on style concentrates on the "natural" ease with which women supposedly express their emotions. They do not need to study rhetoric or employ "long travail et pénible recherche." Their style is an innate gift, always at their disposal. La Bruyère's comments become a recurring element in every debate that seeks to divide writing into feminine and masculine modes. The heroine of Pietro Chiari's novel *Le memorie di Madama Tolot ovvero la giocatrice di lotto,* published in 1754, justifies the daring act of publishing her memoirs in the following way: "Un libro di memorie scritto per mio divertimento, scritto in brevissimo tempo, in quanto abbraccia le azioni mie di soli sei anni, e scritto finalmente per mano d'una donna, non poteva essere un capolavoro dell'ingegno umano ... In esso ebbe più parte la natura che l'arte." [A book of memories written for my own pleasure, in a very short time, even though it describes the events of six years of my life, a product of a woman's hand cannot claim to be a work of human genius ... In it nature played a more important part than art.][11]

Disguised as a compliment, the theory of "natural" gifts for writing sentimental letters ("sentimental" meaning pertaining to emotions) supplied a convenient excuse, a rational explanation why women did not need either a classical education, including rhetoric, Latin or Greek orations, or rules for persuasive writing.[12] In *Social Letters,* Margaret Cavendish complains of the shortcomings of the education devised for women: "in your last letter you advised me to write a book of orations, but how should I write orations, who know no rules in rhetoric, nor never went to school, but only learned to read and write at home."[13] Because of inferior education, she concludes, women will always be at a disadvantage when it comes to a battle of wits with men:

> Women can never have so strong a judgement nor clear understanding, nor so perfect rhetoric, to speak orations with that eloquence, as to persuade so

forcibly, to command so powerfully, to entice so subtly, and to insinuate so gently into the souls of men. (174)

A female letter, limited to the thematics of love, and deprived of the access to rhetorical tools, buried a woman author under the looming figures of mistress, mother, and wife. On the literary scene it occupied a celebrated though inferior position in the hierarchy of the overall epistolary production. In Fritz Nies's words,

> 'naturel', 'aisance', 'négligence', 'absence de recherche', et 'bagatelles' sont des mots clés qui constamment servent à caractériser ces lettres tant admirées. Il semble que la plupart des mots-clés cités—mots, qui dans le dernier tiers du XVIIe siècle, commençaient à caractériser la lettre féminine—soient ceux qui d'une façon générale, servaient à définir les genres mineurs. (1001)

> ['natural,' 'ease,' 'negligence,' 'lack of research,' 'trifles' are the key words used for characterizing these letters that command so much admiration. It seems that most of these key words quoted here, words that in the last decade of the seventeenth century began to refer to feminine letters, were the words that were usually applied when defining minor genres.]

Thus the campaign of praise directed at women's letters succeeded in a double movement: it managed not only to exclude women from "serious" literary endeavors but also to marginalize their contribution to the epistolary production.[14]

Male epistles, on the other hand, were not subjected to any "natural" restrictions of content or style. Men, by virtue of their varied interests and thorough education, could write letters on a diversity of subjects. Thomas Gisborne notes that

> Letters which pass between men, commonly relate in a greater degree to actual business. Even young men, on whom the cares of life are not yet devolved in their full weight, will frequently be led to enlarge to their absent friends on *topics not only of interesting nature, but also of a serious cast:* on the studies which they are respectively pursuing, on the advantages and disadvantages of the profession.[15]

The "serious cast" and "interesting nature" allowed men to transform familiar letters into collections of letters tailored for publication, following in the steps of Cicero, Pliny the Younger, Seneca, and Petrarch. The difference between these epistles and female letters lies not only in the subjects they embrace—politics, literature, art, philosophy, religion, as opposed to the themes of love exploited in female letters—but also in the center of attention that in male epistles shifts to the letter writer. The non-egoistical "I" of female letters, always defined against the "you" of the addressee, changes into an egoistical "I" which attracts all attention to itself. This can be seen, for example, in Petrarch's *Le familiari*. The priority of art over nature implied by Petrarch's reediting, revising, and even inventing letters to nonexistent recipients plays a crucial role in La Bruyère's theory. Although men lack the "natural" gifts for writing from the heart, they have "esprit," which allows them to reproduce that writing at will. In addition, they have access to all the rhetorical tools and traditions, and therefore they excel in the art of persuasion and the art of imitation.

Herbert W. Benario sees Tacitus's style as being closely modeled on Cicero's, and asks:

> But why is the style so different from all else by Tacitus? The ability and capacity to write in various styles, almost as it were, to change clothes, were the marks of a trained rhetoritician, who realized that different genres of literature required different garbs.[16]

No wonder that the Abbé Cotin, educated in the classical tradition, boasted of "the stylistic consciousness which enabled him to write in a myriad of manners and genres."[17] And Jean-Michel Pelous, praising Count de Guilleragues for his extraordinary skill in imitating a female voice to perfection in *Lettres portugaises,* claims that what motivated Guilleragues to undertake this challenge was his desire "to prove himself as a writer of versatility, equally at ease in both serious and light genres" (563).

What transpired then from the commentaries on letter writing first elaborated by contemporary literary theories and later on repeated in conduct material, was a clear-cut opposition between the male and female modes of writing. That opposition was organized as follows:

MALE: ESPRIT = MIND/ARTIFICIAL/LITERARY
FEMALE: HEART/NATURAL/NON-LITERARY

Its function, just like the separation of social spheres into male and female, was to confine women to one category while allowing men a privileged position of moving freely between both. In addition to his own territory, a male writer could always enter the realm of the feminine appropriating the female voice by virtue of rhetorical tools and imitative skills.

Lettres portugaises, published in France in 1669, provides a practical illustration of that theoretical premise. It marks a milestone in the development and the direction of epistolary fiction because, as soon as it appeared, contemporary critics hailed it as the model of feminine epistolary writing. This short novel consists of five letters supposedly written by a Portuguese nun, Mariane, to her French lover, an army officer, who, after a brief love affair, had left her and returned to France. *Lettres portugaises* offered to the reading public a woman's passionate outburst that both dissected and celebrated unrequited love. It presented the image of a female victim, seduced and abandoned by her lover, an image that reinforced the dependence of a woman on a relationship with a man: Mariane's existence relied on her role as the unfortunate mistress of the French officer. The style of her letters was erratic and repetitious, defying the rules of composition and rhetoric. But it was precisely

> these excesses, these faults, these violations of traditional rhetoric that proved their authenticity. Confused speech disturbing the logical order of syntax was considered to be the natural expression and the surest sign of passion, the mirror of the disordered state of the soul.[18]

Since women lacked education and were inferior to men in reason, what logically followed was their superiority in the domain of passion and its expression.[19] Both the content and the style of *Lettres portugaises* then complied with the theoretical assumptions that underlined the ideal of female epistolarity. Its appearance confirmed the earlier critics' (Du Boscq and the Abbé Cotin) belief in women's particular talents for a spontaneous and uncontrolled expression of sentiment, and provided a veritable proof for La Bruyère's theory.

The authorship of *Lettres portugaises* went undisputed until the beginning of our century. The debate whether its author was a real nun (a certain sister Mariana Alcoforado) or Racine's friend, Count de Guilleragues, is far from over. For instance, Peggy Kamuf's psychoanalytic reading (1982) of Mariane's letters establishes without a doubt the nun as the author, challenging the critics whose interpretation of the stylistic and linguistic aspects points to Guilerragues' authorship (F. C. Green, [1926], Leo Spitzer [1953]).

A brief look at the critical arguments in that debate will provide an illustration of the tenacity of the theoretical clichés with regard to female and male modes of writing. Critics who accept Guilleragues as the author of *Lettres portugaises* praise his skill in imitating the female voice so perfectly. In *Told in Letters* (1966) Robert Day writes:

> The reader has been presented with page after page of the most rarefied subjectivity.... Another striking feature of the letters was the Nun's absence of control—an absence so carefully contrived that its artifice went unnoticed until recently. The style was carefully calculated to give the

impression that the Nun was dashing her unpremeditated thoughts down on paper as fast as they came.[20]

In *The Beginnings of the Epistolary Novel in France, Italy, and Spain* (1939), Charles Kany, who regards *Lettres portugaises* as a series of genuine letters written by the Portuguese nun, and only translated by Guilleragues, notes:

> The first French version, made in 1669 by Pierre Girardin de Guilleragues, displays a typically feminine style ... [Mariane] writes as she feels and her mood often changes from sentence to sentence. The sincerity with which she bares her soul permits the reader to follow closely the stages of faith, doubt, and despair through which the heroine passes.[21]

Both Day and Kany reproduce faithfully La Bruyère's separation of letter writing into male and female domains, quoting wit, artifice, and literariness as the male qualities, and natural, i.e., nonliterary, effusions of the heart as feminine.

The crimes Mariane committed against the law of genre in the name of passion ("les fautes commises contre les lois de genre," Pelous, 559), her disregard of the formal and stylistic rules governing epistolary composition, her apparent ignorance of rhetoric, contributed to creating a new law of epistolary genre suitable for women. As long as the epistolary voice was confined to the thematics of passion and expressed it in a spontaneous way, it was a priori feminine. As Isabelle Landy-Houillon observes in the Introduction to the 1983 edition of *Lettres portugaises*, "la lettre d'amour, tout au moins de type portugais, ne peut être que féminine, même sous la plume d'un homme" [a love letter, in particular the Portuguese kind, could not be but feminine, even if written by a man].[22] Due to its immense popularity in Europe, in particular in France (21 editions in six years) and England (the English translation of 1687 ran into tenth edition by 1740) *Lettres portugaises* represented the absolute height of the female epistolary expression, thus providing an ideal for imitation. Madame de Sévigné referred to it as "a Portuguese," meaning an affectionate letter whose "passionate folly can only be justified by love itself."[23]

However, in the fervor of praising the characteristics that imposed the desirable restrictions of content and style on female letters, the creators and supporters of the literary theories disregarded two elements that would later come to signify grave risks to the execution of the law of decorum. These two elements were: the letter's transgressive potential, and the all-conquering force of unbridled passion. In the *Lettres portugaises* a letter plays a double role. Its explicit function is that of a repository of sentiment. Letters mean for Mariane pages to be filled with her musings, confessions, resolutions, accusations, and doubts. The very act of writing letters gives Mariane the opportunity to relive her passion, to recreate it in words. It erases the boundaries between reality and the sensual memories, inducing Mariane to revel "in the pleasure of the epistolary contact."[24]

But what is implicit in her story is the practical importance of letters in conducting their love affair prior to the breakup. Since Mariane lives in a convent, presumably strictly guarded from any contact with the outside world, letters are the only way of reaching the outside world, and her lover. Letters facilitate the actual physical contact since they can provide them with information about the time and place of their meeting, or about any sudden or unexpected change of plans. Mariane mentions the invaluable services of Doña Brites who acts as a go-between and smuggles the lovers' letters in and out of the convent. Thus letters are the actual accomplices in the act of transgression—Mariane as a nun who has yielded to the temptation of the flesh, breaks all the imaginable rules implied in the concept of a convent: moral, social, religious. The letter, then, not only narrates passion but promotes it by transcending the convent walls.

The *Lettres portugaises* depicts the overwhelming power of passion, which, in Mariane's words, reduced her to the state of utter confusion: "Je ne sais pas ni que je suis, ni ce que je fais, ni ce que je désire; je suis déchirée par mille mouvements contraires" [I don't know either what I am, or what I do, or what I desire. I am torn apart by a thousand contrary impulses].[25] Passion deprived her of reason: "vous m'avez donné une passion qui m'a fait perdre la raison" (95). That passion disregards and destroys conventions, filial obligations, religious bonds. Mariane breaks the rules of the convent, sacrifices the love of her parents, accepts the loss of her reputation. She is fully aware of it, yet she would rather confront the consequences of breaking the social and moral obligations than conceive of losing her lover. Of all the misfortunes that befell her, his "Ingratitude" is "the worst of [her] misfortunes." Mariane revels in the "grim pleasure" of contemplating sacrifices she would gladly bear for his sake, including the sacrifice of her own life. In spite of the despair she experiences at the thought of never seeing her lover again, she feels gratitude for having known what passion is. The *Lettres portugaises* paints passion as a force that knows no boundaries and is unstoppable. It also implies the power of letters as agents that are capable of unleashing that force and keeping it alive.

The writers as well as the heroines of two early epistolary novels published in England, Mary Hearne's *The Lover's Week* (1718) and Aphra Behn's *Love-Letters between a Noble-Man and his Sister* (1683) follow the model of *Lettres portugaises* in compliance with the law of genre and unite their voices in the spontaneous expression of sentiment.[26] However, in their novels the focus shifts from letter as a repository of passionate outbursts to letter as a useful tool in conducting illicit liaisons. Rather then dwell on the aftermath of a love affair, both novels concentrate on its initial stages in which letters become indispensable agents in initiating and continuing illicit liaisons.

Behn's novel traces the birth and development of a passionate love affair between Sylvia and Philander. Philander is married to Sylvia's sister Myrtilla, so the clandestine nature of their affair forces them to resort to letters as a means of communication. As in *Lettres portugaises*, letters both narrate passion and foster it, by allowing the lovers to avoid the censure of Sylvia's parents and her sister, Philander's wife. As in *Lettres portugaises,* passion is an overwhelming force, sweeping away all the reservations and scruples on Sylvia's part, and marital obligations on Philander's. In one of the letters to Sylvia, Philander envisions an imaginary land of passion in which "there is no troublesome Honor . . . no Parents checking their dear Delights . . . no slavish Matrimonial Ties to restrain their nobler Flame. No Spies to interrupt their blest Appointments."[27] Even though Sylvia paints a rather grim image of a woman who yielded to temptation and calls herself "a poor, lost Virgin languishing and undone, sighing her willing Rape to the deaf Shades and Fountains, filling the Woods with Cries, swelling the murmuring Rivulets with Tears" (217), her "Rape" is preceded by the adjective "willing," and as she confesses in another letter to Philander, she is "fond of being undone" (223).

The attempts of Sylvia's parents and Philander's wife to separate the lovers prove futile, and the lovers, defying social conventions and obligations, escape to "sanctuary in a small cottage near the sea shore" (281). One of Sylvia's last letters to Philander seems a rather bold refusal to conform to worldly censure:

> Love has arm'd my Soul, and I'll pursue my Fortune with that Height of Fortitude as shall surprise the World; yes, Philander, since I have lost my Honor, Fame, and Friends, my Interest, and my Parents, and all for the mightier Love, I'll stop at nothing now, if there be any Hazards more to run, I'll thank the spiteful Fates that bring 'em on, and will even tire them out with my unweary'd Passion. Love on, Philander, if thou darst, like me . . . nothing shall take one Grain of Love from my resolved Heart, nor make me shed a Tear of Penitance for loving thee. (277)

Sylvia considers herself stronger than Philander in facing the hostility of the world. She is determined to remove all the obstacles which

2: Letters as a Means of Liberation for Female Correspondents 63

society and its conventions placed on her way to happiness with her lover.

The heroine of Mary Hearne's *The Lover's Week*, like Sylvia, is resolved on having a lover of her own choice. She refuses to accept the husband chosen for her by her aunt. In six letters to her friend, Emilie, Amaryllis narrates her love story. In them she includes or mentions the letters sent to or received from her lover. These letters, as she herself points out, enabled them to communicate in spite of her aunt's vigilance, and eventually helped them to devise a plan of escape to a quiet place in the country where they can enjoy each other's company. Like Mariane and Sylvia, Amaryllis knows that she has exposed herself to the world's censure, yielding to "a passion so violent that it outwent Consideration."[28] She does not regret it, however, since she has the "Satisfaction that it is for the Man" she likes (88). Like Sylvia,[29] Amaryllis openly defies social conventions:

> had I taken my Aunt's Advice and married the Duke of A____, whom I could never have loved, I had not only made myself unhappy, but my indifference to him should have given him, and all the World Reason to have been very free with my character, and should have undergone the scandal without the Satisfaction. (88)

Behn's and Hearne's novels focus on the depiction of passion in much the same way as the *Lettres portugaises*.[30] They also represent passion as a force propelling the heroines to transgress social norms and conventions. However, they allow their protagonists to enjoy the forbidden fruits of their rebellion, and represent them as heroes, not victims. Janet Todd marvels at the unabashed vigor and candor which accompany descriptions of these illicit passions: "Women writers like Behn and Manley presented irregular loves and bigamous marriages as part fictional, part nonfictional, with a sparkle quite missing from the later accounts of unwedded sex and illigitimate births."[31] Unlike Mariane, abandoned by her lover, Sylvia and Amaryllis remain with their lovers and retain their love, at least, until the end of the narrative. Any possibility of punishment on account of having engaged in an illicit love affair is thus removed. The final letters of both Sylvia and Amaryllis are defiant declarations against the social order to which they are expected to conform.

Letters become accomplices in those acts of rebellion. Both novels emphasize the indispensability of a letter as a means of clandestine communication. Letters travel freely between lovers, and, apart from one instance in Behn's novel, the attempts to intercept them prove unsuccessful due to the ingenuity of the messengers and the lovers themselves. In fact, the ways in which letters are smuggled in and out, and the methods used to divert the watchfulness of the guardians, are described in most minute detail. In one of her letters to Philander, Sylvia relates the moment of terror she experienced when his letter was delivered to her:

> I have at last recover'd Sense enough to tell you, I have receiv'd your Letter by Dorillus, and which had like to have been discover'd; for he prudently enough put it under the Strawberries he brought me in a Basket, fearing he should get no other opportunity to give it to me . . . there were some Leaves of Fern put at the Bottom between the Basket and the Letter which by good fortune came not with the Strawberries, and after a Minute or two I took up the Basket, and walking carelessly up and down the Garden sat down till my Mother had eat her Fill of Fruit, and gave me an Opportunity to retire to my Apartment and open your Letter. (219)

This account of how Sylvia managed to have the letter delivered in her mother's presence sounds almost like an instruction in deceit.

In creating a letter of passion as a feminine domain, the law of genre wanted to restrict and to exclude women from the literary territory. However, it proved to be a blessing in disguise since the letter of passion paradoxically played a liberating role not only in fiction but also in real life.[32] It opened the public sphere for women writers and allowed them to contest openly the restrictions imposed on them by social conventions. Even though the female epistolary voice was limited to the expression of sentiment, it was nevertheless heard and acknowledged. Using fictional love letters as a means of entering the public sphere, Behn, Hearne, and Haywood (among many others) managed to achieve public success and recognition, and were able to become professional writers. Virginia Woolf celebrated Behn as the first woman in England who earned her living by her pen:

> She was a middle-class woman with all the plebeian virtues of humour, vitality, and courage; a woman forced by the death of her husband and some unfortunate adventures of her own to make a living by her wits. She had to work on equal terms with men. She made, by working hard, enough to live on. The importance of that fact outweighs anything that she actually wrote . . . for here begins the freedom of the mind, or rather the possibility that in the course of time the mind will be free to write what it likes.[33]

Thus women writers launched out into the writing business with the support of the supposedly harmless—in terms of public exposure—love letters.[34] As Eliza Leslie's vehement attacks demonstrate, as late as 1859, women writers, following in the footsteps of their literary predecessors, were exploiting the literary potential of love letters:

> Then there are young ladies born with the organ of letter-writing amazingly developed, and increased by perpetual practice, who can scarcely become acquainted with a gentleman possessing brains without volunteering a correspondence with him. And then ensues a long epistolary dialogue on nothing, or at least nothing worth reading or remembering . . . Sometimes there are attempts at moralizing or criticism, or sentimentalizing—but nothing is ever elicited that, to a third person, can afford the least amusement or improvement, or excite the least interest. Yet, strange to say, gentlemen have been inveigled into this sort of correspondence, even by ladies who *have made business afterwards selling the letters for publication, and making money out of them.* And such epistles have actually been printed. We do not suppose they have been read. The public is very stubborn in refusing to read what neither amuses, interests, or improves, even when a publisher is so weak as to print such things. (*Behavior Book, a Guide and Manual for Ladies as Regards Their Conversation, Manner, Dress . . . etc.*, 163, my emphasis)

What clearly irks Leslie here is that the love letters she refers to do not seem to be sincere expressions of passion, but rather a cynical exploitation of passion, in which heart serves purely monetary purposes. The love letter appears then to be a stumbling block of significant proportions at the intersection of the private and public domains—a perfect plan to create a restrictive genre gone wrong.

Around 1720, the spirit of gay abandon evident in the adventures of Sylvia and Amaryllis, whose letters celebrate their new-found freedom from family ties, begins to fade, giving way to a sense of concern about the social consequences of clandestine communications. Montesquieu's *Lettres persanes* examines the efficacy of control over feminine letters. The scene in his novel is a harem, apparently an antithesis of a convent, yet not unlike it in many respects. Like a convent, a harem denotes an enclosed space reserved for women whose security is strictly guarded (by eunuchs, not by nuns)—"security," in this case, meaning prohibition of any contact with the outside world. Whereas a convent seeks to channel women's interests and sentiments into the service of God, a harem serves a similar purpose, substituting a master for God. His mundane needs define the role of women. Since they are to provide pleasure and children for the master, all their thoughts and cares are directed towards maintaining physical attractiveness to ensure their master's favor. Thus, a harem represents a locus of unanimous feminine passion, carefully watched to keep it from overflowing.

In the *Lettres persanes,* during the period of Usbek's visit in France, his wives are allowed to express their passion only in the letters addressed to him. In fact, in three letters to Usbek from Fatmé, Zashi, and Zélis, the images of female passion repeat and reinforce each other. Their passion, like their life, is communal, not individual. Fatmé writes to Usbek:

> Je me rappelle ce temps heureux où tu venais dans mes bras; un songe flatteur, qui me séduit, me montre ce cher objet de mon amour, mon imagination se perde dans ses désirs, comme elle se flatte dans ses espérances . . . Qu'une femme est malheureuse d'avoir des désirs si violents, lorsqu'elle est privée de celui qui peut seul les satisfaire. Vous êtes bien cruels, vous autres hommes! Vous êtes charmés que nous ayons des passions que nous ne puissions pas satisfaire.[35]

> [I remember those happy times when you used to come to my arms: a delightful illusion leads me on, showing me the image of what I love so dearly; my imagination loses itself in its desire, and deceives itself by its hopes . . . How wretched a woman is, having such violent desires, when she is deprived of the only man who can appease them. You men are cruel! It delights you that we have passions that we cannot satisfy.][36]

Zashi to Usbek: "Les hommes ne sont exposés qu'aux dangers qui menacent leur vie, et nous sommes, à tous les instants, dans la crainte de perdre notre vie ou notre vertu" [The only dangers that men are exposed to are those that threaten their lives; while we, at every moment, are in fear of losing our lives or our virtue.] (L 47)

Zélis to Usbek:

> La Nature, industrieuse en faveur des hommes, ne s'est pas bornée à leur donner des désirs: elle a voulu que nous en eussions nous-mêmes, et que nous fussions des instruments animés de leur félicité: elle nous a mises dans le feu des passions, pour les faire vivre tranquilles. (L 62)

> [Nature, among other devices she employs for the benefit of men, did not confine herself to giving desires to them alone but decreed that we should have them, and should actively provide them with contentment. She made us feel the heat of passion so that their lives should be quiet.] (128)

But if women can express their passion in the letters to Usbek, that is channel it in the right direction, there is always a possibility of changing that direction and carrying on an illicit correspondence. Usbek's fear of such correspondence is based on the recognition that once a letter exits the private sphere, it is difficult to control its course, and on his belief that women have a "natural" propensity to deceit. Allusions to that propensity are scattered throughout the novel. Eunuch Jaron writes to the First Eunuch: "Je sais comment je dois me conduire avec ce sexe, qui, quand on ne lui permet pas d'être vain, commence à devenir superbe, et qu'il est moins aisé d'humilier que d'anéantir (L 22) [I know how to behave towards this sex, which, if not indulged in its vanity, starts to grow arrogant, and which it is harder to humiliate than to destroy, 70]. Rica agrees with Jaron that it is a difficult task to keep women under control. The French husbands have resigned themselves to their wives' infidelities and do not resort to "the prudent measures taken to protect women in Asia— veils to cover them up, prisons to keep them in, the watchfulness of the eunuchs" (L 55). They doubt whether the physical constraints and surveillance over women would bring desirable results and believe that too strict control might even aggravate the situation by "sharpening the sex's wits" (L 55). Usbek, however, has full faith in the efficacy of physical supervision and gives the Chief Eunuch absolute power over the seraglio to suppress any signs of unrest or disobedience, encouraged by Usbek's absence and a temporary suspension of his immediate authority. Hence, he orders interception and careful examination of every letter that leaves the seraglio. The seraglio turns into a place ruled by terror: "Il ne nous est plus permis de nous parler; ce seroit un crime de nous écrire: nous n'avons plus rien de libre que les pleurs" (L 156) [We are no longer allowed to speak to each other; it would be a crime to write; the only freedom we are allowed is to weep, 277], writes Roxana to Usbek.

Usbek's victory over the seraglio seems unquestionable, yet the last two letters tinge it with a sense of defeat. Usbek learns about the deceitful conduct of his beloved wife Roxana, who, despite the vigilance, managed to deceive the Chief Eunuch, and carried on a love affair with a young man of her choice. Usbek experiences pain and deep disappointment: pain because he loves her, disappointment because he had an absolute trust in Roxana, a trust based on her chastity and abhorrence of sexual contact evident during their first encounter. Now he realizes that Roxana's pretended virtue was only "le voile de sa perfidie" (L 159) [a veil that covered treachery, 279]. Usbek is informed about Roxana's infidelity first by a letter from Solim, and immediately afterwards by a letter from Roxana herself. Roxana acknowledges her guilt, but does not express any remorse. On the contrary, she is proud of having outwitted Usbek's jealousy and the stern measures taken by the eunuchs to control the seraglio. She has taken poison to escape Usbek's vengeance, thus depriving him of the satisfaction of seeing her punished. Roxana's defiant words echo Sylvia's rejection of social conventions:

Non! J'ai pu vivre dans la servitude, mais j'ai toujours été libre: j'ai réformé tes lois sur celles de la Nature, et mon esprit s'est toujours tenu dans l'indépendance ... Tu étais étonné de ne point trouver en moi les transports de l'amour. Si tu m'avais bien connue, tu y aurais trouvé toute la violence de la haine. Mais tu as eu longtemps l'avantage de croire qu'un coeur comme le mien t'était soumis. Nous étions tous deux heureux: tu me croyais trompée, et je te trompais. Ce langage, sans doute, te paraît nouveau. (L 161)

[No: I may have lived in servitude, but I have always been free. I have amended your laws according to the laws of nature, and my mind has always remained independent ... You were surprised not to find me carried away by the ecstasy of love; if you had known me properly you would have found in me all the violence of hate. But you had for a long time the benefit of thinking that a heart like mine was subject to you. We were both happy: you thought that I had been deceived, while I was deceiving you. Such language is new to you, no doubt.] (280–81)

Roxana cites her love of freedom as the underlying motive of her rebellion against Usbek's authority. That view is consistent with a theory then current concerning woman's nature according to which, in addition to the inherent propensity for deceit, women were endowed with a spirit of independence.[37] Roxana dies but her suicide is a sign of victory rather than defeat, an act of ultimate self-assertion in which she claims the right to govern her desires and her body. Her voice, which mocks Usbek's desire to possess and control her, "discloses the woman's subversive textual and sexual activity."[38]

Lettres persanes, then, present a highly complex and ambivalent picture of the configuration that links women and letters to passion and control. If men, in order to retain their authority, need to repress female passion, can the physical control of the communication between the private and public spheres guarantee its successful repression? Is such a control at all possible, taking into account the woman's deceitful nature and the subversive potential of a letter? Montesquieu seems to pose these questions, and poses them in a particular social and historical context. As Rica notes in the letter to ***, "L'amour fait retentir ce tribunal. On n'y entend parler que de pères irrités, de filles abusées, d'amants infidèles et de maris chagrins" (L 86) [The court reverberates with love; all you hear of is enraged fathers, deceived daughters, faithless lovers, and dissatisfied husbands, 167]. Clearly, it is this love (read "passion" or sexuality) that is at stake here, and its social consequences that become the matter of concern. Montesquieu mentions "fathers, daughters, husbands" referring thus to the family structure and its failure to achieve stability because women, in the name of passion, neglect their duties as daughters and wives ("enraged fathers, dissatisfied husbands"). Uncontrolled expression of female passion, such as depicted in *Lettres portugaises,* or *The Letters between a Noble-Man and his Sister,* signals danger and has to be curbed. But here a clash of laws occurs: love letter as the feminine form sanctioned by literary theories versus love letter condemned by conduct material as a means of undesirable communication that fosters illicit liaisons, and defies parental authority, a grave threat to the social order.

Elizabeth Haywood's *The Letters from a Lady of Quality to a Chevalier,* 1721, is an attempt at reconciling the two conflicting views.[39] *The Letters* is a collection of thirteen letters and several billets-doux written by "a lady" to "a chevalier" (both remain nameless till the end of the narrative). The first letter informs us (and the chevalier) that she is married to a loving, albeit, dull husband. Her letter is a response to the chevalier's letter, for its "persuasive Eloquence" weakens her resolve not to engage in an illicit correspondence. The next nine letters trace the development of their love affair, focusing on the lady's moods and sentiments, in the vein of *Lettres portugaises.* She describes the novelty and joy of their clandestine meetings, suffers a spell of jealousy, rejoices at his renewed proclamations of eternal love, and experiences a moment of horror, fearing the disclosure of their liaison to her husband. The last three letters, written two years later, mourn the chevalier's departure for England and the inevitable loss of his affection: "full of the hopes of the future Grandeur, you go in search of Fame and Honour, while I am left to mourn this Loss of mine" (79). Like Mariane, Haywood's heroine revels in dissecting verbally every moment spent with her beloved; she recollects his every word, gesture, glance, and dwells on those memories with morbid delight. And as in the case of Mariane, a love affair for the woman ends in grief and abandonment while the man goes on to live an exciting new life.

But whereas the *Lettres portugaises* focused on the depiction of female passion and the aftermath of a love affair, *The Letters* explores the role of the male letter in igniting and keeping that passion alive. It is the chevalier's letter that draws the lady into the correspondence leading to their love affair (in Behn's and Hearne's novels the heroines had already fallen in love with their lovers when the correspondence began). The figure of an epistolary seducer is drawn here according to the tenets of literary theories with regard to male and female epistolary writing. He uses all the literary devices needed for successful persuasion; she rewrites the dictates of her heart. Eventually, the chevalier, equipped with the arsenal of persuasive rhetoric, wins her trust and dispels any doubts she might have had about the sincerity of his sentiments:

> The letter you writ to me this morning, seems to have more Gallantry than Sincerity—the Style appears more studied, and the Sentiments are expressed in a Manner which carry a greater share of Art than Nature—What is your Design? Is it not better for us both to continue as we are? I love my husband—yet when you desire me with that persuasive Eloquence, I confess, I have now no longer power to refuse you! (7)

She is aware of her shortcomings as a female reader confronted with a male writer and knows that it is hard for her to distinguish between art (literary skill in simulating sentiments) and nature (genuine love): "But suppose I could bring myself to imagine that that Soul-enchanting softness of your *Style* was wholly owing to your *Wit* and *Love* had the least sharing in dictating your Expressions, what should I be the better?" (13). The wit, the eloquence, and the persuasive style are the literary means at a man's disposal. It is the power of the written word that creates female passion: "How much more dangerous it is for my Honour and Peace that I should *read* than *hear* you" (13, my emphasis). A letter, "a testimony of affection," as she calls it, offers a continual renewal of passion. Written words can be reproduced and read over and over again. And the clandestine nature of such correspondence adds the excitement of the forbidden: "In such a correspondence as ours, to take away the Mystery, is to take away the Merit" (20).

But in spite of the apparent submission to the transports of passion and the loss of control over her life, the heroine retains a measure of practical common sense in conducting the correspondence. Although she seems to be engrossed in the vicissitudes of her love affair, she devotes much time and thought to its practical side, namely, to ensure smooth communication between herself and her lover. She is the one who arranges for their letters to be safely delivered and provides detailed instructions as to how it should be done:

> And if you must—and if you will (in spite of all my Intreaties to the contrary) continue to write to me, you will find a Bit of Paper, inclosed in this which will direct you how I may receive your Letters with more security, than if sent to our House: for tho' your Servant has taken all the imaginable Caution in the Delivery of them, and has hitherto been seen by none who have had Cunning or Curiosity enough to pry into the reasons of his coming, yet I have a Chambermaid, who is a little related to my Husband . . . I shall be infinitely more at ease, if, for the future, you follow my Directions, and making the Superscription to another, deceive even the very person whose hands I take it from. (14)

Her greatest fear is to be discovered by her husband, and the only occasion on which she reproaches her lover is when she thinks that, due to his negligence, her husband might suspect them: "Had you not any of my Letters in your pocket, which by some accident you might drop?" (68). And, in fact, like Montesquieu's Roxana, she manages to carry on the correspondence and deceive her husband successfully till her lover's departure. Like Roxana, Behn's Sylvia, and Hearne's Amaryllis, she resorts to letters as a means of escape, in her case, from a dull and conventional marriage into a world of excitement and daring. Usbek's fear of illicit correspondence was based on the letter's transgressive potential on the one hand, and the theory of the female "natural" propensity to deceit, on the other. Here another dangerous factor appears in the figure of an epistolary seducer. Haywood's novel shows that Usbek's concern about a letter's route once it leaves the private/domestic sphere is justified.

In presenting to the reading public a heroine who wrote passionate love letters according to the tenets of the literary theories regarding the female and male epistolary writing, Haywood complied with one set of rules. But as a writer/translator who had to fulfill the obligations and conventions prescribed by society, she had also to comply with the demands of conduct material. Therefore, *The Letters* are followed by "A Discourse concerning Writings of this Nature by Way of Essay." Here Haywood adopts the voice of a conduct book's author. Rather than insisting on physical control over letters—interception of letters and careful scrutiny of female letters, such as presented in Montesquieu—Haywood appeals to internal discipline, dictated by common sense. She begins the essay by pointing out the inconveniences and risks involved in carrying on an illicit correspondence, such as the one conducted by her heroine. Continual fear of discovery, carefully planned arrangements, and constant precautions make a woman's life miserable: "Yet what is all this Circumspection, this Watchfullness, this Guard over every action, Word, and Look, but a continual Slavery, which, methinks, a Soul design'd for Liberty should scorn" (6). It is ironic that Haywood quotes "Liberty" as the reason against clandestine correspondence, since it is precisely the lack of freedom that drives women to engaging in clandestine communication.

Moreover, says Haywood, writing letters often leads to the triumph of passion over reason. It is conducive to passionate thoughts and desires for two reasons. Firstly, it is much easier for women to write about passion than to talk about it, since "Paper can not blush" (6)—that is, a woman restrained by natural bashfulness in conversation with a man, would not feel the same restraint in writing to him.

Secondly, male letters have long been known to have the power of conquering female hearts. As in the poem:

> The Pen can furrow a fond Female's Heart,
> And pierce it more than Cupid's talk'd of Dart:
> Letters, a kind of Magick Virtue have,
> And, like strong Philters, human Souls enslave.
>
> (6)

While spoken words may easily be forgotten, letters "will remain perpetual Monitors" of affection. The contemplation of the author's wit, his elegant style, the beauty of his sentences, will, in turn, lure the reader into the contemplation of the author's person, and the absent writer will be persistently present in the mind of the reader. Passion becomes the "Master" and once a woman allows that to happen she walks "the Path to Ruin" (8). A woman has to remember that she is continuously judged by "Custom" and "Religion," and, unfortunately for her, "the Esteem of the World" should "weigh down all other motives" (12). Thus an unhappily married woman should resign herself to her fate rather than engage in an illicit correspondence. Look at our heroine, says Haywood, and the torment of mind the affair caused her:

> The Lady, whose Letters I have taken the liberty to translate, tho' she has been cautious enough in expressing any thing (even in those the most tender among them) which can give the Reader an Assurance she had forfeited her Virtue; yet there is not one, but what sufficiently proves how impossible it is to maintain such a Correspondence, without an Anxiety and continual Perturbation of Mind, which I think a Woman must have bid farewell to her Understanding, before she could resolve to endure. (14)

Having expounded the pros and cons of such a correspondence in case of a married woman, Haywood concludes that, in spite of all the apparent attractions, it is not worth the trouble. The final paragraph of "The Essay" ends with the following piece of advice for her female readers:

> There is nothing a Woman can do more to the prejudice of her Peace of Mind, her Honour, and her Reputation, than the encouraging a Correspondence of this kind: nor can any Motives whatever, that shall induce her to it be reconciled to Reason or Prudence. (29)

"Reason" and "Prudence," nominated here as the two basic virtues, seem to be the guiding principles in Haywood's writing. Like the astonishingly practical heroine, who tries to fit a love affair into her marriage, not willing to sacrifice one for the sake of the other, Haywood wants to reconcile two conflicting sets of demands imposed on a woman writer—to present an epistolary novel complying with the literary expectations to have it published, and at the same time not to transgress social conventions and expose herself to the attacks of her reading public. The false note one detects in the novel, i.e., the incongruous combination of passion and practicality, reflects the preposterous situation of a female epistolary writer who is forced to reconcile the irreconcilable. By mimicking the heroine, Haywood offers female readers and female writers a strategy for survival. The emphasis with which she talks about "Custom" and "the Esteem of the World," which should outweigh any other values, demonstrates her awareness of the importance of conventions if one strives for acceptance on either the social or the literary scene, and of how the two scenes are entwined.

Haywood's dilemma whether a woman should appear to be a creature of prudence or of passion, in other words, reason or heart, reflects the heated debate which reverberated throughout Europe in the eighteenth century: "La donna, cioè, è essenzialmente sentimento o ragione?" [Is woman in essence a creature of feeling or reason?][40] Toward the end of the eighteenth century reason scored a victory over heart, and cautious calculation over spontaneity. As Fiorella D'Alia notes "le donne colte emergono come figure decise a lottare sempre contro ogni elemento passionale" [educated women emerge as figures bent on fighting any temptation of passion] (30). The sensibility of the heart was perceived as an obstacle to reason ("la sensibilità del proprio cuore è uno scoglio per la loro ragione") since it allowed the flesh to control the spirit.[41] Impulsive acts of frivolity, vanity, and flights of fancy—former attributes of femininity—give way to cautious calculation, prudence, and common sense.

Although the victory of reason over heart (cf. the slogan of the Italian feminists' in the 1970s—"facciamola finita col cuore" [let's wipe out the heart]) initiated a number of positive changes for women, e.g., in the field of education, and did away with the stereotype of a female victim of emotions, one cannot help but reflect on the motives underlying that victory.[42] Did reason win because it meant acting with restraint and not yielding to the impulses of uncontrolled desire? Did it win because writing and acting from the heart proved to be a trap in domestic situations while resorting to reason and self-control could save fathers and husbands a lot of problems and turn the domestic sphere into a place of emotional stability and rational decisions?

Haywood's case triggers these doubts since it highlights the conflict between the spontaneous expressions of love, officially sanctioned by the law of genre, and the risks of breaking the law of decorum through passionate purports. Her clumsy efforts to appease both censors result in a compromise: including a text as a censoring mechanism. A reader who has read the novel and might feel encouraged to experience by herself the joys of an illicit love affair, will find a guide in an accompanying text that will convince her not to do it. Thus both censors will remain satisfied: the novel written according to the law of genre will keep its status as pure fiction, and the conduct essay will expound the impropriety of imitating it in real life.

Haywood's own literary career reflects the significant role played by these two censors. Her commercial success as a writer of bold amatory fiction, with feisty and sexy heroines, brought upon her severe attacks of renowned contemporary critics and writers, forcing her to undergo a literary conversion. A contrite confession and profuse apology for her early lifestyle of pleasure and promiscuity (probably more textual than carnal) as well as a change from sentimental to domestic fiction restored her public respect and esteem.[43] Haywood, in Janet Todd's words, "becomes a Magdalen figure who reforms into sentiment" in order to please the reading public and to adjust her image to the demands of the current market.[44] The gradual shift in Haywood's works from "sex to sentiment" began around 1730 and continued until 1740, when she reached a fully respectable and socially laudable position as a mature lady editor of the journal "Female Spectator" (1744–46), giving advice to young women. *The Letters*, offering its readers the voice of prudence that overbears the voice of passion, is the first step, although not yet completely satisfying, towards "domesticating" a woman writer.

3
Clarissa—Woman Writer and Reader in an Epistolary Web

IN *THE EPISTOLARY NOVEL* (1933), GODFREY SINGER QUOTES A BLURB from the *Journal of Literature* of 1734 on *Letters from the Marchioness de M . . . to the Count de R . . .* , a series of love letters translated from the French by Mr Humphrey and published in England in 1734.

> If any Love-Letters may be rank'd with the celebrated ones of Abelard and Eloise, those of a Religious Portuguese Lady, and those of Chevalier de Her__they are these of the Marchioness de M__to Count de R__. They have the Fire, the Turn, the Spirit, and easy Air of those we have mention'd; they furnish us besides with this useful lesson, that Guilty Love must expect to meet with unhappy Consequences.[1]

In his own commentary on this quotation Singer notes:

> Particularly notable in this criticism, aside from the lofty comparison to the classic love letters of the day, is the indication that here we have a love story in letters behind which there is to be found a moral impulse, something of that same moral impulse later to be found, indeed, in the art of Samuel Richardson. The final letters of this volume are marked by a passionate outpouring of tragic writing which not only tells us of the separation of lovers forever, the despair of the Marchioness, and her weariness of life, but also makes clear the feeling that *such are just punishments of illicit love*. (51, my emphasis)

Both the author of the blurb and Singer situate the novel in the same category as *Lettres portugaises* or Haywood's *Letters from a Lady of Quality to a Chevalier* in terms of tone and theme—the spontaneous expression of female passion through letters.

However, as both authors note, the *Letters . . .* introduce a novel element, namely, the emphasis on the disastrous consequences of illicit love, thus issuing a warning against the uncontrolled flow of female passion. The heroine of the *Lettres portugaises* claimed that her passionate love affair, despite its unhappy ending, made her life worthwhile. The heroines of Behn and Hearne cherished the sense of freedom acquired through love affairs and acclaimed letters as an indispensable means of conducting them. The readers heard only their voices united in a triumphant defiance of social conventions. There were no editorial or authorial intrusions to comment on the heroines' behavior. Haywood's *Letters from a Lady of Quality to a Chevalier* demonstrates a slight shift towards expounding the social significance of breaking these conventions, although the emphasis in the essay following the narrative falls on the practical inconvenience of conducting an illicit, in this case, extramarital affair, rather than moral evil. Consequently, clandestine communication is viewed more in terms of a pragmatic hazard than of a breach of ethics.

The *Letters from the Marchioness de M . . . to the Count de R . . .*, as both the blurb's author and Singer point out, marks a step further towards the explicit exposition of social consequences of uncontrolled passion. The difference between *Lettres portugaises* and the love letters published seventy years later lies in the moral lesson included in the narrative itself that the transgression of the social conventions has to be punished. Singer conveniently omits all the social implications of that transgression, and elevates it to the moral category, that is the category of sin and punishment. In view of the redefined roles for women, rebellious heroines like those of Hearne, Behn, or Haywood can no longer proclaim their desire for independence and remain unpunished—they will have to make room for the heroines of Richardson who will expound the "moral impulse" and prove the futility of female efforts to rebel against or escape from the bonds of familial structure. In this sense, Richardson's novels will provide an antidote to "these women's poisons" ("these women," that is, among others, Behn, Manley, Haywood, who appeared on Richardson's black list of "infamy"[2]).

Since a letter is an indispensable agent in sustaining the infamous liaisons, it will have to undergo a close scrutiny and a necessary metamorphosis—women's letters will cease to function as a means of transgression and will become a tool of controlling communication. The novel in which this metamorphosis takes place is Richardson's *Clarissa*. *Clarissa* reenacts the shift from the transgressive to the manipulative role of a female letter, and establishes the cause-and-effect relationship between the role played by a female letter in a familial structure and the need to control it. It also rationalizes the importance of textual censors and shows why the process of reading a novel accompanied by a simultaneous analysis of its content, in other words, a guide to its "correct" reading, could prove a golden mechanism of unobtrusive surveillance.

3: Clarissa—Woman Writer and Reader in an Epistolary Web

Carolyn Flynn claims that Richardson's novels exemplify the male attempt to keep female sexuality in check. She links Richardson's preoccupation with the control of women to the fear of uncontrollable female sexuality, always present although rarely explicit in eighteenth-century fiction:

> they [women] were purer than men, sublime in nature, yet at the same time more susceptible to temptation. Through a careful program of checks and balances, 'punctilio' Richardson called it, society insured the purity of its women. Not without reason, for women, by nature of their inherent frailty, the evil that lies in the bone, were ever in danger of sliding down to their naturally low level. The sentimental woman, the artificial product of sublimation and repression, had to be guarded by her family and husband, matronized by her children, bound in the hoops and rules, to keep social morality properly fixed ... Unless carefully checked by parents or guardians, the young woman would surely succumb to her own nature.[3]

Thus "punctilio" plays a major role in the struggle for a perfect system of domestic surveillance.

My claim is that in *Clarissa* this struggle is fought on the territory of correspondence. Letters shape the structure of the novel not only because the author was intent on depicting "the hearts of the writers while wholly engaged in their subjects," but also because letters become both subjects and objects of control.[4] The control of female letters thus constitutes the theme of the novel. That control will function on two levels. One is purely physical and includes interception and inspection of female letters. Its chief objective is to keep under surveillance the letter writer. This pattern of controlling female communication is already present in Richardson's *Familiar Letters on Important Occasions* where Richardson advocates strongly the parental supervision of female correspondence and warns young women against the disastrous consequences of too much independence:

> I have known several young ladies of your age impatient of the least control, and think hardly of every little contradiction; but when, by any unadvised step, they have released themselves, as they call it, from the care of their try'd friends, how often have they had cause to repent their rashness.[5]

The physical control system of female correspondence imposed within the familial structure employs authority figures as censors to guard and protect young women from breaches of punctilio. "Evil communication corrupts good manners"—such is the title of a sermon mentioned by Richardson in *Familiar Letters* (51), and it could be regarded as a justification of that surveillance network.

Richardson is aware, however, that purely physical control of letters may be inadequate, or inefficient, since male letters have the power to manipulate female readers and eventually bring them to ruin. Only the utmost prudence exercised by women can keep them out of trouble since "men are deceitful, and always put the best side outwards; and it may possibly, on the strict inquiry, which the nature and importance of the case demands, come out far otherwise than it at present appears" (27). To demonstrate the male deceit, *Clarissa* explores the second level of control. It is what I call a manipulation through text because it relies on women being not only literal writers and but also literal readers. Since they use heart rather than mind for guidance, they are unable to interpret and decipher the literary devices and tricks employed by male correspondents. The bag of tricks available to men involves forgery, falsification, and use of rhetoric to persuade, convince, and imitate. La Bruyère's division into the male and female modes of writing provides a handy basis for that manipulation.

I propose to explore *Clarissa* as a text in which a female letter writer and a female letter reader move within those two control systems in order to act out the corruption of manners by "evil communication." *Clarissa* epitomizes the precepts regarding female correspondence set out in conduct material, and develops fully the figure of an epistolary seducer, that had so far existed in only a somewhat rudimentary form. Two sources crucial for such a rereading of *Clarissa* are conduct material (including Richardson's own *Familiar Letters on Important Occasions*) and La Bruyère's theory of male and female modes of writing letters.[6] Clarissa and her epistolary adversary Lovelace will act as representatives of those modes and the ensuing epistolary duel between them will constitute the first part of the novel.[7] The second part, which begins with the aftermath of Clarissa's rape, will retrace the details of that duel, "unfolding" Clarissa's tale in an effort to disentangle the epistolary web responsible for the breakdown in the familial control system. The ubiquitous editor and his comments serve as a textual crutch to support the reader every time doubts prompt him to stumble, and emphasize the conduct-like character of the novel.[8]

Clarissa's first letter to Miss Howe begins with the words "our family." From the very beginning, then, Clarissa is situated within the family structure and identified as a daughter, niece, and sister. She is obliged to conform to the rules imposed on the family by the authority figures, that is, her father, brother, and uncles. Any attempt to bypass or disregard these rules will constitute a transgression that, in Richardson's world, belongs to the category of moral offence. In one of the letters to Miss Howe, Clarissa speaks of "the sin of prohibited correspondence" (I, 222). A sin inevitably precedes a fall; the sin of correspondence will lead to the fall into and through communication.

The origin of Clarissa's sin is to be found in her love of independence and her love of writing. It is the latter that prompted her to embark on the correspondence with Lovelace; "I love writing," she admits in a letter to Miss Howe, "and those who do are fond, you know, of the occasions to use the pen" (I, 15). That correspondence, even though approved by her father, uncles, and brother, is nonetheless carefully monitored by the whole family. There is nothing private about it, and Clarissa obediently accepts the conditions set up by her family:

> As every one had heard his manner of writing commended, and thought his narratives might be agreeable amusements in winter evenings, and that he could have no opportunity particularly to address me in them, since they were to be read in full assembly before they were given to the young gentleman, I made the less scruple to write. (I, 15)

The Harlowe household functions according to the conduct book precepts so that nothing that concerns the communicative links with the outside world is left to chance. Clarissa has not only to keep all the letters written to her by Lovelace, but also to make copies of her letters to him, to enable a constant surveillance of their content. Her escritoire and the key to it become objects of particular importance. Clarissa describes the visit of her mother to her room in the following way: "Clarissa, give me his letters and the copies of yours . . . I besought her to take the key of the private drawer in my escritoire, where they lay. She took all his letters and the copies of mine, and withdrew to read them" (I, 106).

Although her mother's inspection did not find anything amiss in Clarissa's correspondence with Lovelace, Clarissa was prohibited from continuing it, since the family's interest demanded that she should marry "the rich Mr Solmes." Clarissa's mother, acting on the orders of the father, makes that prohibition very explicit: "As I know, your father would have no patience with you, should it be acknowledged that you correspond with Mr Lovelace, or that you have corresponded with him since the time that he prohibited you to do so; I forbid you to continue such liberty" (I, 109).

From that moment on, Clarissa's correspondence with Lovelace will be a double breach of filial duty: she not only disobeys her father's order to discontinue the epistolary exchange with Lovelace, but also acts against the family interest by refusing to marry Mr. Solmes. Her correspondence with Lovelace encourages her determination to oppose the family's plan, and gives her support by keeping her informed about all the decisions and goings-on in her own household. Clarissa, confined to her room, deprived of the services of her faithful maid, Hannah, relies on Lovelace's letters to provide her with information and advice:

> This man, somehow or other, knows every thing that passes in our family. My confinement, Hannah's dismission, and more of the resentments and resolutions of my father, uncles, and brother than I can possibly know, and as soon as the things happen, which he tells me of . . . he is excessively uneasy upon what he hears . . . he solicits me to engage my honour to him, never to have Mr Solmes. (I, 153)

Clarissa's correspondence with Anna Howe serves the same purpose; Anna not only sympathizes with Clarissa's ordeal at home, but also encourages Clarissa not to give in, and instructs her how to deal with her family: "I have no patience to see you thus made the sport of your brother's and sister's cruelty; I urge you by all means to send out of their reach all the letters and papers you would not have them see" (I, 430). Anna perceives the danger of discovering the illicit letters and the repercussions of that discovery. She is fully aware of the value letters have as material documents to be used against either their writer or their addressee.

Anna's and Lovelace's letters to Clarissa subvert the authority and rules of the Harlowe family, and support Clarissa's struggle for independence. No wonder, then, that each attempt at communication is regarded as transgression, and each letter as a danger signal. James Harlowe decides to take further steps and tighten the controlling grip:

> You are forbidden likewise to correspond with the vile Lovelace; as it is well known you did by means of your sly Hannah. Whence her sudden discharge. As was fit. Neither are you to correspond with Miss Howe; who has given herself high airs of late; and might possibly help in your correspondence with that detested libertine. Nor in short, with anybody without leave. (I, 144)

Clarissa's room is constantly searched for paper and ink, her accomplices in the crime of communication. As Clarissa writes to Miss Howe, "I must write as I have opportunity, making use of my concealed stores; for my pens and ink (all of each that they could find) are taken from me" (II, 33).[9] The anxiety, caused by the suspicion that in spite of all the precautions Clarissa might still manage to smuggle letters in and out of the house, makes Clarissa's family devise the plan of sending her to the house of her uncle. The control of letters is the predominant issue in that plan, as Clarissa's brother, James, explains in a letter to Clarissa:

> I will honestly tell you the motive for your going . . . it is that they may be sure that you shall not correspond with anybody they do not like (for they find from Mrs. Howe, that by some means or other you do correspond with her daughter, and through her, perhaps, with somebody else). (I, 323)

That decision, which will cut off any ties Clarissa has with the outside world, pushes Clarissa into the desperate act of accepting Lovelace's offer and leaving her parents' house.

Clarissa's flight proves the inefficacy of the physical control of correspondence exercised in the Harlowe household, implying the inefficacy of visible censorship, in general. What Richardson, however, needs to do at this point, is to explain why it is bound to fail. The failure of the control system is caused in part by the support provided for Clarissa by her confidante, Miss Howe, but the main culprit is the art of Lovelace's writing. Throughout her illicit correspondence with Lovelace, Clarissa has a premonition of danger; she questions the wisdom of her resolution to carry on that correspondence:

> For my own part, I am very uneasy to think how I have been drawn on one hand, and driven on the other, into a clandestine, in short, into a lover-like correspondence, which my heart condemns. It is easy to see, if I do not break it off, that Mr Lovelace's advantages, by reason of my unhappy situation, will every day increase, and I shall be more and more entangled. (I, 138)

Brought up according to conduct book precepts, Clarissa knows that a clandestine correspondence with a man can only lead to a disaster. Anna Howe shares her view, and warns her against the intimacy to which a clandestine correspondence necessarily leads:

> By your insisting that he should keep the correspondence private, it appears that there is *one secret* which you do not wish the world should know; and he is the master of that secret. He is indeed *himself*, as I may say, that secret! What an intimacy does that beget for a lover! How is it distancing the parent! (I, 57, Richardson's emphasis).

Lovelace, "the master of the secret, the secret himself," will force himself like a wedge between Clarissa and her family until their separation is complete. Clarissa has a vague sense of something in Lovelace's letters that does not ring true:

> I found in the afternoon a reply to my answer to Mr Lovelace's letter. It is full of vows of gratitude, of eternal gratitude is his word, among others

still more hyperbolic ... such language looks always to me, as if the flatterer thought to find a woman a fool, or hoped to make her one. (I, 459)

Clarissa does not pursue further her suspicions regarding the sincerity of Lovelace's writing, and in spite of the above reservations accepts Lovelace's letters at face value.

Lovelace's letters, however, should not be accepted at face value, since Lovelace is a male letter writer; that is, he inhabits the male domain of esprit/artificial/literary. Like Clarissa, he has an exceptional "knack at letter writing" (I, 24), but his "knack," contrary to Clarissa's, results from art, not nature. In fact, the very first letter written by Lovelace in the novel, and addressed to John Belford, reveals the literary aspect of his letter writing; the style of the first line "In vain dost thou and thy compeers press me to go to town" is explained and commented on by the editor (or the author?) in the following way: "these gentlemen affected what they called the Roman style (the wit, the *thee* and the *thou*) in their letters" (I, 82, Richardson's emphasis). Lovelace thus establishes the link with the literary epistolary tradition, and declares that "art" will induce Clarissa to trust and love him: "Well says the poet: He who seems virtuous does but act a part / And shews not his own nature but his art" (I, 183).

Lovelace's letters to Clarissa follow a careful plan laid out in his letter to Belford. Lovelace's objective is to lure Clarissa away from her family, and, having Clarissa in his power, force her family to "come creeping to me and bring that sordidly imperious brother to kneel at the footstool of my throne" (I, 187). Lovelace stages a twofold campaign to make his plan work; firstly he must win over Clarissa; secondly he must infiltrate the Harlowes' household to set up his own controlling network within it, "an engine, whose springs I am continually oiling" (I, 183). The first step in his campaign is to attract Clarissa by means of his skill as a writer. His letters, witty and amusing descriptions of his travels abroad, evoke in Clarissa deep admiration for their writer and his literary talent. Clarissa justifies that admiration in a letter to Anna Howe:

> You have seen some of these letters, and have been pleased with his account of persons, places, and things; and we have both agreed that he is no common observer upon what he has seen. My sister herself allowed that the man had a tolerable knack of writing and describing; and my father, who had been abroad in his youth, said his remarks were curious, and showed him to be a person of reading, judgment, and taste. (I, 15)

Lovelace's writing establishes him as a man of "reading, judgment, and taste" in contrast to Solmes, whose letters reveal him to be a man of inferior understanding and gross manners; "I have Solmes's answer," writes Clarissa to Anna Howe; "he had certainly help in it. For I have seen a letter of his; as indifferently worded, as poorly spelt. Yet the superscription is of his dictating, I dare say; for he is a formal wretch" (I, 210).

Once Lovelace's intellectual superiority over his rival is proven, he can present himself as Clarissa's ally, supporting her fight against the marriage with Solmes. Lovelace acts out the role of a loyal friend, enraged at Clarissa's treatment by her family, and eager to save her from her predicament. Clarissa, first with some hesitation, later with more trust, accepts his proclamations of friendship and honorable intentions:

> So uneasy is he for fear I should be prevailed upon in Solmes's favour; so full of menaces, if I am, so resenting the usage I receive; such protestations of inviolable faith and honour; such vows of reformation; such pressing arguments to escape from this disgraceful confinement—O my dear, what shall I do with this Lovelace? (I, 287)

He wins her trust completely by promising to engage his family to assist Clarissa in her predicament.

> He then pressed me to receive a letter of offered protection from Lady Betty. He said, that people of birth stood a little too much upon punctilio; as people of virtue also did: else, Lady Betty would write to me. (I, 229)

The reference to "punctilio" unerringly strikes the right chord in Clarissa's reaction. The magic word of conduct book vocabulary assures Clarissa that Lovelace is like her in observing the rules and regulations of social conventions, and Clarissa does not have to fear any impropriety on his part.

Of course, she does not know that at that point Lovelace's plotting extends beyond the epistolary art and is directed at gaining access to the Harlowe household and supervising it from within. Lovelace's "watchful spy" establishes himself in the Harlowe household as a confidant of the family, a trustworthy and loyal servant. Lovelace boasts of his skill in performing that operation:

> The dear creature [Clarissa] has tempted him, he told them, with a bribe (which she never offered) to convey a letter (which she never wrote) to Miss Howe; he believes, with one inclosed (perhaps to me); but he declined it: and begged they would take no notice of it to her. This brought him a stingy shilling; great applause and an injunction followed it to all the servants, for the strictest lookout, lest she should contrive some way to

send it—And, about an hour after, an order was given him to throw himself in her way; and (expressing his concern for denying her request) to tender his service to her, and to bring them her letter; which it will be proper for him to report that she has refused to give him. Now seest thou not, how many good ends this contrivance answers? (I, 219)

And, in fact, this master stroke of Lovelace's plotting leaves Clarissa totally helpless in his hands. In consequence, Clarissa is forbidden any communication with Anna Howe, her only true friend; Clarissa's loyal servant, Hannah is dismissed, and the only person she can turn to is Lovelace's spy. Through him Lovelace is able to monitor every new development in the Harlowes' household and prepare his next move accordingly; thus, the Harlowes have only an illusion of being in charge while it is really Lovelace who controls the situation. Now he needs only to convince Clarissa to escape from her father's house and Clarissa will be totally at his mercy.

Fearing Clarissa's resistance to such a serious breach of punctilio, he decides to engage Anna Howe in the campaign of persuasion. He convinces Anna that it is important for Clarissa to leave her father's house in order to avoid marriage with Solmes. Anna Howe, taken in by his argumentative skills, becomes his advocate almost against her will, and lends him her voice. In Anna's letter to Clarissa, written on March 23, only the handwriting is her own; the content is dictated by Lovelace:[10]

> He was so very far from intending to intimidate you, he said, that he besought me not to mention one word to you of what had passed between us; that what he had hinted at, which carried the air of menace, was owing to the fervour of his spirits, raised by his apprehensions of losing all hope of you for ever; and on a supposition that you were to be actually forced into the arms of the man you hated. But would you throw yourself, if you were still farther driven, into any other protection, if not Lord M.'s, or that of the ladies of his family, into my mother's, suppose; or would you go to London to private lodgings, where he would never visit you unless by your leave, he would be entirely satisfied. (I, 320)

Clarissa reads exactly what Lovelace wants her to read since Anna transcribes faithfully his every word. Clarissa then is acquainted with Lovelace's plans and his intentions in an indirect way, and her response is much less guarded than it would have been if he had addressed her directly. To achieve further credibility in Anna's eyes Lovelace stages an affair with a young girl, Rosebud. Knowing Anna's inquisitive nature, he prepares a scene that not only absolves him of any dishonorable conduct towards the girl, but even makes him appear

3: Clarissa—Woman Writer and Reader in an Epistolary Web

a champion of domestic bliss and noble intentions. Anna reports the whole affair to Clarissa (as Lovelace hopes she will) and cannot help but praise his conduct:

> I am almost afraid for your heart, when I tell you that I find, now I have got to the bottom of this inquiry, something noble come out in this Lovelace's favour. I could not endure to change any invective into panegyric all at once, and so soon. We, or such as I at least, love to keep ourselves in countenance for a rash judgement, even when we know it to be rash. Everybody has not your generosity in confessing a mistake. It requires greatness of frank soul to do it. So I made still a further inquiry after his life and manner, and behaviour there, in hopes to find something bad: but all uniform! (I, 444)

Anna's letters, contrary to her intentions, become a most effective weapon in Lovelace's hands since they elicit the desired response from Clarissa without her even realizing that her critical friend is being manipulated by Lovelace.

Lovelace's plotting at this point becomes so complex that the editor/author feels it necessary to intervene and explain to the reader what is really happening. If both Clarissa and Anna are incapable of reading Lovelace correctly, maybe the reader will follow their example and will let Lovelace engulf her in his snares? A word of warning follows:

> Perhaps it will be unnecessary to remind the reader, that although Mr. Lovelace proposes (as above) to Miss Howe that her fair friend should have recourse to the protection of Mrs. Howe, if further driven; yet he had artfully taken care, by means of his agent in the Harlowe family, not only to inflame the family against her, but to deprive her of Mrs. Howe's, and of every other protection, being from the first resolved to reduce her to an absolute dependence upon himself. (I, 320)

It is worth noting here that the editorial intrusions nearly always refer to Lovelace's actions and are meant to clarify his intricate plottings for the reader. These intrusions attest to Richardson's preoccupation with the correct response of his female readers whose naivety, he believes, will lead them straight into Lovelace's literary traps. Richardson's presence in the text as the benevolent mentor of young women underlines *Clarissa*'s character as a conduct book and emphasizes the importance of a text as a censoring device used in the process of reading. Behn or Hearne let their readers interpret their texts for themselves, and even Haywood added her commentary as an afterword, not as an insistent interruption of the text.

Ensured of Anna's support, Lovelace can draw Clarissa further into his game of deception, this time appealing to Clarissa's feminine "heart," sensitive to suffering. His letters abound in detailed descriptions of his physical and moral sufferings for her sake and are interspersed with exclamation marks, witnesses of his agitation: "All last Sunday night he was wandering about the coppice and near the back door. It rained; and he has got a great cold attended with feverishness," reports Clarissa to Anna. She responds to his letter in the way he expects her to:"I can't help saying I am sorry he has suffered for my sake" (I, 396). His next letter to her exploits that sympathy even further: "What is to become of me! How shall I support this new disappointment! No new cause! On one knee, kneeling on the other, I write! My feet benumbed with midnight wandering!" (I, 408). Clarissa cannot help feeling grateful for what appears to be sincere interest in her welfare: "Treated as I am treated by my friends, it is dangerous to be laid under the sense of obligation to an addresser's patience; especially when such a one suffers in health for my sake" (I, 394).

Lovelace's artful writing, like the male art of feigning passion, serves the purpose of deceiving the naive woman, guided by "heart" rather than "mind." Lovelace manages to evoke in Clarissa all the sentiments which tip the scales in his favor—admiration of his writing, gratitude for his disinterested help in her cause, pity for his suffering on her behalf, and respect for his apparent regard for her wishes. His talent at manipulating Clarissa through letters accounts for the successful operation of "seducing her away" (II, 214). Driven to despair by her family's insistence that she marry Solmes, encouraged by Anna, who inadvertently stands by Lovelace's side, and mellowed by his assurances of honorable assistance, Clarissa writes to him about her decision to escape. She realizes almost immediately the impropriety of her rash step, "that all punctilio is at an end the moment I am out of my father's house" (I, 93), and tries to revoke her decision. It is too late, and, once sent, "the letter is out of her power" (II, 72). Her frantic efforts to call off the escape are useless. Whereas Lovelace controls his language, Clarissa loses control of her own writing. It is at that moment that she realizes her own powerlessness and the futility of trying to match Lovelace's contrivances. Clarissa's words sound like an excerpt from a conduct book: "How one step brings on another with this encroaching sex! How soon may a young creature, who gives a man the least encouragement, be carried beyond her intentions, and out of her own power! (II, 76). It is the prohibited correspondence that allowed Lovelace to talk her into fleeing her parents' house and left her unprotected at the mercy of a man, as Clarissa writes to Anna:

> Take care how you fall into my error; for that *begun with carrying on a prohibited correspondence;* a correspondence which I thought in my power

3: Clarissa—Woman Writer and Reader in an Epistolary Web

to discontinue at pleasure. My talent is scribbling; and I the readier fell into this freedom, as I found delight in writing. (II, 185, Richardson's emphasis)

Thus, Clarissa from the depth of her grievous experience voices the warning preached again and again in the conduct material. But that warning is only a hint of the horrors that await her.

Until the moment of her flight, Clarissa was controlled as a writer by her family, who intercepted and inspected her letters, and as a reader by Lovelace, who manipulated her mind. Once she accepts Lovelace's "protection," she becomes "a puppet" in his hands; he controls her both as a letter writer and as a letter reader. As in her father's house, every attempt to communicate with the outside world is closely watched, and her correspondence remains the object of control. Lovelace takes over the parental function of supervising her letters and regards it almost as his duty, since freedom of expression cannot be allowed in a woman's correspondence. Lovelace then identifies himself with Clarissa's father/guardian and assumes his role:

> This perverse lady keeps me at such a distance, that I am sure something is going on between her and Miss Howe, notwithstanding the prohibition from Mrs. Howe to both: and as I have thought it some degree of merit in myself to punish others for their transgressions, I am of opinion that both these girls are punishable for their breach of parental injunctions. And as to their letter-carrier, I hold myself justified to have him stripped and robbed, and what money he has about him given to the poor; since if I take not his money as well as letters, I shall be suspected. (II, 507)

Lovelace resorts to the same methods of surveillance as those applied in the Harlowe family: interception, spying, continuous supervision of writing materials:

> A master-key, which will open every lock in this chest, is put into Dorcas's hands; and she is to take care, when she searches for papers, before she removes anything to observe how it lies, that she may replace all to a hair. Sally and Polly can occasionally help to transcribe. Slow and sure with such an Argus-eyed charmer must be all my movements. (II, 507)

As in the Harlowe household, the incoming and outgoing letters are objects of interest and preoccupation. In a letter to Belford, Lovelace gives a detailed account of a fight he had with Clarissa over a letter she tried to send to Anna Howe, and explains why that letter is to him so vital:

> But thinkest thou that I will not make it the subject of one of my first plots to inform myself of the reason why all this commotion was necessary on so slight an occasion as this would have been, were not *the letters that pass between these ladies of a treasonable nature.* (III, 2, my emphasis)

The arrival of a letter for Clarissa causes instant commotion: "And here, just now, is another letter brought from the same virulent little devil. I hope to procure transcripts from that too, very speedily" (III, 496), and a few days later, "O, Jack! I am sick to death, I pine, I die for Miss Howe's next letter! I would bind, gag, strip, rob, and do anything but murder to intercept it" (III, 497).

But Lovelace's abilities to control Clarissa's correspondence go far beyond the mere interception of letters—Lovelace, a male writer proficient in artifice, can also forge them. While previously Lovelace resorted to his rhetorical skills to adapt his epistolary voice to the demands of the situation, that is, to elicit the required response in his reader, Clarissa, now he demonstrates his ability to edit letters or write "in a myriad of styles," like his literary forefathers—the Abbé Cotin and Guilleragues.[11] Lovelace edits his cousins' letters to Clarissa because "if properly worded, [they] might be necessary to shew her as matters proceed" (II,155). And, of course, Clarissa's response is again predictable: "You may believe my dear," she writes to Miss Howe, "that these letters put me in good humour with him. He saw it in my countenance, and congratulated himself upon it" (II, 279). Lovelace presents Clarissa with a letter from Mr. Doleman which Clarissa sends immediately to Anna for her perusal. That letter, which evokes in Clarissa feelings of gratitude for Doleman's efforts to find her a suitable lodging in London, is nothing but a skilful forgery by Lovelace, who boasts of his talent in a letter to Belford:

> Thou knowest the widow; thou knowest her nieces; thou knowest the lodgings; and didst thou ever read a letter more artfully couched than this of Tom Doleman? Every possible objection anticipated! Every accident provided against! Every tittle of it plot-proof! Who could forbear smiling to see my charmer, like a farcical dean and chapter, choose what was chosen for her. (II, 314)

Lovelace's plan is now to persuade Clarissa to take lodgings of his choice, pretend that they are married, and make Clarissa his mistress. As he explains to Belford, "If I can have her without marriage, who can blame me for trying?" (II, 222). Doleman's letter induces Clarissa to accept the house in London, and thus to fulfill Lovelace's wish.

Since Anna's letters may prove injurious to his plan and uncover his treacherous designs, he intercepts all of them, and forges them to

3: Clarissa—Woman Writer and Reader in an Epistolary Web 89

provide Clarissa only with such information as might facilitate his task. Lovelace describes step by step his techniques to make the forgeries as perfect as possible:

> But did I not tell thee that I provide for everything. That I always took care to keep seals entire, and to preserve covers? Was it not easy then, thinkest thou, to contrive a shorter letter out of a longer; and to copy the very words? . . . Miss Howe's hand is not a bad one, but it is not so equal and regular. That little devil's natural impatience hurrying on her fingers, gave, I suppose, from the beginning her handwriting, as well as the rest of her, its fits and starts, and those peculiarities, which, like strong muscular lines in a face, neither the pen nor the pencil can miss. (III, 428)

Thus, Anna writes to Clarissa only what Lovelace "permits her to write" (III, 428).

In answering Anna's letters on Clarissa's behalf, Lovelace takes great pains to avoid arousing in her any suspicion. Clarissa's letters, intercepted by Lovelace, serve as models for imitation: "having therefore so good a copy to imitate I wrote, and taking out that of my beloved, put under the same cover the following short billet: inscriptive and conclusive parts of it in her own words" (III, 435). The effect of these forgeries is Lovelace's complete triumph over Clarissa. Supported by what she believes to be Anna's views about Lovelace's conduct, she lets down her defenses and accepts Lovelace's proposals at face value. Only a rash step on Lovelace's part, an unguarded moment of passion, revealed during the outbreak of fire, opens her eyes to the real nature of his tricks. Thus while Lovelace's writings managed to camouflage successfully his real intentions, his behavior reveals them clearly.[12]

Clarissa, finally convinced of his base character, flees the "vile house" (III, 357) and hides at Mrs. Moore's in Hampstead. Clarissa hopes that her ordeal is over:

> As I have escaped with my honour, and nothing but my worldly prospects, and my pride, my ambition, and my vanity, have suffered in this wreck of my hopefuller fortunes, may I not still be more happy than I deserve to be? And who knows but that this very path into which my inconsideration has thrown me, strewed as it is with briars and thorns, which tear in pieces my gaudier trappings, may not be the right path to lead me into the great road to my future happiness; which might have been endangered by evil communication. (III, 337)

But the "sin of prohibited correspondence" cannot be expiated so easily. Lovelace finds her hiding place and arrives there prepared to execute his original plan of "having Clarissa without marrying her." Once again, letters play an important part in his scheme. Equipped with forgeries of his relatives' correspondence, Lovelace uses them as proofs of their marriage and of Clarissa's erratic behavior. The letters gain him the support of Mrs. Moore, who assists him in carrying Clarissa away. This time Clarissa will not be able to get away. Lovelace's brief note to Belford contains a mission-accomplished message: "And now, Belford, I can go no further. The affair is over. Clarissa lives. And I am your humble servant, R. Lovelace" (IV, 48).

Up to this point the reader has been able to unravel Lovelace's epistolary web through his letters to Belford and through the editorial intrusions in places where that web became too intricate to disentangle. Now it is Clarissa's turn to do the unraveling. The reader witnesses the entire story backwards, the "unfolding" of Clarissa's story, executed by the victim herself. Lovelace's letters serve as documents that can be traced back to the place of their origin, that is, to their writers. Dates and places, pieces of information characteristic of letters, have material value as they enable Clarissa to situate them in time and space and thus verify their credibility. "Lovelace, I shall find out all your villainies in time," she vows (IV, 67), and indeed she sets out to execute the painstaking task of unveiling Lovelace's epistolary deceits. Clarissa writes to Lady Betty Lawrence asking her if "you wrote a letter, dated, as I have a memorandum, Wednesday, June 7, congratulating your nephew Lovelace on his supposed nuptials" (IV, 211); to Mrs. Hodges, to verify the existence of Captain Tomlinson, whose letters Lovelace used as proofs of his good rapport with Clarissa's uncle; and to Anna, to check the letters that presented Lovelace in a favorable light. The result of those inquiries is, of course, the devastating truth that Lovelace acted according to a carefully prepared plan, moving step by step to achieve his goal. Clarissa ponders that truth with bitterness:

> When I reflect upon all that has happened to me, it is apparent that this generally supposed *thoughtless* seducer, has acted by me upon a regular and preconcerted plan of villainy. In order to set all his vile plots in motion, nothing was wanting, from the first, but to prevail upon me, either by force or by fraud, to throw myself in his power . . . For never was there as I now see, a plan of wickedness more steadily and uniformly pursued than *his* has been, against an unhappy creature who merited better than *him*. (IV, 223, Richardson's emphasis)

Clarissa's sad reflections on Lovelace's perfidy are complemented by the reflections of the editor, who advises his less attentive readers to go

3: Clarissa—Woman Writer and Reader in an Epistolary Web 91

back to earlier letters and reread them in order to grasp the enormity of Lovelace's deceptions:

> The attentive reader need not be referred back for what the lady nevertheless could not account for, as she knew not that Mr. Lovelace has come at Miss Howe's letters; particularly that in vol. III, Letter IX. which he comments upon in Letter XXIV. of the same volume. (IV, 263)

That slow process of "unfolding" Clarissa's tale serves two purposes: the first is to retrace and repeat the pattern of Lovelace's epistolary strategies, to draw the reader's attention to the minutiae of those strategies, and thus to imprint indelibly on the reader's mind the image of Lovelace as a perfidious epistolary seducer. The second is to demonstrate the inefficiency with which Clarissa reads and writes letters. Clarissa fails to read Lovelace's letters correctly because, as a woman, she is not prepared to deal with male cunning and rhetorical skills, partly because of naiveté, "natural" to her sex, and partly due to her limited education. Colonel Morden voices that opinion in a conversation with Lovelace:

> He said that men had generally too many advantages from the weakness, credulity, and inexperience of the fair sex: that their early learning, which chiefly consisted in inflaming novels, and idle and improbable romances, contributed to enervate and weaken their minds. (V, 171)

Lovelace shares Morden's opinion and almost pities Clarissa for her naiveté:

> This dear lady is prodigously learned in *theories*. But as to *practices*, as to *experimentals*, must be, as you know from her tender years, a mere novice. Till she knew me, I daresay, she did not believe, whatever she had read that there were such fellows in the world, as she will see in you four. (II, 444, Richardson's emphasis)

Lovelace considers himself more evil than the most perfidious character ever created in fiction. Thus he claims that Clarissa's knowledge derived from books does not protect her from real-life encounters.

Clarissa is an incompetent reader because she applies the rules of familiar letter writing to reading male letters. She looks for heart and expression of genuine sentiments where there is only the mind employed to counterfeit those sentiments. Lovelace cynically praises the familiar letter writing to Clarissa because he knows that this is the only kind of writing she practices and is able to comprehend:

> I proceeded therefore—That I loved familiar letter writing, as I had more than once told her, above all the species of writing; it was writing from the heart (without the fetters prescribed by method or study), as the very word *correspondence* implied. Not the heart only; the soul was in it; the mind impelling sovereignly the vassal fingers. (III, 198, Richardson's emphasis)

In his description of correspondence Lovelace uses exactly the same words as La Bruyère when he extols the superiority of feminine epistolary writing over male letters. Lovelace puts to practice what La Bruyère only implied in his theory, namely that men are capable of imitating the feminine writing as well as using "the fetters [chains] prescribed by method and study." The access to those "fetters" accounts for his success in winning over Clarissa and seducing her away from her family. Clarissa's failure to see through his epistolary artifice is then a direct cause of her fall.

The unfolding of her story also proves her to be an inefficient letter writer. The only instance when Clarissa's letter achieves its purpose is the letter written to Lovelace about her decision to leave her parents' house. But this is precisely the one letter she should never have written. All the other letters, which aim at persuading others to assist her, fail in their mission. Solmes does not take "no" for an answer, her uncle sides with her parents rather than with her; Lovelace follows her to Hampstead in spite of her entreaties to leave her alone; her family does not believe her when she begs their forgiveness in view of her grave condition. Her sister's letter sounds bitterly ironic when juxtaposed with Clarissa's failures as an effective, persuasive writer: "Sister Clary,—I wish you would not trouble me with any more of your letters. You always had a knack of writing; and depended upon making every one do what you would when you wrote. But your wit and folly have undone you" (V, 22). Suspended between two systems of letter control, physical and textual, Clarissa has no space to move. Everything she writes turns against her and exposes her vulnerability.

As the epistolary duel between Lovelace and Clarissa makes clear, Lovelace's "knack" for writing differs essentially from Clarissa's not only in its origin (artifice versus nature) but also in efficacy. His letters are missives/missiles that hit the target. They make people do what he wills them to do; Clarissa's only describe actions.[13] Lovelace's letters act while Clarissa's react to them. The dichotomy between the two modes of epistolary writing is apparent in Lovelace's description of Clarissa's response to Anna's letter:

> It is easy for me to perceive that my charmer is more sullen when she receives, and has perused, a letter from that vixen than at other times.

3: Clarissa—Woman Writer and Reader in an Epistolary Web

But as the sweet maid shows, even then, more of *passive grief* than of *active spirit,* I hope she is rather lamenting than plotting. (II, 294, Richardson's emphasis)

While Lovelace uses his letters for plotting, Clarissa uses hers for lamenting; his express "active spirit," hers "passive grief."

The metaphors which refer to Lovelace and Clarissa underline the gap between them, i.e., the gap between "art" and "nature," "wit" and "heart," "literary" and "non-literary." The reader is thus reminded over and over again that Lovelace is the aggressor/addresser, Clarissa the aggressee/addressee (the term "addresser" is Lovelace's, I, 187). Anna Howe calls him "a curl-pated villain, full of fire, fancy, and mischief; an orchard-robber, a wall climber, a horse-rider without saddle or bridle" (I, 307). Lovelace is a "fowler" who sets up snares to "ensnare this single lark" (II, 210).[14] He is "a spider" (II, 202), "a panther" (II, 372), "a hound" (II, 242)," a pernicious caterpillar, that preys upon the fair leaf of virgin fame," "the fretting moth, that corrupts the fairest garment," "the eating canker worm, that preys upon the opening bud" (IV, 62). Clarissa, on the other hand, is "a feather blown by the wind" (II, 47), "a broken lily" (IV, 44); Clarissa and Anna are two "reeds supporting each other" (III, 122). In other words, Clarissa is "the lady scrupulously strict to *her* word, incapable of art or design" (II, 370, Richardson's emphasis), Lovelace "the head to contrive, the heart to execute, the plottingest heart in the world" (III, 61). Literal Clarissa is no match for literary Lovelace.

What is significant about this contrast is that it is by no means unique. It is universal, not an exception but the rule. Thus it is not the confrontation between Lovelace and Clarissa, but between a Lovelace and a Clarissa. Lovelace situates himself within the tradition of "addressers." He calls himself "a universal lover" (I, 89). "Is there but *one* Lovelace in the world?"—asks Lovelace of Belford (II, 221, Richardson's emphasis), drawing attention to the popularity of a rake, a figure long established in the literary tradition: "And are not lovers' oaths a jest of hundreds years' standing?" (III, 70). He has to use the strategies of a rake not to act "out of character." As he explains in a letter to Belford: "Were I to take thy stupid advice, and marry, what a figure should I make in the rakish annals!" (II, 484). Thus, Lovelace, "a master of arts in love" (II, 314), is a continual source of fear and horror to parents who try to shield their daughters from the likes of him, and a continual danger to the stability of a familial order. Lovelace prides himself on having acquired that status: "Had I been a military hero, I should have made gunpowder useless; for I should have blown up all my adversaries by dint of stratagem, turning their own devices upon them. But these mothers and fathers—Lord help 'em!" (II, 242).

Although Lovelace is the main plotter and letter manipulator in the novel, he is by no means the only one. Two other male characters demonstrate the ability to manipulate women by letters. Belford, asked by Clarissa to send her those letters of Lovelace which would bear testimony to his dishonorable intentions, decides to comply with her request. But loyal to Lovelace even when his sympathy seems to be totally engaged by Clarissa, he edits the fragments sent to Clarissa to cover up Lovelace's crude frankness and frivolity of expression:

> I have actually delivered to the lady the extracts she requested me to give her from your letters. I do assure you that I have made the very best of the matter for you, *not* that conscience, but that friendship, could oblige me to make. I have changed or omitted some free words. The warm description of her person in the *fire scene,* as I may call it, I have omitted. (V, 19, Richardson's emphasis)

As Lovelace's letters before, now Belford's editing affects Clarissa's reading and Clarissa reads a version considerably toned down by a male editor. Despite his noble character and intentions, Belford's complicity puts him in the same category as Lovelace, that of "universal" plotters.

The other person whose letters significantly affect Clarissa's fate is a certain Mr. Brand, a subservient acquaintance of the Harlowe family. To ingratiate himself into the wealthy family, and thus to ensure financial profit, he writes a letter that misrepresents Clarissa's relation to Belford, and accuses her of encouraging the addresses of yet another libertine. Although the letter is pompous and poorly written, it nevertheless gains credence in the Harlowe family. Having found a confirmation of Clarissa's fall, and thus an excuse for their own implacability, the Harlowes continue to remain unmoved by Clarissa's pleas for forgiveness. Belford, in a letter to Lovelace, comments on the harm it caused: "I ran through your letters, and the copy of that of the incendiary Brand's (by the latter of which I saw to what cause a great deal of this last implacableness of the Harlowe family is owing)" (V, 195). The manipulative character of the letters of Brand and Belford reinforces the sense of the irresistible power of male letters.

If Lovelace stands for a universal epistolary seducer, Clarissa represents a universal epistolary victim. Exceptional as she may be in her beauty, accomplishments, and virtues, she cannot escape the role allotted her by tradition. As Lovelace succinctly puts it, "when all's done, Miss Clarissa Harlowe has but run the fate of a thousand others of her sex" (IV, 52). Anna Howe, pondering Clarissa's ordeal, repeats the same conclusion: "Thus happy in all about you, thus making happy all within your circle, could you think that nothing would happen to you, to convince you *that you were not to be exempted from the common lot?*" (III, 14, Richardson's emphasis). Thus Clarissa is just another name added to the already substantial list of female victims. In Belford's words, her name only "swells the guilty list" (III, 269).

Just as Belford's and Brand's epistolary manipulations complement Lovelace's machinations to underline their universal character, Clarissa's defeat in the epistolary battle is complemented by that of Anna Howe. If Clarissa becomes the victim of male epistolary art, Anna is a potential victim. In the early stages of her correspondence with Clarissa, she is just as vulnerable to Lovelace's tricks as Clarissa is, and actually becomes Lovelace's advocate. Later her letters, just like Clarissa's, forged and edited by Lovelace, become a valuable weapon which he uses unscrupulously and efficiently against Clarissa. Thus Anna in spite of her protestations of independence and hatred of male domination, is only "a puppet dancing on a wire" (II, 298). But Lovelace goes even further than that and actually plans a campaign to get her into his power. "That's a charming girl! Her spirit, her delightful spirit!—not to be married to it—how I wish to get that lively bird into my cage! how would I make her flutter and fly about!—till she left a feather upon every wire" (IV, 383). He lays out the details of that plan in a letter to Belford but eventually decides to abandon it: "I had once thoughts of revenging myself on that vixen. But I think— let me see—yes, I *think*, I will let this Hickman have her safe and entire" (IV, 494, Richardson's emphasis). At this point the editor refers the reader to Letter XXXIV of volume III, to ponder Lovelace's perfidy once again. Anna avoids Clarissa's fate not because she is more careful or less naive than Clarissa but because Lovelace chooses not to ruin her. However, she is a potential victim, since "no one would have saved her" if Lovelace "had decreed her fall" (II, 299).[15] Anna and Clarissa then demonstrate the powerlessness of women in a confrontation with an epistolary rake and prove that "no woman is love-proof or plot-proof" (II, 483).

Is there then any way of shielding women from deceitful male practices, of saving "paragons of virtue" from "devils of contrivances?" (III, 272). *Clarissa* suggests that one possible way is a complete dependence on parents or guardians.[16] Clarissa writes a whole sermon on the necessity of that dependence:

> There are other duties, you say, besides the filial duty: but that, my dear, must be a duty prior to all other duties; a duty anterior, as I may say, to

> your very birth. Can there be a stronger instance in human life than mine has so early furnished, within a few months past, of the necessity of the continuance of a watchful parent's care over a daughter: let that daughter have obtained ever so great a reputation for her prudence? Is not the space from sixteen to twenty-one that which requires this care more than any time of a young woman's life? For in that period do we not generally attract the eyes of the other sex, and become the subject of their addresses, and not seldom of their attempts? And is not this period in which our conduct or misconduct gives our reputation or disreputation, that almost inseparably accompanies us throughout our whole future lives? And when our dangers multiply both from *within* and *without,* do not our parents know that their vigilance ought to be doubled? At *every* age on this side of matrimony (for then we come under another sort of protection, though that is far from abrogating the filial duty) it will be found that the wings of our parents are our necessary and most effectual safeguard from the vultures, the hawks, the kites, and other villainous birds of prey that hover over us with a view to seize and destroy us the first time we are caught wandering out of the eye or care of our watchful and natural guardians. (II, 327–28, Richardson's emphasis)

Clarissa's view reverberates over and over again through the voices of Anna, Mrs. Howe, the Harlowes, even Lovelace, who asserts the parents' right to educate and control their daughters (III, 326). When deprived of that control, Clarissa yearns for it and searches for its substitute:

> *Paternal,* poor lady!—Never having been, till very lately, from under her parents' wings, and now abandoned by all her friends, she is finding out something *paternal* and *maternal* in every one, to supply to herself the father and mother her dutiful heart pants after. (IV, 379, Richardson's emphasis)

If parental control is such an iron safeguard against all the dangers awaiting innocent girls in the "wide, wide world," if every character in the novel claims its necessity, if Clarissa herself talks about it in a conduct book manner for pages and pages, what, a reader will ask, makes her reject it in the first place, and why would she choose the dangerous path of independence? Richardson answers that question— the censor's accusing finger points to Clarissa's first clandestine letter to Lovelace.

The moment when Clarissa decides to continue her correspondence with Lovelace, in spite of her parents' prohibition, determines the course of events and seals her fate. Clarissa's efforts to pinpoint the very beginning of her fall always lead her back to that moment. "As for your first fault, *the answering his letters*" (my emphasis, II, 175)

3: Clarissa—Woman Writer and Reader in an Epistolary Web

writes Anna to Clarissa; Clarissa refers to it as "fatal step" (IV, 268), "fatal error" (V, 319), "unhappy rashness" (V, 320), "unhappy step" (V, 321). Lovelace also looks back to it as the step which enabled him to execute his plan: "She blames herself for having corresponded with me, a man of free character; and indeed whose *first* view it was to draw her into this correspondence; and who succeeded in it by means unknown to herself" (II, 219, Richardson's emphasis). But even though the success of his plan depended on that correspondence, Lovelace, himself, condemns it, and blames Clarissa for having agreed to it. He, "the tempter," turns into "the accuser" (II, 219), and ponders the risks involved in marrying a woman tainted by "the sin of prohibited correspondence":

> But then, as I have often reflected, how had I known, that a but blossoming beauty, who could carry on a private correspondence, and run such risks with a notorious wild fellow, was not prompted by inclination, which one day might give such a free-liver as myself as much pain to reflect upon, as at the time it gave me pleasure? (IV, 96)

The "fatal error" is irrevocable, as subsequent events demonstrate. Clarissa cannot escape its consequences, and her ruin can only be resolved in her death.

Numerous critical studies on *Clarissa* exalt her death, and view it as a rebellion against the social order. For Eagleton, for instance, it is "a political gesture, a shocking, surreal act of resignation from society whose power system she has seen in part for what it is" (74). Carol Flynn holds a similar opinion and claims that "marriage will not cure all; death will not testify to her shame but to her triumph" (141). According to Flynn, the fact that Richardson lets Clarissa die rather than marry her seducer proves that Richardson was able to transcend the conventions of his day:

> In Richardson's world, the fallen woman is a wretched creature doomed to a bad end. Yet his own Clarissa transcends the conventions he employs. She avoids the traditional paths awaiting her: she does not take to the streets, does not marry her seducer, and does not become pregnant. (143)

But such interpretations distort the novel's expressed goal, which is to "warn the inconsiderate and thoughtless of the one sex, against the base arts and designs of the other."[17] Viewed in the light of conduct material, Clarissa's fall is irredeemable, at least on earth. Clarissa's lost reputation cannot be restored by penitence or pity. Neither Clarissa nor Lovelace can envision a future life together: over them looms the shadow of their sins against punctilio. Lovelace writes about his reservations to Belford:

> And what a couple of old patriarchs shall we become, going on in the mill-horse round; getting sons and daughters; providing nurses for them first, governors and governesses next; teaching them lessons their father never practised, nor which their mother (as her parents will say) was much the better for! And at last when life shall be turned into the dully sober stillness, and I become desirous to forget all my past rogueries, what comfortable reflections will it afford to find them revived, with equal, or probably greater trouble and expense, in the persons and manners of so many Lovelaces of the boys; and to have the girls run away with varlets, perhaps not half as ingenious as myself. (IV, 385)

Lovelace is afraid of the bad example they will furnish for their children, and so is Clarissa:

> *Were* I to marry him, what a figure should I make, preaching virtue and morality to a man whom I had trusted with opportunities to seduce me from all my own duties!—And then, supposing I were to have children by such a husband, must it not, think you, cut a thoughtful person to the heart, to look round upon her little family, and think she had given them a father destined, without a miracle to perdition? ... And after all, who knows but that my own sinful compliances with a man, who would think himself entitled to my obedience, might taint my own morals, and make me, instead of a reformer, an imitator of him? For who *can touch pitch and not be defiled?* (IV, 441, Richardson's emphasis)

Clarissa fears for the moral standard of her immediate family but she also fears for the moral standard of her household. How will she, a woman whose reputation is irrevocably lost in society, preach virtue to others, her servants and dependents, whose moral education depends on her? How will she be able to govern and teach them if she cannot quote her own conduct as an example? The pedagogic ramifications of her misconduct play no little part in Clarissa's musings about her future:

> One of my delights was, to enter the cots of my poor neighbours, to leave lessons to the boys, and cautions to the elder girls: and how should I be able unconscious, and without pain, to say to the latter, fly the delusions of men, who had been supposed to have run away with one? (IV, 442)

The sin of prohibited correspondence turns Clarissa into an imperfect mistress of a household, a mistress who has lost all claim to authority based on virtue and unstained reputation, and she is painfully aware of it. Apart from marriage with Lovelace, which Clarissa rejects as a possible solution, Clarissa weighs two other possibilities: marriage with her old suitor who renews his offer after having learned of Clarissa's misfortune, and life as a single woman.[18] She rejects both after a careful scrutiny of what that life would be like:

> The single life, at such times, has offered to me, as the life, the *only* life, to be chosen. But in *that,* must I not *now* sit brooding over my past afflictions, and mourning my faults till the hour of my release? And would not every one be able to assign the reason why Clarissa Harlowe chose solitude, and to sequester herself from the world? Would not the look of every creature who beheld me appear as a reproach to me? And would not my conscious eye confess my fault, whether the eyes of others accused me or not? (IV, 442, Richardson's emphasis)

Rather than regard her death as a rebellion against the social order, we should consider it as an act of compliance with that order, a willing and conscious escape not from the social conventions, but from the consequences of breaking those conventions. Ian Watt emphasizes Clarissa's awareness of that breach: "But there is also more than a hint that what Clarissa cannot face is not so much what Lovelace has done or what the world may think about it, but the idea that she herself is not wholly blameless" (75). Belford compares the character of Calista, the heroine of Rowe's play *The Fair Penitent,* with Clarissa, and concludes that Calista is not a real penitent because "her character is made up of deceit and disguise. She has no virtue; is all pride; and her devil is as much *within* her, as *without*" (V, 61, Richardson's emphasis). Clarissa, of course, is all honesty and purity. But although Clarissa's intentions are always noble and virtuous, her execution of those intentions breaks the law of filial obedience. She falls by allowing the evil from "without" to penetrate "within."

By making a letter the agent responsible for that penetration by evil from without, Richardson invests it with an almost magical power—the power to destroy innocent young creatures like Clarissa. The elevation of the letter to an instrument of destruction cannot, of course, be innocent. If, as Terry Eagleton claims, our interest should focus on what fiction "does rather than on what it mirrors "(4), we should turn our attention to what *Clarissa* does on the level of letters. First of all, *Clarissa* limits, if not rules out completely, the possibility of any free correspondence by women, since that correspondence becomes an object of strict surveillance in a familial structure. Men are able to control communication carried on by women from within the private sphere by virtue of the authority bestowed on them by the social order; they are entitled to intercept, read, or interpret any letter that might contain the slightest implication of indocility. Female correspondence ceases to be a private matter between writer and addressee; it becomes a matter of public concern within the family structure. An attempt to escape the family structure is rarely successful, since the control system will bring the letter back. Thus, Richardson practically erases the figure of an autonomous female correspondent and her access to letters as means of free communication.

Secondly, by creating the figure of an omnipotent epistolary seducer, he cancels out a female letter reader who would be competent enough to see through and deal with male artifice. A letter becomes for men a weapon used unscrupulously and efficiently against women. *Clarissa* then segregates the functions of letters according to gender: men are able to exploit the manipulative and persuasive potential of a letter; women can use letters effectively only as vehicles of description. Clarissa's letters, totally inefficient as means of persuasion, have value as testimony to her ordeal. Anna Howe encourages her to turn her letters into a story:

> You are, it seems (and that too much for your health), employed in writing. I hope it is in penning down *the particulars of your tragical story.* And my mother has put me in mind to press you to it, with a view that one day, if it might be published under feigned names, it would be of as much use as honour to the sex. And then, she says, your noble conduct throughout your trials and calamities will afford not only a shining example to your sex, but at the same time, *a fearful warning to the inconsiderate young creatures of it.* (IV, 500, my emphasis)

The resolution of the epistolary entanglement in *Clarissa* thus brings us to a clear-cut division of the letter's function: the power of action is reserved for male letters, the power of description for female letters.[19]

Does Richardson then leave any space for a female letter writer besides that of a scrupulous chronicler of male perfidy? Yes, but it is a strictly defined space. Anna Howe resurrects Clarissa's ghost from before the fall, and reconstructs her daily occupations. In that "ghostly" portrait Clarissa excels of course in all sorts of domestic virtues, proves to be a perfect mistress of her household, "an excellent economist and housewife." She is also an accomplished letter writer who "takes delight" in the familiar style, suitable for women because of "the gentleness of their minds, the delicacy of their sentiments, and the liveliness of their imagination" (V, 463). But those familiar letters are directed only to the father figures/censors themselves: "the pious Dr. Lewen, the worthy Dr. Blome, the ingenious Mr. Arnold." The correspondence with these men serves educational purposes since, as Anna remarks, "to their conversation and correspondence she owed many valuable acquirements" (V, 464). That correspondence occupies a strictly defined time slot in her daily schedule. Clarissa devotes to her "epistolary amusements" only the morning hours "she saved from rest" (V, 476). Clarissa has to snatch moments to write letters since they are a marginal activity among the much more important household duties prescribed for women. The posthumous Clarissa will obediently copy models from familiar letter manuals and parrot what has already been said for her, taking care that her writing not interfere with her household duties. As her successor in *Sir Charles Grandison*, Harriet Byron, observes:

> I am told that she writes finely, and is Madame de Sévigné to her correspondents. I hope to be one of them. But she has not, I find, suffered her pen to run away with her needle, nor her reading to interfere with that housewifery which the best of judges hold so indispensable in the character of a good woman.[20]

Richardson then successfully relegates female letter writing to the margins of literary activity. Clarissa's trajectory from the pedestal through the fall to death parallels the trajectory of a female writer who wants to use letters as means of communication and apply the law of genre, that is, use heart and spontaneity to conduct correspondence with men. In *Clarissa* the conflict between the law of genre and the rules of conduct clearly reaches a definite resolution: the law of genre has to surrender to the law of decorum. That defeat will have long-lasting consequences in terms of narrative patterns that shape epistolary fiction and its heroines. They can either write letters directly to their censors, or pay with life for any "uncensored" ventures into the territory of correspondence with men.

Richardson owed his success in providing a model plot for an epistolary tale of seduction and betrayal to the perfection with which he appropriated the female voice. "Although Richardson was obviously not a woman writer," notes Janet Todd in *The Sign of Angellica*,

> his early pretence in his epistolary novels that he was merely editing female texts, as well as the apparent autonomy he gave letters to women, made it seem that a female voice was actually present, while his centralising of female subjectivity, his concern for the problems of seduction, marriage and moral discrimination were typical of women writers ... Richardson represented the subjective, personal, domestic and internal ... in his didactic mode [he] made no claims to authorial power. (141–42)

And yet this apparent lack of claim to authorial power on Richardson's part was a brilliant strategic maneuver that mobilized the disciplinary principle of tact to obscure and cover up the movements and functions of control mechanisms. The apparent siding with women and their concerns, rendered authentic through the use of female voice, effectively masked his own role in imposing censorship on unruly sentiments. Like the rhetoric of idealizing women that supplanted the rhetoric of hostility, Richardson's identification with a sentimental heroine undercut any possibility of rebellion. While Usbek's Roxana acted with a full awareness of the oppressive terror reigning in the harem and thus had a just cause to fight, Richardson's female audience heard only Clarissa's sad tale. The benevolent editor, whose wordly wisdom and fatherly concern for her misfortunes guided them through the book, was bound to elicit their respect and admiration. Creating a bond of sympathy between his heroine, himself, and his female readers, Richardson hoped to enlist their support in banning clandestine correspondence and to shift the emphasis from "the past offence" to "the future disorder."[21] In Clarissa's story, he adjusted the punishing measures to the new disciplinary tactics which proposed "against a bad passion, a good habit; against a force, another force, but it must be the force of sensibility and passion, not that of armed power" (106).

4
Female Epistolary Strategies in *Evelina, Lady Susan,* and *Lettere di una novizia:* The Tactics of Caution, Convention, and Cliché

Richardson's legacy regarding correspondence, set forth in *Clarissa,* subjected letters by women to a system of censorship that displayed all the characteristics of being perfect. Nothing was left to chance. Under the magnifying glass of worry every little detail received equal consideration. The outcome of applying that system both in life and in epistolary fiction was the complete narrative paralysis of an autonomous female letter writer. Could there be a female epistolary voice after Richardson and if so, how would it have to adjust to fit the Richardsonian image of female correspondence?[1] In his study on the epistolary fiction in the late eighteenth century in England, Frank Black observes that "Richardson's ingenuity in exploring the possibilities for variation within the type he invented left comparatively little for his followers beyond tame imitation."[2] I would argue that "the tame imitation" was one of the few strategies that allowed women writers to remain present on the literary scene, protecting them from attacks on their reputation and irreparable injuries to their careers.[3] Writing in Richardson's protective shadow was more an act of social conformism than of purely literary imitation. Arabella, the heroine of Charlotte Lennox's *The Female Quixote* (1750), finds out from her mentor that, if she wants to succeed on both social and literary fronts, she has to follow the footsteps of Richardson,"an admirable writer of our time" who "has found the way to convey the most solid instructions, the noblest sentiments, and the most exalted piety in the pleasing dress of a novel."[4] The lesson that Lennox teaches Arabella "reflects the changing of the female novel," which from now on "will serve as a conduct book, colluding with the new ideology of femminity and teaching the sentimental image of womanhood" (160).

In order to conform to that ideology, the female writers of epistolary novels needed to rethink and redefine the use and function of letters.

That redefinition affected in turn the applicability of narrative patterns. Letters could no longer act as a means of orchestrating the events in the story, as paper messengers that assisted in escapes, clandestine meetings, and illicit love affairs, since the transgressive schemes promoted by such correspondence challenged the social order and contested the validity of rules existing in a familial structure. If a heroine permitted herself to be drawn into clandestine epistolary exchange, the censor of decorum, in the name of moral instruction, demanded her severe punishment. The necessity of conveying that message resulted in a total rigidity of form, imposing a preexisting plotline that allowed no room for deviation. In his classificaton of letter narratives, François Jost distinguishes what he calls "la lettre drame," in which the plot progresses through letters, addressed by the protagonist to his/her adversary.[5] The letters constitute an essential component of the plot since they dominate and manipulate the events in the novel, and the fate of the protagonists. This type of epistolary fiction, thematically linked to the tale of seduction and betrayal, dominated two-thirds of the eighteenth century.

And it was this fiction that the Richardsonian shadow pushed to the margins of popularity. Instead, a new narrative configuration moved to the center of attention. That new form corresponded to François Jost's, a "static/passive type," where the plot progresses in letters, not through them. Letters serve merely as repositories of sentiments and impressions that the protagonists, the central figures in the novel, share directly with their confidants. Since the confidants are of only secondary importance, and their comments usually appear only as echoes of their replies scattered throughout the protagonists' letters, the novel becomes a monologue in letters. Jean Rousset refers to it as a "journal camouflé" [camouflaged journal] where the epistolary form is nothing else but appearance.[6]

The shift from letters as a means of constructing the story to letters as only a medium to accommodate it, marked the tendency towards further control and eventual elimination of potential risks posed by uncensored correspondence. A number of women writers between 1750–1790 resorted to the passive type in order to satisfy both the censors of decorum and the censors of genre, since a letter was still highly favored as a typically feminine mode of expression. Frances Sheridan, greatly admired by Johnson and Richardson, made her heroine, Sidney Bidulph, tell her story in a series of long letters to an absent female friend (*Sidney Bidulph*, 1761). Frances Brooke used descriptive letters in *The History of Lady Julia Mandeville* (1763). Anne Fuller's *The Convent* (1786) employed letters "From the Same to the Same" practically substituting a letter for a diary. In Clara

Reeves's *Two Mentors* (1783) letters circulated only between two confidantes. Letters then had no other function than to describe—what and how they described remained still within the permissible boundaries of the law of genre, since the descriptions focused on sentiments and made no claim to art.

A subtle change, however, was waiting in the offing, a change that began by gradually replacing passion with modesty, and excess with temperance. That change was necessary to accentuate "that the femininity conveyed in the writer and the heroine was the natural state of woman; the novel that delivered it, however crafted, was artless, modest and sincere" (Todd, 145). In terms of writing and reading letters, that change had gone even further. The principle of spontaneity and the guidance of the heart, two elements that proved to be so injurious to female correspondents in the epistolary fiction, became targets of critique and gave way to caution and the guidance of mind. In the subsequent part of this chapter I will examine the strategies used by women letter writers who participated in executing that shift. Assuming that Richardson remains the idol of feminine epistolary fiction, I will show how three women build their own narratives around his statue. Whereas their writing strategies seem to comply with both the law of decorum and the law of genre, their stories subvert the accepted rules and beat the censors at their own game. The texts I have chosen are: Fanny Burney's *Evelina,* whose heroine applies a tactics of caution in her epistolary ventures, Jane Austen's *Love and Freindship* and *Lady Susan,* in which the heroines use the tactics of convention, and Guido Piovene's *Lettere di una novizia,* a novel whose protagonist applies the clichés of female epistolary style to draw the readers within and without the novel into a game of interpretation.

EVELINA AND IDOL CARESSING

Among the post-Richardsonian epistolary productions of the 1770's Black chooses two novels worthy of consideration and places them in two categories according to gender. Discussing Smollett's *Humphrey Clinker,* he praises the "new vigor given to the epistolary form" which the author achieves by "placing the pen for most of the time in masculine hands" (1). Fanny Burney's *Evelina* tops Black's list of respectable "feminine compositions" as a novel whose "peculiar merit" lies in bringing the "novel back to the depiction of manners, in a rich and realistic picture of London society of the 1770's, with a foreground occupied by a heroine so human that one could believe in her" (2). Evelina is pretty, naive, chaste, and modest. But what adds to her credibility as "a human heroine" is the use of letters as a form of self-expression, a form considered appropriate for young girls, and by the same token, for female writers, as Black notes: "Many young ladies seem to have felt with the authoress of *Sophia; or, the Embarrassed Wife* that letters were the 'most easy for a first attempt,' and often the initial essay led to further experiments in the same form"(8). *Evelina* thus scores points on two counts: first, by selecting the appropriate form to accommodate the content; secondly, by aspiring to attain Richardsonian ends. Black's criteria coincide with the opinion of the eighteenth-century critics who praise those two elements in a review of *Evelina* published in 1778: "This performance deserves no common praise, whether we consider it in the moral or literary light. It would have disgraced neither the head nor the heart of Richardson."[7] Fanny Burney herself acknowledged indebtedness to her literary predecessors in the preface to *Evelina*, though she did it with a great deal of caution:

> To avoid what is common, without adopting what is unnatural, must limit the ambition of the vulgar herd of authors: however zealous, therefore, my veneration of the great writers I have mentioned, however I may feel myself enlightened by the knowledge of Johnson, charmed with the eloquence of Rousseau, softened by the pathetic powers of Richardson, and exhilarated by the wit of Fielding and humour of Smollett, I yet presume not to attempt pursuing the same ground which they have tracked; and whence, though they may have cleared the weeds, they have also culled the flowers; and, though they have rendered the path plain, they have left it barren.[8]

Burney's critics have been apt to point out precisely what were her borrowings from other authors. Marjorie Dobbin sums it up: "In brief, from Richardson, Burney copied the epistolary style, the use of feminine perspective, and a plot that dealt with feminine problems."[9] How closely did Burney imitate the Richardsonian epistolary model, and to what end? To continue Burney's own metaphor, what plants did she decide to leave on the "barren path" laid down by her famous predecessor? In order to answer these questions we must focus on two issues: first, the correspondents in the story, their sex and age, and how these factors relate to the kind of letters they write; secondly, the function letters have within the novel, i.e., whether they affect the plot or merely recount it. The exploration of these issues will help us understand how Burney's text both used and subverted the Richardsonian model.

Evelina tells a story of a seventeen-year-old orphan who leaves the quiet village of Berry Hill, where she has lived with her benefactor, Mr. Villars, an elderly country parson, to go to London in the company of Mrs. Mirvan, and her daughter, Maria. Evelina's arrival in London marks an important change in her life—she has to find her way in the world of fashion and intricate social conventions, a world totally alien to an unsophisticated and naive girl. In the course of the story, Evelina manages to learn the rules of etiquette, resolves the problems of her birth and heritage (she finds her father and persuades him to accept her as his legitimate daughter and heir), and makes an extremely good match, accepting Lord Orville, an impeccably eligible man of society—no small achievement for an eighteenth-century Cinderella.

Evelina consists of 84 letters, 54 of which are written by Evelina to her benefactor and guardian, Mr. Villars, 11 from Villars to Evelina, and 6 from Evelina to her friend and confidante, Maria Mirvan, and a few letters that pass between Mr. Villars and Lady Howard, Mrs. Mirvan's mother. Thus, the two main correspondents are Evelina and Mr. Villars. Evelina uses letters to share with Mr. Villars the events of her new life. She writes to him minute accounts of every moment spent away from him, describes her impressions, joys, and disappointments as she promises in her first letter from London: "I shall write to you every evening all that passes in the day, and that in the same manner as, if I could see, I should tell you" (15). Her letters, then, appear to be nothing more than a journal with a specific addressee.[10]

But we should not overlook the fact that Mr. Villars is Evelina's legal guardian, and, as such, "the source of all permission."[11] Evelina cannot be a spontaneous and reckless or artless writer. She has to choose her writing strategies carefully in order to win his consent to her proposals, or to persuade him to accept her decisions. In Julia Epstein's words, Evelina's letters are

> emissaries to her guardian: they plead the case without offending her judge. Although Evelina claims to be sending her guardian a minutely detailed journal, a comprehensive account of her "entrance into the world" in fact, she maintains the selective privilege of the creative artist throughout her narrative. She writes from the angle from which she chooses Villars to view her adventures; she adopts a discourse of innocence arrested and then tutored; and he reads ultimately only what she wants him to know.[12]

Her deception is so transparent that the reader cannot help but perceive it, even though Villars does not.

Evelina's first letter to Villars illustrates her tactics. Evelina needs his permission to be able to accompany the Mirvans on their trip to London. She opens the letter with the description of gaiety and happiness that the Mirvan household radiates (a veiled allusion to the normal family life she is participating in for the first time in her life).

She then proceeds to present him with her request. Although she is the one who wants to go, she makes it sound as if she were writing on behalf of her friends, who urged her to do it: "I am desired to make a request to you. I hope you will not think me an encroacher; Lady Howard insists upon my writing! Yet I hardly know how to go on . . . But these dear ladies are so pressing!" (13). Farther on, Evelina alternates assurances of her filial love and obedience with references to the attractions that await her in London, were she allowed to go, not the least of which is the opportunity of sharing the Mirvans's domestic bliss:

> However, pray don't suppose that I make any point of going, for I shall hardly sigh, to see them depart without me, though I shall probably never meet with such another opportunity. And, indeed, their domestic happiness will be so great,—it is natural to wish to partake in it. (13)

What Evelina does not mention, but what Villars is bound to infer from the last sentence, is her craving for a normal family life, something she never had as an orphan despite all the affection bestowed on her by Villars. Only a totally unfeeling person could remain unmoved by her entreaties. And Villars, of course, relents, as Evelina had hoped he would: "To resist the urgency of entreaty, is a power which I have not yet acquired" (14).

Throughout her correspondence Evelina uses her innocence and ingeniousness to protect her from the attacks of the world but also as a strategy in negotiations. Her letters abound in proclamations of her artlessness, intellectual inferiority, lack of linguistic skills, and awkwardness of expression; "Adieu, my dear Sir, pray excuse the wretched stuff I write; perhaps I may improve by being in this town, and then my letters will be less unworthy your reading" (17). She appeals to her correspondent's sympathy and pity and by evoking them manages to achieve her goals. Unlike Clarissa, who trusted her rhetorical skills and the power of her pen, Evelina approaches writing with caution and distrust. The supposed spontaneity and naturalness of her letters exist only in the image of herself created for her addressees ("innocent as an angel, and artless as purity itself," in Villars's words, 9). Evelina learns that she lives in a "world so deceitful, where we must suspect what we see, distrust what we hear, and doubt even what we feel" (244). Although the plot of *Evelina* appears to progress in letters, and not by means of letters, Evelina herself is the force motivating the plot. If her applications to Villars were unsuccessful, the movement of the novel would be arrested. Her letters not only describe, but also plead and persuade. Thus, Evelina, like Clarissa, unfolds her tale but, unlike Clarissa, "the feather blown in the wind" (*Clarissa*, II, 47), she turns that tale into her advantage.

Evelina, following Richardson's prescriptions, writes letters only to her guardian and legal protector, in other words, to a father figure, and to Maria, her friend and confidante. Both Maria's mother and Villars know and approve of this correspondence. There is only one letter in the novel which Evelina writes independently, so to speak—a letter to Lord Orville. That episode is significant since it is probably the most obvious link between *Clarissa* and *Evelina*. Fearing that the rude and disrespectful behavior of her cousin towards Lord Orville might cost her the irretrievable loss of his "good opinion" (234), Evelina decides to write him a letter with a brief explanation and apology for the unpleasant incident. Evelina acts on the spur of the moment; she does not have either time or opportunity to consult anyone about the rightness of her decision. However, immediately after she has dispatched the note to Lord Orville's residence, she is besieged by doubts. She transcribes the note first in a letter to Maria and, only after a certain period of reflection, to Villars:

> I fear for your disapprobation; yet I should not be conscious of having merited it, but that the repugnance I feel to relate to you what I have done, makes me suspect I must have erred. Will you forgive me, if I own that I *first* wrote an account of this transaction to Miss Mirvan?—and that I even thought of *concealing* it from you?—Short-lived, however, was the ungrateful idea, and sooner will I risk the justice of your displeasure, than unworthily betray your generous confidence. (Burney's emphasis, 234).

That lengthy preamble with its humble and contrite tone is to soften the blow: "You are now probably prepared for what follows—which is a letter—a hasty letter, that, in the height of my agitation, I wrote to Lord Orville" (234). Like Clarissa, Evelina, aware of the risks involved in writing to a man, wants to stop the letter from reaching Orville:

> I applied to the maid of the house to get this note conveyed to Berkley-square; but scarce had I parted with it, before I regretted having written at all; and I was flying down the stairs to recover it, when the voice of Sir Clement Willoughby stopped me. As Madame Duval had ordered we should be denied to him, I was obliged to return upstairs; and after he was gone, my application was too late, as the maid had given it to the porter. (235)

Also like Clarissa, Evelina learns that once sent "the letter is out of her power" (*Clarissa*, II, 72), and liable to all sorts of mishap. And in fact, that letter causes Evelina a great deal of suffering and almost ruins her prospects of marrying Lord Orville. Willoughby intercepts the letter and sends Evelina a reply in the name of Lord Orville. Evelina reads it avidly and in haste, and misconstrues its message. A letter to Maria describes her initial reaction:

> The moment the letter was delivered to me I retired to my own room to read it; and so eager was my first perusal, that—I am ashamed to own,—it gave me no sensation but of delight. Unsuspicious of any impropriety from Lord Orville, I perceived not immediately the impertinence it implied,—I only marked the expressions of his own regard; and I was so much surprised, that I was unable for some time to compose myself, or read it again:—I could only walk up and down the room, repeating to myself, "Good God, is it possible?—am I then loved by Lord Orville?" (242)

But the moment of infatuation passes as Evelina reads the letter the second time, now much more critically and attentively.

The second "perusal" reveals it to be frivolous and disrespectful: "I could not find one sentence that I could look at without blushing; my astonishment was extreme, and it was succeeded by the utmost indignation" (242). Through the process of painstaking rereading and interpretation, Evelina manages to pinpoint the improprieties contained in the letter; "the clandestine air given to it, by his proposal of sending his servant for my answer, instead of having it directed to his house," the reference to a design in Evelina's "sweet commencement of correspondence," and "a mortifying freedom of style" (245). Evelina reproaches herself for having let her partiality and regard for Orville affect her judgment as a reader, and blind her to the obvious tone and content of his letter; "Never, never again will I trust to appearances;—never confide in my own weak judgement;—never believe that person to be good and amiable! What cruel maxims are we taught by a knowledge of the world" (241). She decides that the best way to manifest her indignation would be to leave the letter unanswered.

In the letters to Maria she probes her own feelings for Orville, and the pain that each thought of him causes her, but does not have the courage to disclose the whole affair to Villars. Eventually, however, his kindness and affection disarm her, and she pours out her heart to him. Having read the letter three times, Villars comes to the conclusion that Orville must have been intoxicated when he wrote it, since it is impossible for "a man who had behaved with so strict a regard to delicacy" to "thus wantonly insult a modest young woman" (252). However, rather than leave the letter unanswered, suggests Villars, Evelina should have enclosed it in an empty cover, and have returned it to him again; such a resentment would at once have become *your* character, and have given him an opportunity, in some measure, of clearing his own. He could not have read this letter the next morning without being sensible of the impropriety of having written it. (252)

Villars' advice repeats almost verbatim an excerpt from Richardson's *Familiar Letters on Important Occasions* where a young lady who receives a letter from an importunate suitor "should return it unopened or in a blank cover."[13]

The affair with the letter gives Evelina the opportunity to ponder the dangers of autonomous correspondence for young women, and the evils of concealment. A brief sermon, with Clarissa's ghost peeping over Evelina's shoulder, follows:

> This conversation, though extremely affecting to me at the time it passed, has relieved my mind from much anxiety. Concealment, my dear Maria, is the foe of tranquility; however I may err in future, I will never be disingenuous in acknowledging my errors. To you and to Mr. Villars I vow an unremitting confidence. (253)

Evelina vows never to carry on a correspondence with any young man not sanctioned by permission from her guardian. When Lord Orville, already as her future husband, asks Evelina to write to him during her stay in town, she recoils from him with horror : "Can you indeed desire, my Lord, that I should, a second time, expose myself, by an unguarded readiness, to write to you?" (337). She also learns the importance of her own signature and the risks involved in allowing that signature to fall into undesired hands. In answer to Willoughby's explanation and apology for the forgery of Orville's name, Evelina sends him an unsigned note of acknowledgment, thereby depriving it of any manipulative potential.

Evelina's subtitle, "A Young Woman's Entrance into the World," points to its educative character and pragmatic end. In Julia Epstein's words "*Evelina* serves as a guide-book for young women; lacking a guide to the confusing byways of social etiquette for unmarried women, Evelina composes one for herself as she goes."[14] For Kristina Straub, *Evelina* "is an instruction book. Evelina's entrance into the world is an entrance into sexual maturity and an introduction to the rituals and institutions that will define the quality of her experiences as a woman."[15]

An important part of these rituals is the ability to deal with writing and reading letters. *Evelina* essentially repeats Richardson's message: young women should be allowed to carry on a correspondence only with their guardians, or confidantes approved by parents. They should never venture to start an epistolary communication with young men, no matter how decorous their manners might seem. A signed letter constitutes a weapon capable of ruining a woman's reputation, and in consequence, destroying every chance of her happiness. The incident with the forged letter could be read as the plot of *Clarissa* in miniature. Had Willoughby been successful in his attempt to draw Evelina into a clandestine correspondence, she might have shared Clarissa's fate. But Evelina avoids that fate precisely because she proves that she has learned the lesson conveyed in *Clarissa*, a lesson of distrust towards male letters. It is the vivid recollection of male epistolary artfulness, depicted in conduct material and novels, that makes her reject the first interpretation of Orville's letter, and search for a key to decode its true meaning.

But despite the apparent repetition of the Richardsonian warnings, *Evelina* marks an important shift in the tactics of female letter writers and readers, namely, from spontaneity to calculated strategies in both writing and reading. Those strategies include the anticipation of the recipient's response, the effective use of stereotypical images to lead the reader in the desired direction, interpretative skills that make it possible to spot false notes and linguistic/stylistic improprieties. The frequent references to the acts of reading and writing demonstrate the significance of those acts in the life of a young woman. As Epstein argues:

> Letter writing in *Evelina* is a synecdochic gesture: it stands, in miniature, for the tenuous and danger-fraught communication process between authority and its charge, between the empowered and the powerless. A well-behaved young woman, Evelina knows, must be innocent and artless, and the "art" of letter-writing—that accomplishment for cultured ladies we looked at in chapter 1—should reflect this. But innocence and artlessness get Evelina continually in trouble, so self-preservation demands that she replace those traits with experience as fast as she can.[16]

Thus, Evelina replaces spontaneity with caution, and for writing from the heart, she substitutes writing organized according to the dictates of the mind. Evelina abandons her plan of writing to Villars each evening to acquaint him with the events of a particular day, supposedly because she finds it "impractical" but she might have another reason for that change: the need for a certain distance and the time to reflect and organize her thoughts. Evelina admits that she does not want to write in those moments of her life when passion dominates reason: "I could not write yesterday, so violent was the agitation of my mind" (352). Burney then does not follow the Richardsonian model in which all the letters flow from the heart "so that they abound not only with critical situations, but with what may be called *instantaneous* descriptions and reflections."[17] "The instantaneous descriptions" give way to descriptions where reflection and critical evaluation come to the fore.

Evelina also proves to be a cautious and fastidious reader, capable of passing fair judgment on the text and its writer. She demonstrates her abilities when dealing with the letter forged by Willoughby in Orville's name, and later on, when she receives a letter from Willoughby with the explanation of the forgery. She decides to keep this letter secret from Orville to prevent a conflict between the two rivals. Her summary of Willoughby's conduct manifests her common sense and her choice of reason over passion:

> What a strange letter! how proud and how piqued does its writer appear! To what alternate *meanness* and *rashness* do the passions lead, when reason and self-denial do not oppose them! The rudeness of his manner of writing to me, springs from the same cause: the proof which he has received of my indifference to him has stung him to the soul, and he has neither the delicacy nor forbearance to disguise his pleasure. I determined not to show this letter to Lord Orville, and thought it most prudent to let Sir Clement know I should not. (370)

Evelina's reading is informed by suspicion and prudence, as opposed to Clarissa's reading, informed by trust and literalness. Evelina quotes reason and self-denial as the values atop her list, while retaining the appearance of naturalness and spontaneity, expected of a young woman. Burney's success as an author parallels Evelina's success in society because Burney herself applied the strategies taught in *Evelina*. In a brief biographical note, Reginald Brimley Johnson observes that "the book as a whole is attractive because of its spontaneity. It is as natural and impulsive as [Evelina's] journals, and as truthfully reflects her own impressions."[18] Like Villars, Burney's critics accepted the appearance for truth, proving the efficacy of Evelina's and Burney's writing strategy. Evelina does not defy the law of decorum, she does not "overturn the social order; what she achieves is a measure of personal autonomy and control within the confines of 'acceptable' social behavior for women."[19] Burney then instructs her female public that a way to enter the society is to comply with its conventions, but it is a conscious compliance, ruled by constant guardedness and diplomacy.

Lady Susan and Idol Smashing

If Burney apparently conformed to the Richardsonian epistolary model, and loudly acknowledged his position as a revered idol, Jane Austen appeared less than respectful towards her literary predecessors. In Annette Hopkins's words, in Austen's early epistolary pieces (usually referred to with the slightly derogatory term "juvenilia"):

> There is imitation of predecessors, and contemporaries aplenty, but it is not the sort of imitation usually found in the work of the author of sixteen. There is no burning of incense to literary idols, but there is a good deal of idol smashing. And the demolition, it must be acknowledged, is carried on with the hand of justice rather than mercy.[20]

Hopkins's essay belongs to a slim group of articles that consider Austen's epistolary pieces with regard to preceding letter fiction. The bulk of criticism concerning *Love and Freindship* and *Lady Susan* focuses on them in the light of her future production. John Halperin, for instance, regards them as

> precursors of what was to follow. The juvenilia are precocious and sometimes amusing but they are by no means brilliant, as those who view them with passionate hindsight like to make out—nor are they more than intermittently entertaining. They are chiefly interesting in illuminating for us Jane Austen's first struggles to find a literary voice of her own.[21]

They are discussed as "intimations of the major novels."[22] In her extremely perceptive "Plots and Possibilities: Jane Austen's Juvenilia," Patricia Meyer Spacks relates the creation of characters and plot designs in the juvenilia to Austen's mature works: "As the young writer tests imaginative possibility, she foretells principles of plot-making she will later choose to follow."[23] These comments all concentrate on the juvenilia as a springboard necessary for Austen to make a leap into the future.

Those rare articles that link the juvenilia with the preceding literary tradition usually consider them in terms of thematic connections, or search for elements of burlesque and ridicule. A notable exception is Julia Epstein's article, "Jane Austen's Juvenilia and the Female Epistolary Tradition," an attempt to study systematically "the particular letter form Austen inherited and its relation to her early use of epistolary narrative and female narrative voices."[24] Epstein explores the paradox inherent in the definition of a familiar letter—its claim to absolute spontaneity and artlessness while concealing "its nature as a written artifact, a composed and studied discourse" (402), and shows how Austen exposes that paradox both in her private letters and in the juvenilia. She claims that Austen's epistolary pieces reveal a conscious reaction to the image of a female letter writer propagated in the eighteenth century, and to the limitations imposed on female letters by literary theories and conduct material.

Building on Epstein's analysis, I would like to focus on two issues essential for a fuller understanding of the evolution of that image: the female letter as an object of male manipulation, and the competence of female writers and readers in epistolary exchanges. That analysis, however, entails constant retrospection in order to trace the features that connect Austen's epistolary fiction with its predecessors and distinguish it from them. The intertexts for my reading of Austen will be *Clarissa* and *Evelina,* texts that engaged in a dialogue with each other, and which were bound to provoke Austen's reaction. If *Evelina*'s tactics could be called defensive—showing how to avoid the traps involved in epistolary communication unobtrusively, without offending the high and mighty and breaking social conventions, Jane Austen's *Love and Freindship* and *Lady Susan* could be called offensive—how to conquer a hostile world by means of writing and reading.

Love and Freindship deconstructs the female letter as a locus of male power. Both its title *Love and Freindship* and subtitle "Deceived in Freindship and Betrayed in Love," place the novel within the sentimental epistolary convention and suggest the continuation of the Richardsonian tradition of tales of seduction and betrayal. The novel consists of fourteen letters written by Laura to her friend's daughter, Marianne, and one letter written by Isabel, Marianne's mother. This letter contradicts the tenets of the epistolary convention—Isabel asks Laura to share with Marianne "a regular detail of the Misfortunes and Adventures of her life" to provide her with a moral lesson for the future.[25] Laura, claims Isabel, can safely engage in correspondence now, since having reached the age of fifty-five she is safe "from the determined Perseverance of disagreable Lovers and the cruel Persecutions of obstinate Fathers" (1). Since she is past her prime as a conventional heroine Laura's letters are safe from any attempt to control or manipulate ("disagreable Lovers and obstinate Fathers"). Her letters perform only a narrative function; they serve as a vehicle for recounting the story of her life. Laura is the only person in charge of her script; she breaks up the narrative at random to pick it up in the continuing letter. Since the narrative covers events that have already happened, her letters have no material value as documents to be intercepted or used against her.

In fact, in Laura's life, letters never played any significant role as means of communication or objects of control. Laura mentions only one instance when a letter was sent to convey a message, but she immediately undercuts the possibility of its being an object of interest:

> Unwilling to intrude our society on him unexpected and unthought of, we wrote a very elegant and well penned Note containing an account of our destitute and melancholy situation and of our intention to spend some months with him. As soon as we had dispatched this letter, we immediately prepared to follow it in person. (23)

Since Laura and Sophia did not give Sophia's relatives any time to reply to their letter, but followed it immediately themselves, the act of sending the letter becomes completely pointless.

As in the incident with the letter, Laura seems to operate on two levels: the level of convention (understood as a set of behavioral rules) and the level of rebellion against that convention. The former is reflected in the conventional situations and the language she uses, the latter in her actions. Laura wants Marianne to adopt her strategy, in order to resist the limitations imposed on women. Laura's strategy aims to reject passivity as the way of behavior for women, and to undertake action. The proper reaction of a young lady in any disagreeable situation was to faint: "Ah, what could we do but what we did! We sighed and fainted alternately on the sofa" (19). But as Laura points out, although fainting on the sofa was fairly safe, fainting in the park brought a fatal end to her friend, Sophia. Laura's letters are a warning to Marianne against "fainting fits which though at the time they may be refreshing and agreable, yet beleive me, they will in the end, if too often repeated and at improper seasons, prove destructive to your constitution . . . One fatal swoon cost Sophia life" (40). "Frenzy fits," on the other hand, continues Laura, "are much better since it is an exercise to the Body, and if not too violent, is conducive to Health in its consequences. Run as often as you chuse, but do not faint" (40). If convention requires women to faint, i.e., to be completely passive in unpleasant situations, why not try a frenzy fit, which, at least, provides the body with some physical activity? Austen clearly perceives convention as an ideological construct which prescribes a set of rules within which a heroine is supposed to move. Laura accepts them on the verbal level, but rejects them on the level of acting; hence the discrepancy between what she says or writes and what she does.

Lady Susan, a short epistolary novel, first published in 1871, but written probably around 1793, is for Brian Southam "remarkable for its portrayal of a central figure quite without sympathetic or appealing qualities, a heartless schemer and adventuress."[26] Frank Black calls Lady Susan "a hard, self-seeking woman of the world, a scheming coquette" (106). Both critics agree that Lady Susan has odd qualities for a heroine of an epistolary novel; she lacks "sympathetic inclinations"; she is guided by mind rather than heart; she is capable of manipulating people; in short, she is more a Lovelace than a Clarissa.

Lady Susan is fully aware of her "oddity" in the society she belongs to. She knows that to be accepted by that society means conforming to its conventions. Therefore, she uses language to construct a façade behind which she can hide her real personality. Lady Susan is a widow, not rich enough to live the life of affluence she craves; in order to achieve it, she has to secure a wealthy husband. She resorts to the manipulation of people around her by using her verbal skills. Like Lovelace, Lady Susan is very proud of her abilities to practice artifice by means of language: "I trust I shall be able to make my story as good as hers. If I am vain of anything, it is of my eloquence. Consideration and Esteem as surely follow command of Language, as Admiration waits on Beauty."[27] She despises the passivity and emotional weakness of her daughter, Frederica, since she perceives both the dangers and the inefficacy of such an attitude:

> I never saw a girl of her age, bid fairer to be the Sport of Mankind. Her feelings are tolerably lively, and she is so charmingly artless in their display as to afford the most reasonable hope of her being ridiculed and despised by every Man who sees her. (77)

Frederica's actions are ineffective—she writes one letter that could alter her wretched situation, but since she believes in the God of Truth, not the God of Art, she fails to achieve anything, and it is her mother who profits from it by employing her manipulative skills. Unlike Frederica, Lady Susan refuses to be "the Sport of Mankind," and prefers to ridicule and despise men, instead of being ridiculed and despised.

The first two letters, written by Lady Susan, give a sample of her literary talent. The first letter, addressed to her brother-in-law, is written in the feminine style in which emotions flow naturally from the heart. Lady Susan, after having created a scandal during her stay with some friends, desperately needs the invitation from her brother-in-law. Not a word, however, is breathed about the real reason for her visit; her haste to visit them is attributed to her emotional needs:

> My kind friends here are most affectionately urgent with me to prolong my stay, but their hospitable and cheerful dispositions lead them too much

into Society for my present situation and state of mind; and I impatiently look forward to the hour when I shall be admitted into your delightful retirement. I long to be made known to your dear little Children, in whose hearts I shall be very eager to secure an interest. (2)

Sure that her brother-in-law will accept those declarations at their face value, Lady Susan ruthlessly ridicules the rhetoric of sensibility in the letter to her friend and confidante Mrs. Johnson, giving her readers a sense that "they are reading an anti-conduct book."[28] In this letter she reveals the real reasons for her removal to Churchill, which changes from a place of "delightful retirement" in the first letter, to "that insupportable spot, a Country Village" in the second (7). The little children whose affection she craved in the first letter become a means of securing her sister-in-law's affection:

I mean to win my Sister-in-law's heart through her children. I know all their names already, and I am going to attach myself with the greatest sensibility to one in particular, a young Frederic, whom I take on my lap and sigh over for his dear Uncle's sake. (18)

Lady Susan's strategy in making letters a means of manipulating people consists in using the rhetoric of sentiment to subvert cliché situations. The efficacy of her writing lies in the gap between the assumption of transparent truth and artlessness on the part of her addressee, and the actual use of that assumption to produce the appearance of truth. If, in her friend's words, "facts are such horrid things" (146), language is there to transform them into a more palatable reality for her interlocutor. And Lady Susan proves to be a mistress of such transformations. Writing, then, for her means action, not a passive reaction to or reflection of reality. Lady Susan does not "unfold her tale"; she constructs it herself. She is capable of adapting rhetoric to the demands of the situation. As Barbara Horwitz notes, "on the occasions when she is addressing those respectable adversaries, she speaks their own language, the language of conduct books" (181). Like Lovelace, she carefully plans her every move and selects the best strategy to execute her plans. With her brother-in-law, her strategy is to appeal to his pity and sympathy by references to her recent bereavement, and to highlight the concern for her daughter's future. With Reginald, it is the manifestation of serenity and quiet gentleness. She monitors the results of her conquest in a letter to Mrs Johnson:

It has been delightful to me to watch his advances towards intimacy, especially to observe his altered manner in consequence of my repressing by the calm dignity of my deportment, his insolent approach to direct familiarity. My conduct has been equally guarded from the first, and I never behaved less like a Coquette in the whole course of my life, tho' perhaps my desire of dominion was never more decided. I have subdued him entirely by sentiment and serious conversation, and made him I may venture to say at least *half* in love with me, without the semblance of the most common-place flirtation. (37, Austen's emphasis)

With her own daughter, she uses the pressure of silent contempt rather than an open demand that Frederica accept "a marriage from which her heart revolted." "Instead of adopting so harsh a measure," Lady Susan merely proposes "to make it her own choice by rendering her thoroughly uncomfortable till she does accept him" (26).

For Lady Susan truth is in the eye of the beholder, so she provides the clues that will enable him to construct that truth along her guidelines. If Reginald expects her to be a perfect sister, mother, and household manager, Lady Susan supplies him with all the necessary elements to fulfill his expectations. "I know," claims Reginald in a letter to his father,

> that Lady Susan in coming to Churchill was governed only by the most honourable and amiable intentions. Her prudence and economy are exemplary, her regard for Mr Vernon equal even to *his* deserts, and her wish of obtaining my sister's good opinion merits a better turn than it has received. As a mother she is unexceptionable. Her solid affection for her Child is shewn by placing her in the hands, where her Education will be properly attended to; but because she has not the blind and weak partiality of most Mothers, she is accused of wanting Maternal Tenderness. (55, Austen's emphasis)

Lady Susan's words guide Reginald's perception of her person in the desired direction. All her strategies seem to work: she receives the invitation from Mr Vernon, makes Reginald fall in love against his inclinations and propose to her, and renders Frederica's life totally miserable. But at some point her plans go awry. Lady Susan loses Reginald and has to accept the second best on her list of possible choices, Sir James Martin, previously designated as her daughter's husband, a man "contemptibly weak," but very rich and sure to be a gullible partner.

The mix-up in Lady Susan's plans comes from a rather unexpected quarter—the competence of her female adversaries in decoding her rhetorical constructs. Lady Susan, as a skilled writer, finds her match in Mrs. Vernon, her seemingly harmless and unassuming sister-in-law. Sure of captivating her brother-in-law, Lady Susan is "afraid of his wife" (15). She admits defeat in her campaign designed to win Catherine's affection and good opinion: "I wanted her to be delighted at seeing me—I was as amiable as possible on the occasion—but all in vain—she does not like me" (15). Mrs. Vernon recognizes Lady Susan for what she is—a woman who uses her physical attractiveness, charming manners, and verbal skills to secure a respectable position in society. "She is clever and agreable," writes Catherine Vernon to her mother, "has all that knowledge of the world which makes conversation easy, and talks very well, with a happy command of Language, which is too often used I beleive to make Black appear White" (21). Part of the challenge for Lady Susan—besides a relatively easy task of deceiving all the male characters in the story—is to deal with the fierce opposition to her designs which she encounters in the persons of Catherine Vernon and her mother.

Lady Susan thus presents a clash between what Deborah Kaplan calls "two networks" of women who "are also teams in competition with one another," a team of competent writers (Lady Susan and Alicia Johnson), and a team of competent readers (Catherine Vernon, her mother, and Mrs. Manwaring).[29] Men play the role of pawns in that game, necessary but insignificant means of achieving social respectability. Austen emphasizes their lack of individual characteristics by giving them the same first names. Reginald de Courcy is the son of Reginald de Courcy. Lady Susan's late husband's name was Frederic Vernon, and "little Frederic" Vernon is the son of her brother-in-law. The repetition of those first names points to their interchangeability on the marriage market, as long as they have money and title. In *Lady Susan* Austen creates a world in which men, to use Lovelace's metaphor, are "puppets" in women's hands. "Mr Vernon lived only to do whatever he was desired" (167). Reginald, like his father, has little to say about his own future. His sister and mother have already chosen and approved of Frederica as his future wife. Reginald's mother assures her daughter that "when Reginald has recovered his good spirits, *we* will try to rob him of his heart once more, and I am full of hopes of seeing their hands joined at no great distance" (161, Austen's emphasis). As the narrator informs us, "Frederica was therefore fixed in the family of her Uncle and Aunt, till such time as Reginald De Courcy could be talked, flattered, and finessed into an affection for her" (171). Lady Susan agrees to release Reginald from her dainty hands without further ado because she is already planning to secure for herself Sir James. Thus, she emerges from the matrimonial campaign in almost full victory, with a wealthy and tractable husband and a respectable social position.

Lady Susan reverses completely the system of epistolary exchanges presented in *Clarissa*. Men not only cease to dominate it but become interchangeable objects in the epistolary games devised and controlled by women who have all the rhetorical power to plot and manipulate. Clarissas turn into Reginalds, and Lady Susans replace Lovelaces. The Conclusion to *Lady Susan,* written as authorial narrative, offers the author's comment on further developments in the lives of the protagonists. Deborah Kaplan claims that the Conclusion "undermines the subversiveness of that part of *Lady Susan* which is told in letters." But, asks Kaplan, "why does Jane Austen subvert its own subversion?" (171). In Kaplan's opinion, the epistolary part of the novel "expresses the perspective of Austen's women's culture" but

> the text endows women's networks with more power than they had in Austen's actual life. At the heart of *Lady Susan* lies the fantasy that the discourse of one woman to another has magic power: women writing and speaking to one another are doing and becoming. (172)

The Conclusion, in Kaplan's opinion, undercuts that illusion of power since "the narrator who subtly champions the world of the patriarchal culture, portrays the female characters' machinations as unthreatening and amusing little events" (173). She claims that Austen, living within the patriarchal culture, could not allow her characters to realize their "rebellious desires" to challenge the existing social order and reject its power structures.

But why would Austen present those rebellious desires? Merely to bask in a momentary glory and have a foretaste of power? And why did she give up the epistolary form after *Lady Susan?* The answer to these questions may lie not in Austen's efforts to reproduce the actual reality, to which Kaplan refers her conclusive remarks, but in her desire to produce it by means of fiction. By introducing the person of an impartial narrator whose voice comments on the story, the characters, and their future, Austen draws the readers' attention to the fictionality of the epistolary part of the novel. The author's voice can tell us what will happen to the protagonists, because it has the ability to enter their minds. Thus we learn that Mrs Vernon's "anxiety on the subject made her press for an early visit to London," that "With a heart full of the Matter, Mrs Vernon waited on Lady Susan," and that she "was then convinced of what she had only suspected before that she might have spared herself all the trouble of urging a removal [of Frederica to the Vernons], which Lady Susan had doubtless resolved on from the first"(167). The author does not assume the role of the letters' editor but of their creator.

By pointing to the fictionality of *Lady Susan,* of its characters and their letters, Austen unmasks the fictionality of its epistolary predecessors, whose creators, in the guise of editors, presented illusion with "all the éclat" of truth.[30] The female letter, reduced to the object of control and manipulation in *Clarissa,* Evelina's spontaneous and naive outpourings in letters, and the female letter elevated to the agent of manipulation in *Lady Susan,* then belong to the same category, the category of letters rooted in fiction, not in "real life."[31] Austen's Conclusion subverts not her own narrative, but the epistolary narratives before her because it calls into question two aspects emphasized over and over again by Richardson. The first is the appeal to universality and immutability of epistolary relations in *Clarissa.* If Lady Susan is no more than a figment of Austen's imagination, so are Lovelace and Clarissa of Richardson's. They are not autonomous beings, as Richardson would have us believe: their existence and actions depend wholly on the will of their creator. Secondly, Austen challenges the claim of epistolary narratives to "represent real life," as the basis for their instructional qualities. By the same token, she undermines the principal motive for publishing the bulk of epistolary novels in the eighteenth century: the use of authentic documents, letters, to provide examples and warnings for the reading public. Reading novels was justified only, if it meant instruction, not enjoyment. We recall Richardson's disappointment and dissatisfaction with his audience who read *Clarissa* for the sake of the plot, not for the moral in *A Collection of the Moral and Instructive Sentiments.*[32] And instruction, to be effective, demanded the backup of "real life." Austen's finger directed at the fictionality of Lady Susan's correspondence makes us reflect back on her epistolary predecessors, and question the validity of the instructional claims based on real life representation.

Austen's juvenilia also demonstrate the breakdown of communication through letters. In *Love and Freindship,* writing a letter becomes a pointless, mechanical gesture. In *Lady Susan,* letters obscure, deceive, and manipulate, rather than inform, clarify, and negotiate. Writing and reading letters become exercises in encoding and decoding the duplicity of epistolary discourse, oscillating between spontaneity and calculation, unembellished truth and convenient lies, sincerity and pretense. Letters function as agents in the competitive games for domination between men and women, and are inscribed in that manipulative web. Epistolary fiction promotes these games, exploiting the letter's potential as a means of control and manipulation. In Richardson's world women are losers in that game; Burney's Evelina uses the tactics of caution to hold her ground; in Austen's world men become dupes of female artifice. And in the epistolary world of Laclos, "liaisons dangereuses" allude to any kind of epistolary exchange, since letters are a means of destruction in both camps. Thus "letters do not provide an arena for true communication. Instead, epistolary clichés condition and conventionalize possible forms of expression."[33] The noticeable decline of the epistolary form, particularly among well-known women writers at the end of the eighteenth century, may be attributed not to "the dissatisfaction with the epistolary form," as Black claims, but to the dissatisfaction with the clichés that pervade that form.[34]

RITA AND THE UTILIZATION OF IDOLS

The decline of epistolary fiction at the end of the eighteenth century, however, does not mean that the stereotyped image of letters propagated in that fiction has ceased to exist. On the contrary, its existence has proved to be hard to erase long after *Clarissa* or *Les Liaisons dangereuses* lost their grip on the reading public. The possibility of using letters as agents in power games (for example, Edgar Allan Poe's "The Purloined Letter") draws attention to the importance of interpretation. If writing and reading letters prove to be dangerous activities because of a whole range of misuses and abuses of letter-texts, it is necessary to develop accurate interpretative skills. Guido Piovene's novel, published in Italy in 1941, *Lettere di una novizia*, demonstrates how the clichés that grew out of the eighteenth-century epistolary fiction affect the reading and interpretation of letters by women.

Two major critics of Guido Piovene's works, Pietro Pancrazi, and Tibor Wlassics, place *Lettere di una novizia* within the eighteenth century epistolary tradition, notably, that of Richardson and Laclos.[35] Piovene's novel shares with its predecessors not only the use of letter as a narrative form but also the moral stance underlying the meditation on the human condition. It confronts "la malattia morale," [moral sickness] and offers "l'anatomia di un delitto" [the anatomy of a murder].[36] But while Piovene's literary forefathers professed a moral truth by inserting themselves between the narration and the reader, Piovene offers no such comfort. In his case "la ricerca della verità" [the search for truth] seemingly leads nowhere, as the truth remains buried under layers and layers of narration equally inaccessible to the internal and external readers. Like peeling an onion, the act of reading Piovene's novel leaves the readers tearful, with discarded layers of narration lying around an empty center.

In Wlassics's words the novel constitutes "un guscio vuoto, una maschera senza un volto dietro di essa" (176) [an empty shell, a mask behind which there is no face]. But it is precisely this shell and the process of its creation that attract Piovene, as he points out in his own comment: "il contenuto di quello che fanno [i personaggi] è dunque da biasimare; il metodo, direi la forma, è degno di riflessione"[37] [The substance of all their actions is therefore worthy only of blame: but the way in which they act, the mode of their behaviour, is something worth thinking about].[38] The shell/form is the correspondence that involves Rita Passi, a young novice soon to become a nun, her mother, the mother superior, two priests, don Giuseppe Scarpa, and don Paolo Conti, and a young neighbor, Michele Sacco. Since the only access to truth lies in the letters that circulate among the protagonists, the task of both internal and external readers is to use letters as a means of solving the jigsaw puzzle of Rita's personality and her life. The plot of the novel consists of actions/decisions that result from the acts of writing, reading, and interpreting letters.

The aim of Rita's correspondence with the priests is to enlist their help in leaving the convent. Her letters must create such a version of "truth" that would persuade them to fulfil her wish. Don Scarpa remains unmoved by her pleas for assistance but don Conti yields to them and arranges her escape into a hiding place. Her brief stay in hiding ends in a tragedy. Frightened by the prospect of returning to the convent, Rita kills an elderly servant sent to bring her back, and dies in prison shortly after the trial for murder. Thus Don Conti's decision to accept Rita's letters as an expression of truth triggers the events that lead to a tragic ending. His decision signals both Rita's triumph as a skillful writer, capable of manipulating her reader's response, and don Conti's failure as a reader unable to decode the artifice of her texts. Michele Sacco, a young man who rushes to assist Rita when she tries escape the scene of her crime, is another victim of the art of epistolary persuasion.

Lettere di una novizia then is a novel about an interpretative fiasco, a fiasco that, I argue, stems from the application of literary clichés to the reading and interpretation of Rita's letters. My reading of Piovene's novel will focus on the construction of Rita as a text/shell behind which there is no other referent than other texts and the readers' perceptions of them. Consequently, my analysis will substitute the moral problematics as the theme of the novel for the problematics of the text and will explore the meandering of a reading process rather than the meandering of an evil mind.[39] I see Piovene's debt to the eighteenth-century epistolary fiction not only in using the epistolary form but also in using the clichés that grew out of it, in particular, the literary clichés surrounding the figure of a nun and the female letter writer. There are two sets of clichés at work. The first revolves around the typical characteristics of a feminine letter, as defined by the law of genre. According to that law, a woman's letter is a candid and spontaneous expression of sentiment and presents unembellished truth, since women lack talent and education to practice artifice. The second regards the figure of a nun and the connotations that image evokes in a reader acquainted with the classics of Italian literature, as we might assume in the case of don Scarpa and don Conti. Ironically, then, a cliché, itself a literary artifact, becomes a tool that manipulates the acts of writing and reading texts, a tool that creates fact out of fiction, as happens in Rita's case.

For critics of reader-response theory the act of reading means the interaction between "the text and the reader."[40] The term "interaction" implies active participation in that act on the part of both, the text and the reader. While it is relatively easy to imagine the willingness of the reader to be active in the reading process, it is more difficult to perceive participation by the text. Umberto Eco explains it in the following way: "Un testo è una macchina pigra che esige dal lettore un fiero lavoro cooperativo per riempire spazi di non-detto o di già-detto rimasti per così dire in bianco, allora il testo non è che una macchina presupposizionale" [A text is a lazy mechanism which demands from a reader an extensive cooperation to fill in the blanks of the non-said or of the already-said; hence a text is nothing other than a mechanism based on assumptions].[41] In order for that "lazy mechanism" to work, the author of the text, like any good strategist, must be able to predict the reactions of his adversary—the reader, and organize the textual strategies accordingly. The means at the author's disposal include: language, a given lexical and stylistic tradition, and literary and cultural background. Wolfgang Iser subsumes all these elements under one heading, "the repertoire," which "consists of all the familiar territory within the text. This may be in the form of references to earlier works, or to social and historical norms, or to the whole culture from which the text has emerged" (69).

Literary clichés constitute a significant part of the repertoire. Cliché is commonly understood as "a hackneyed phrase or idea." But the banal and repetitive character that turns a cliché into a derogatory term of common parlance accounts for its usefulness and indispensability in the act of reading and interpretation. The act of interpretation requires the reader to move among the mixture of new and old elements. Cliché, "with its déjà vu effect,"[42] provides the reader with the familiar ground, easily identifiable, thus enabling him "to meet the challenge of the new by reducing it to the old."[43]

Cliché performs a number of functions in the reading process, as Ruth Amossy explains:

> It activates the reading process on the most varied levels. It plays an important part not only in an immediate deciphering, but also in reading

operations such as the constructional and/or intellectual identification and critical reflection. As an automatized figure, the cliché insures an illusion of transparency, a passage through the discourse towards the 'referent'. As the bearer of a stereotyped meaning, it presents a picture conforming to the reader's conception of what is read. The cliché grounds discourse in truth and helps to persuade the addressee, bringing about an adherence or solidarity of the mind.[44]

Since cliché belongs to earlier discourses, literary or social, continues Amossy, it is "a site of active intertextuality" (37). "Le cliché, comme la citation est toujours senti comme un emprunt: ils constituent tous deux la reprise d'un discours antérieur."[45] [The cliché, like a quotation, bears a mark of a borrowing since both of them always recall prior discourses]. It appeals to the reader's memory, requiring constant retrospection to locate recognizable models and identify them, and close attention to their handling by the text. A reader first lets himself be seduced by a cliché, but later on, there comes a moment of reflection, reexamination, and denunciation. This happens, for example, in Agatha Christie's *The Murder of Roger Ackroyd* where Christie uses the stereotyped image of a reliable narrator to lull the reader's suspicions and to direct his attention to anyone but the narrator-murderer. The moment of reflection and reexamination ruptures the sense of complicity established between the readers and the stereotyped image, and allows them to confront the cliché vis-à-vis the text, and to identify its purpose. Failure to do so will result in a faulty interpretation.

Rita Passi constructs herself as a mosaic of literary clichés in the hope that their irresistible appeal will affect the reading and interpretation of her letters, and consequently, guarantee the success of her writing strategy. The image of a beautiful young girl, forced against her will to become a nun, and to suffer the constraints of life in a convent, brings to our minds a host of literary memories: Mariane from *Lettres portugaises*, Diderot's Susanne from *La religieuse*, the nun of Monza from Manzoni's *I Promessi Sposi*, and Verga's Maria in *Storia di una capinera*, to name only a few. In each case letters play an important role in the story. I propose to focus on Manzoni's Gertrude and Verga's Maria since the popularity of both novels in Italy made them what Eco calls "sceneggiature-motivo, schemi abbastanza flessibili, del tipo 'la fanciulla perseguitata' dove si individuano certi attori (il seduttore, la fanciulla), certe sequenze di azioni (seduzione, tortura), certe cornici (il castello tenebroso)"[46] [plots with fairly flexible schemes, of the "damsel in distress" kind where one can isolate certain actors [the seducer, the girl], certain sequences of events [seduction, torture], certain frameworks [a murky castle]. They became, in other words, literary stereotypes familiar to an Italian reader.

Gertrude, the nun of Monza, occupies two entire chapters of *I Promessi Sposi*. Born into a prince's family, Gertrude is destined from birth to become a nun, in order to leave intact the whole property to her brother, heir to the family title. Frightened by the prospect of becoming a nun, Gertrude decides to write a letter to her father, begging him to change his mind. She never gets a direct response; however, her family ignores her completely, and makes her feel rejected and unloved. In need of affection, Gertrude writes a love letter to a page who appears to be sympathetic to her predicament. Her father intercepts the letter which he uses so effectively against Gertrude that she has only one choice: to yield to her family's wishes. She expresses her total subjection to her father's will in the third letter, which destroys forever her dreams of freedom and opens the door to the convent. Her passionate nature, however, needs an outlet: Gertrude becomes mistress of a "scellerato," and his accomplice in the murder of a nun. Thus, a young, innocent girl turns into a ruthless, immoral woman whose beauty becomes "bellezza sbattuta, sfiorita, e direi quasi scomposta."[47] [a flawed beauty, however, which had lost its bloom and was almost ready to fall into decay].[48] The iron will of Gertrude's father and a complete disregard of her own needs and preferences are thus responsible for her moral fall.

The three letters that appear in the story play an important part. Each of them marks a significant change in Gertrude's life. The first letter, in which Gertrude begs her father to let her leave the convent, becomes the reason for her complete isolation and, in a way, sets in motion the sequence of events that lead to tragedy, since her loneliness prompts her to write the fatal love letter to the page. Thus, the first two letters become objects of manipulation in her father's hands and assist him in his cruel plans. The third one, which dutifully parrots her father's wishes, serves as a document to remind her that her decision is irrevocable. The narrator does not include the letters; he only reports their content. That correspondence, however, follows closely the Richardsonian scheme in which epistolary transgression leads to a downfall.

Maria, the heroine of *Storia di una capinera,* shares Gertrude's fate in many respects. Like Gertrude, Maria is forced to enter the convent against her inclination. The decision is made by her stepmother, who wants her own daughter to marry well and be rich. When Maria takes the veil, her stepsister marries Nino, the man Maria has fallen in love with. Her stepmother's cruelty, her father's indifference, and Nino's betrayal cause Maria so much pain that she dies of a broken heart. Maria's letters, long and spontaneous descriptions of her sufferings, have no other function than to tell her sorrowful tale. Like the songs of the "capinera" from Verga's preface to the novel, they remain a sound, heard but unheeded. In both novels, then, we encounter the same recurring elements: beautiful, innocent girls turned nuns against their will, cruel parents, letters that tell the truth but achieve nothing, and tragic consequences.

Let us now take a closer look at the ways in which Rita Passi makes use of these elements in constructing her texts. In the first letter, addressed to don Scarpa, Rita evokes a series of images that are to ground her text in truth:

> Vi chiedo che questa lettera e le vicende che vi espongo rimangano segrete come tra *penitente e confessore* . . . Vi farò perdere qualche ora di tempo; ma per voi forse non è tempo perduto; anzi è perduto solo quello che non impiegate ad assistere *un'anima che si smarrisce* Ma dovrò invece esporvi, senza pietà per me stessa, anche i suoi aspetti più crudi, giacché sono ricorsa a voi come ad *un medico, a cui bisogna dire tutto.* (13, 14, 34, my emphasis)
>
> [I would ask you to keep this letter, and the thing I am going to tell you about, as a secret between penitent and confessor . . . I am afraid I am going to take up some of your time, but perhaps it will not be really wasted. The only time that is really wasted is that not spent in helping a soul that is going astray. I must reveal even the more crude aspects of it to you, since I have turned to you as to a doctor, to whom one must tell everything.] (1, 2, 25)

Rita establishes the relationships that depend on her absolute frankness and sincerity: penitent and confessor, a lost sheep and a caring pastor, a patient and a doctor. Once she has put herself in a position which requires her to tell the truth and nothing but the truth, she proceeds to a series of images intended to convince the priest of her mother's ill-conduct towards herself. She describes her childhood spent with her paternal grandparents, who, after the death of their son, cared for their granddaughter, and gave her all the affection and attention she needed. But, explains Rita, "[i nonni] mi consideravano una bambina maliconica per l'incuria materna" (15) [my father's parents] regarded me as a rather sad little girl, being without a mother's care, 3]. The mother, continues Rita, was wrapped up in her amorous pursuits, and rarely spent time with her daughter: "la vedevo talvolta con gli occhi e i capelli aridi, la pelle opaca su cui trascorreva il rossore, in tutta la bruttezza della sofferenza amorosa" (15) [I saw her with feverishly dry eyes and hair; her skin waxy and flushed, with that ugly look that people's faces get when they are unhappily in love, 3]. But despite her own indifference towards her daughter, she looked with hatred upon anyone who showed affection for Rita. That hatred was a chief motive in her frequent interventions in Rita's life: "era assorbita dall'odio per quelli che mi accostavano, e che accusava di staccarmi da lei: tanto che spesso interveniva, allontanando un'amica, licenziando una governante, *sconvolgendo la trama della mia quieta e monotona vita.* (15, my emphasis) [she was eaten up by hatred of the people who looked after me and used to accuse them of alienating me from her; so she was always interfering, sometimes to put an end to a friendship, sometimes to dismiss a governess, and so upsetting the smooth course of my quiet and monotonous life, 3]. Rita's references to her childhood build up the image of a docile and highly sensitive child whose life was run by the whims of a despotic and egoistic mother. That image will accompany the reader towards the predictable resolution: Rita's arrival at the convent at her mother's instigation, and the separation from her beloved grandparents. Rita decides never to go back to the emptiness and misery of the life with her mother:

> Perché in quei giorni avevo deliberato did non amare più nessuno al mondo dedicandomi a Dio ... Crebbe in me a poco a poco la tenerezza fisica per l'astinenza, il desiderio di restare per sempre chiusa e senza contatto, l'inclinazione alla pulizia ed al silenzio. (37)

> [For it was at that time that I decided never to love anyone again, but to devote myself only to God ... Little by little I felt a positively physical affection for chastity growing within me, the desire to remain shut away and detached, for ever, a longing for cleanliness and silence.] (27)

Rita's writing strategy is intended to convince the reader that she has no real vocation to become a nun, that her willingness to stay in the convent is the choice of a lesser evil: "Così messa in sospetto, cominciai a meditare sugli avvenimenti trascorsi che mi hanno condotta alla soglia di monacazione, e i dubbi divennero molti" (39) [Once this suspicion was aroused in me, I began to reflect on the events in the past that had led me to the brink of taking the veil, and my doubts increased, 29]. The question she asks the priest "È genuina la mia vocazione?" [Is my vocation a real one? 29] implies the reply she expects from him: "no," since she was forced to enter the convent by her mother's conduct. Rita uses the key elements of the literary clichés: a cruel parent who disregards the child's inclination, and the possible tragedy that may result from it. Rita does not state it openly, but alludes to the impending danger if no one heeds her call for help:

"Ho la impressione del pericolo" (39) [I have a premonition of danger, 29].

But don Scarpa resists the seductive appeal of clichés. Before replying to her letter, he consults the mother superior to find out more about Rita and her relationship with her mother. His experience as an old priest and confessor prompts him to look for the unsaid parts in Rita's life, and the reasons behind her reluctance to reveal them: "Ho pesato la vostra lettera frase per frase; mi sono giovato di tutta l'esperienza che mi consentono i molti anni trascorsi ad assistere le anime degli incerti e dei sofferenti, per meglio intuire anche quello che la vostra penna taceva (48) [I have pondered every sentence of your letter. I have used all the experience bestowed on me by the many years I have spent in assisting the souls of people in doubt and suffering, in order to understand by intuition even the things that your pen has passed over in silence, 35]. And he finds the confirmation of his suspicions in mother Giulietta's answer: "Rita è un'anima buona e ha taciuto scrivendovi i fatti più scandalosi della sua vita familiare" (44) [Rita is a good soul, and in writing to you she passed over in silence the more scandalous facts of her family life, 32]. His reply consists of routine comments, used to resolve doubts concerning vocation: the infallibility of God's judgment, and the consolation of prayer. Don Scarpa thus replies to Rita's clichés by using another set of clichés from the religious repertoire (he advises her to read Saint Augustine and Saint Francis, two examples of doubts experienced and conquered).

Rita's failure to enlist don Scarpa's help does not discourage her from trying again, this time beginning a correspondence with the bishop's secretary, don Paolo Conti. Rita writes to him several letters, each of which reveals some new event in her life. Each letter begins with a promise of absolute truth and the presentation of reasons which made her hide certain parts of her story in previous letters. The motives are always honorable: unwillingness to involve her mother: "Per non essere creduta bugiarda dovrò rivelarvi una parte penosa della mia vita, e mostrarmi vendicativa contro una donna del mio sangue che preferirei perdonare" (73) [Not to be considered a liar, I shall have to reveal a side of my life that is very painful to me, and put myself in the light of behaving revengefully towards a woman relative of mine whom I would rather forgive, 52], or female modesty: "è avvenuto un fatto a cui noi donne diamo tanta importanza" (152) [Something has happened to which we women attach such great importance, 130]. Each letter claims to be an objective reconstruction of facts, painfully torn away from her heart by don Paolo's insistence, almost against her will: "la mia ultima lettera fu una confessione penosa, mi venne strappata da voi" (127) [My last letter was a painful confession. You wrung it out of me, 127]. Rita invokes the same cliché, confessor-penitent, as before, only this time the confessor has an active part, that of an interrogator. Rita makes don Paolo an accomplice in the writing of her text, and thus more susceptible to accepting it at face value: "Devo mettere davanti a voi il mio peccato ... Voi mi leggerete da oggi come se foste in confessione" (128). [I must lay my sin before you ... From to-day on you must read my letters as though this were all in the confessional, 109].

Her letters abound in sordid details concerning her adolescence, the period of her life sketched hastily in the letters to don Scarpa. As before, Rita paints a grim picture of a young impressionable girl in the clutches of an egoistic mother, whose interests and affections revolve around herself and her numerous lovers. Rita plays only the role of a sympathetic ear, a shoulder to lean on in times of crisis, a role which she accepts to prove her propensity for sacrifice:

Sì, dicevo a me stessa, questa è la mia vera missione: assistere quella donna, che certo è debole, ma si sottopone a sua figlia; scoprivo in me una profonda propensione al sacrificio: mi pareva che la mia pelle emanasse luce. (81)

['This is it,' I said to myself,' this is my task—to help this woman, who is certainly weak, but submits to her daughter.' I discovered that I had a profound urge towards self-sacrifice; and it seemed to me that my skin gave off a kind of radiance.] (60)

But to the cliché "innocent girl," "cruel parent," Rita adds another dimension: an innocent girl experiencing her first true love and the mother wrapped up in her sordid love affairs. Rita accentuates the contrast between the sensual nature of the amatory adventures of her mother, and the pure and ideal relation between herself and Giuliano;

Il ritegno con cui mi trattava Giuliano mi faceva credere infatti che il nostro amore fosse l'opposto di quello a cui assistevo ormai con ostilità: un'alleanza di anime tenere e gravi e avverse alla passione ... Il mio pensiero andò verso mia madre, e sentii tanta nausea di tutto quel suo amore, delle sue vicende d'amore. (100, 108)

[In fact, the reserve with which Giuliano treated me led me to believe that our love was the very opposite of the other love of which I was a witness, and by now a hostile one; I believed that ours was an alliance between minds as sensitive as they were grave and averse to passion ... My thoughts turned to my mother, and I felt such nausea for all that preoccupation of hers with love, for all her vicissitudes in love.] (83, 91)

Giuliano's death (accidental in Rita's version, a deliberate murder by Rita in her mother's version) destroys all the plans of living with "a pure heart." Her mother's hatred forces her to enter the convent and stay there forever. Rita uses this part of the story to present herself as a classical victim, "un innocente che non sa come scolparsi" (159) [an innocent person who does not know how to prove that he is not guilty, 138]. She is a typical victim of fate, with everything and everyone against her:

> Cacciata dalla mia casa per capriccio, richiamata per un capriccio, gettata poi per capriccio tra gli avvenimenti più strani, ora mi vedevo distrutta per un capriccio della sorte, che riassumeva tutti quelli della malvagità umana. (160)

> [Driven away from home for a whim, called back again for a whim, and then by a whim thrown into the midst of the strangest adventures, I saw myself ruined, now, by a trick of fate that epitomized the whole range of human malice.] (139)

The reference to the "whim of fate" that governs her life recalls the heroines of Manzoni and Verga, and the futility of any attempt to change their lives. Rita's words echo the words in which Nino, Maria's lover, sums up her life: "Voi siete una vittima ... Voi siete la vittima della vostra posizione, della cattiveria della vostra matrigna, della debolezza di vostro padre, del destino" (40) [You are a victim ... You are a victim of your position, of your stepmother's malice, of your father's weakness, of destiny].

To the spectacular use of clichés, Rita adds a series of appeals to don Conti's moral obligations as a human being, and a priest—appeals which gradually become more and more intense and personal. First she appeals to his duty: "Ora aiutatemi perché ne ho bisogno e perché è vostro dovere" (67) [Now you must help me, because I need it, and because it is your duty, 49]. Then to pity: "Io sono stata franca: salvatemi per pietà" (112) [I have been frank. For pity's sake, save me, 96]. The last appeal contains a veiled threat of suicide:

> È stato l'ultimo tentativo di un'anima, che voleva salvarsi senza macchiarsi di altre colpe. Anche questo è finito. So che, cercando ancora la mia libertà farei la vostra rovina. Smetto di scrivervi per sempre; forse vi è una via d'uscita, ma ho paura di nominarla. (161)

> [It has been the last attempt of a soul trying to save itself without incurring further guilt. This has come to an end. I know that by going on trying to get my liberty I would ruin you. I am giving up writing to you, for ever. Perhaps there is a way out, but I am afraid to call it by its name.] (140)

4: Female Epistolary Strategies 133

Rita plays here the "innocent victim" note, a victim willing to sacrifice one's own life rather than endanger someone else's. The "innocent victim" cliché proves a successful means of persuasion. Don Paolo resolves to help her escape from the convent because "è ingiusto che siate costretta a una vita che vi dà tanta ripugnanza" (163) [it is not just that you should be forced into a life that is so repugnant to you, 140]. The reference to "force" in his reply brings into the reader's mind the tragic consequences of forcing people to act against their inclinations, as in the case of Manzoni's Gertrude or Verga's Maria. Don Conti's action is "un'azione rischiosa ma credo che il compierla sia in armonia col precetto, che ci obbliga a riparare i torti subiti dalle anime che sono ricorse a noi" (164) [It is a risky thing to do, but I believe that it is in keeping with the precept that tells us that we must redress the wrongs suffered by souls that have recourse to us, 141]. The generalizing allusion to "torti subiti" seems to be an echo of "the wrongs" suffered by Rita's literary predecessors: Gertrude and Maria.

Don Conti is not the only character in the novel who responds to Rita's plea for help. Michele Sacco, a young man who occupies the house opposite the one in which Rita is hiding after the escape from the convent, also becomes involved in her affairs. Rita notices the young man pass her house and writes him a letter. That letter is a composite of clichés, skilfully arranged to convey the dominant image, that of a damsel in distress. All the necessary elements are employed. There is a cruel mother who forced her to enter the convent: "Mia madre, unica parente che mi rimanga, mi cacciò fuori di casa a dodici anni come testimonia importuna della sua vita, per chiudermi nel Collegio delle ** a **" (191) [My mother, the only relative I have left, turned me out of the house when I was twelve years old because I was an unwanted witness of the life that she was leading, and shut me up in the convent of the__at__, 162]. There is a priest of loose morals who, pretending to be her friend, arranged her escape from the convent and installed her in that house to give vent to his vile desires:

> Don Paolo Conti mi convinse a tacere e, un paio di giorni prima di mona-cazione, mi ordinò di fuggire e mi nascose nella casa accanto alla vostra sotto la guardia di una donna. Io l'ubbidii perché ritenevo che tutti i suoi consigli fossero diretti al bene perché pensavo a salvarmi dalla minaccia più immediata. Ma appena cominciai a riavermi Don Paolo mi fece cono-scere per quale scopo si era occupato di me e oggi mi annuncia una sua visita in una lettera piena di lusinghe colpevoli che mi ha riempito di ribrezzo. (192)

> [Father Conti convinced me that I should keep silent, and a few days

before I was to take the veil he told me to run away and he hid me in the house next to yours, under the surveillance of a woman. I obeyed him because I thought that all his advice was well meant, and it seemed to me that in this way I would escape from the more immediate threat. By as soon as I began to recover, Father Conti made me aware of the reason why he had taken such interest in me, and to-day I have had a letter from him in which he announces that he is going to pay me a visit; this letter is so full of guilty lures that it has quite sickened me.] (163)

And, of course, besides the two villains of the scenario, there is Michele Sacco, the savior of the persecuted virgin, whose honor and chivalry are at stake, if he does not come to her help:

L'unica mia speranza è di trovare una persona che abbia compassione di me e che mi nasconda a tutti. Non oso chiedervi di essere quella persona; mi sono rivolta a voi perché ho visto voi solo e perché il vostro viso mi è parso quello di onesto. (193)

[My only hope is to find someone who will have pity on me and be willing to hide me from everybody. I dare not ask you to be that person. I turned to you because you are the only person I have seen and because your face seems to be that of an honest man.] (164)

Needless to say, like all damsels in distress, Rita is kept a prisoner "senza carta nè inchiostro" (192) [without paper or ink, 163]. Michele Sacco, like don Conti, cannot resist Rita's plea, and agrees to a meeting: "Riflettendo ancora pensai che nulla poteva accadere di male se avessi dato un minuto di ascolto a una ragazza che aveva chiesto il mio aiuto" (204) [at last, having thought it over, I decided that no great harm could be done if I were to listen for a moment to a girl who had called for my help, 169]. Michele, like Conti, believes Rita to be a victim of fate.

But Rita is not a helpless victim of fate. As far as it is possible to piece together her portrait from the multitude of contradictory statements provided by herself and others, she is an opportunist, willing to use every means at her disposal to satisfy her own desires. Her manipulative skills, apparent in her use of letters, make others respond to her demands. The clash between the image of Rita as the victim, projected through her letters, and the ruthless Rita, who did not hesitate to murder an elderly servant to avoid returning to the convent, becomes evident in Michele's description of the scene, which he witnessed himself:

Quello che vidi poi mi è rimasto impresso e non potrò scordarlo fintanto vivo. Appoggiata di schiena al davanzale della finestra già aperta, gli occhi duri ed immobili, quasi che non si accorgesse nemmeno del nostro arrivo, la ragazza guardava in alto ed in disparte: credetti che fosse strabica; ma il suo era male ben peggiore. I capelli neri, un po' piatti, con riflessi rossastri pesavano scarmigliati sul suo volto paffuto. La contemplammo un attimo con orrore. Notai il vestito, lungo, accollato, antiquato, che non sembrava appartenerle. (205, 206)

[What I saw afterwards remained indelibly stamped on my mind; I shall not forget it as long as I live. Standing with her back to the sill of the open window, her eyes fixed and staring almost as though she hadn't even noticed our arrival, there was the girl, gazing upwards and to one side. At first I thought she was squinting; but then I realized it was something far worse. Her rather flat dark hair, with reddish lights in it, lay tumbled in disorder all round her swollen face. We gazed at her for a moment in horror. I noticed that her dress was long, high-necked, and old-fashioned and evidently didn't belong to her.] (170)

Michele has obviously experienced the shock at the juxtaposition of the two Ritas: Rita, the persecuted virgin (which implies physical beauty, fragility, softness of expression, and grace of movement), and Rita, the killer, cold and unattractive, dressed in old-fashioned, ill-fitting clothes.

The confrontation of text with reality makes us ponder the reasons why don Conti and Michele Sacco failed as the readers of Rita's letters and what made them accept her texts at face value. Oddly enough, don Conti himself claims to be an attentive reader and the allusions to reading and interpretation appear frequently in his letters. For example, he refers to "la seconda lettura di quella lettera a don Scarpa" (64). And yet he allows Rita to draw him into a clandestine correspondence, and continues it against his better judgment. In what is to be his last letter to Rita, he admits that he failed to see through the artifice of her letters:

Con le vostre abili e graduali menzogne avete già saputo condurmi a un rischio grave e immeritato. Respingo con orrore il tentativo della vostra ultima lettera, di associare anche me, come tacito complice, alla colpa commessa col segreto maneggio di questa corrispondenza ... La mia colpa è stata soltanto di non capire ciò che ora mi pare evidente. Le vostre lettere erano sempre bugiarde. Restate in convento, o uscitene, ma non ricorrete al mio aiuto. Non scrivetemi più. Questa è l'ultima lettera. (148, 149)

[By your clever, carefully graded lies you have up till now been able to lead me into taking a very grave and unjustifiable risk. I reject with horror the attempt made in your last letter to involve me also, as a tacit accomplice, in the fault committed in the secret intrigue of this correspondence

> ... My only fault has been my failure to understand what now seems quite evident. Your letters have always been false. Stay in the convent, or if you leave, don't apply for help to me.] (127)

But, of course as we well know, he will relent once more, this time providing Rita with a means to escape and a hiding place, and this decision proves to lead to fatal consequences.

What then does his reading lack, if Rita manages always to get one step ahead of him? The answer to that question may lie in the analysis of the reading process and the role clichés play in it. In the first stage clichés dazzle and seduce the reader with their familiarity, offering the truth ready made for instant acceptance. The next stage, however, should involve a moment of reflection, a pause to "reexamine them, put them in perspective, and denounce them."[49] Both don Conti and Michele Sacco never reach that stage. They project Rita's letters onto the images/texts already preexisting in their minds and fail to see that Rita controls their reading by providing them with only such elements as would create a story she wants them to read. There is no center of truth in the novel because Rita's text/shell skillfully shifts that center into the eye of the beholder/reader. The only truth is the one created in the reading process.

By presenting two kinds of readers, don Scarpa as an incredulous reader who resists the fascination with clichés, and don Conti and Michele Sacca as readers who give in to them, Piovene's novel offers a comment on reading and interpretation, in particular the tenacity of clichés, and the contorted ways in which they affect a text's perception. In her essay "Fiction as Interpretation/Interpretation as Fiction," Naomi Schor discusses the acts of reading and interpretation as "something that is done *in* fiction," rather than something "done *to* fiction."[50] She distinguishes between "an interpreter," i.e., an interpreting critic, and "an interpretant," i.e., an interpreting character. The interpreter is the interpretant's "specular image" who "mirrors his confusions as well as triumphs" (168). "Via the interpretant," says Schor, "the author is trying to tell us something *about* interpretation and the interpreter would do well to listen and take note" (170). Isn't then don Conti's interpretative failure a pretext to pause and reflect on the vicious perfidy of texts that elude the reader in search of truth and render a "correct" interpretation a difficult, if not an impossible, task?[51] If we read as ironic the term "scolaro" applied to don Conti (209), we also have to read as ironic Rita's statement in court: "Non calcolavo l'effetto delle mie lettere; supponevo soltanto che ne avessero uno; avevo grande fiducia che ne nascesse qualcosa di buono per me" (215) [I didn't reckon on the result of my letters. I supposed that they would have some result and I was very confident that it would somehow turn out all for my good, 178]. Rita's proclamation of spontaneity, the hallmark of feminine writing, and her claim that she never intended her letters to be manipulative, is, of course, one more cliché, this time an obvious eye-opener for both external and internal readers.

Rita's words reflect back on epistolary fiction, and offer a comment on the writing strategies of Evelina and Lady Susan. All three heroines seem to accept the social and literary model of female correspondence: Evelina writes long dutiful letters to her guardian, sharing with him every moment of her life; Lady Susan sends affectionate notes to her relatives, demonstrating warm interest in family matters; Rita discloses her religious doubts in the letters to priests. No conduct book writer would find anything amiss in these letters. Yet they all use conventions not to mimic reality but to create it. Their apparent meekness, spontaneity, and naturalness mask their rebellion against the social constraints that hamper their freedom. For each of them truth is in the eye of the beholder and they use language to construct it, projecting through their letters images already preexisting in the minds of their addressees.

5
Deconstructing the Definition of Female Letters as Sentimental, Nonliterary, and Private

O come—blessed Lord—Jesus! And with these words, the last but half pronounced, expired: such a smile, such a serenity overspreading her sweet face at the instant, as seemed to manifest her eternal happiness already begun.[1]

Je n'en sentis plus le battement; et en effet, notre malheureuse amie expira dans le moment même.[2]

[I could no longer feel it beating; in fact our unhappy friend expired at that very moment.][3]

Unable to finish the sentence, she sunk back on her pillow: her countenance was serenely composed; she regarded her father as he pressed the infant to his breast with a steadfast look; a sudden beam of joy passed across her languid features, she raised her eyes to heaven—and then closed them for ever.[4]

Le sort de Mme de Merteuil paraît enfin rempli, ma chère et digne amie; et il est tel que ses plus grands ennemis sont partagés entre l'indignation qu'elle mérite, et la pitié qu'elle inspire. J'avais bien raison de dire que ce serait peut-être un bonheur pour elle de mourir de sa petite vérole. Elle en est revenue, il est vrai, mais affreusement défigurée; et elle y a particulièrement perdu un oeil. (L 175)

[Madame de Merteuil's destiny seems at last, my dear and worthy friend, to have been fulfilled. It is such that her worst enemies are divided between the indignation she merits and the pity she inspires. I was quite right to say that it would perhaps be fortunate for her if she died of smallpox. She has recovered, it is true, but horrible disfigured; more than anything by the loss of an eye.] (391)

5: Deconstructing the Definition of Female Letters 139

Three spectacular deaths of epistolary victims—Clarissa, Mme de Tourvel, and Charlotte Temple—and a no less spectacular disfigurement and disappearance of Madame de Merteuil from the social and literary scene—signaled the inevitable agony and death of "la lettre drame" at the end of the eighteenth century, not only in England but also in France and America.

Susanna Rowson's *Charlotte Temple,* published in America in 1791, proves that even the author's voice could not protect the heroine from the tragic consequences of unsupervised correspondence. Charlotte, an innocent English schoolgirl, attracts the attention of an American officer, Montreville. She accepts his letter and answers it, and this step leads to her ruin and death. Charlotte disregards her mother's admonition that "I should never read a letter given me by a young man, without first giving it to her" (31). Montreville's letter has the power to "awaken new emotions in her youthful bosom" (32), and from that moment on her fate is sealed. Although *Charlotte Temple* is an attempt to discard the letter form and replace it with third-person narration, its plot follows faithfully the tenets of epistolary fiction, since the events in the story revolve around that ominous letter and the fatal consequences of Charlotte's reply. Here the plot turns on the letter being used solely as a tool of manipulation and destruction in the hands of an artful seducer (among whose numerous literary forefathers are Lovelace and Valmont), wreaking havoc on the virtue and the lives of innocent creatures, totally unprepared for traps set for them by innocuous-looking, yet deadly "paper-messengers."[5] It is worth noting that Rowson does not actually quote Montreville's letter or Charlotte's answer, probably relying on her readers' ability to supply the clichés that make up their content. Montreville's second letter to Charlotte, quoted in its entirety, dispels any illusions of a happy ending that Charlotte might have harbored in her naive bosom. As might be expected, Charlotte dies broken-hearted after giving birth to an illegitimate daughter, and Montreville lives an unhappy life, tormented by the painful memories of their encounter.

Rowson's novel reads almost like a conduct book because of its frequent interruptions of the narrative to warn the female audience about the dangers of clandestine correspondence, and the artful traps laid by merciless seducers: "My bosom glows with honest indignation, and I wish for power to extirpate those monsters of seduction from the earth" (29). The editor of letters in the epistolary fiction who intervened in footnotes to point out faults and suggest remedies, is here supplanted by the direct voice of the author. But despite this structural change, the message remains the same as in conduct books or epistolary fiction, namely, that any unsupervised correspondence for women entails tragic consequences.

Unsupervised letter writing becomes a reprehensible activity, linked to the notion of sin. This connection is clear in Clarissa's comment on the "sin of prohibited correspondence" as the cause of her rape and untimely death. It is echoed by Mme de Tourvel's reference to Valmont as "auteur de mes fautes" (L 161) [the author of my sins]. Rowson, too, insists on the irreparable consequence of one rash act: "Charlotte had taken one step in the ways of imprudence: and when that is once done, there are always innumerable obstacles to prevent the erring person returning to the path of rectitude" (36). But in the world of punctilio a sin of rashness requires punishment. The victims have to be punished for having disobeyed the conduct-book precepts, and the aggressors/addressors for their libertine practices. In both cases death becomes the appropriate resolution in novelistic terms. Victims "expire" quietly, surrounded by friends, at peace with the world and their consciences; seducers die a violent death in duels, tormented to their last breath by the memory of their vile deeds. Mme de Merteuil, being a woman-aggressor, loses not her life but, even worse, her beauty and her social position, and ends up an outcast in a foreign country.

In one way or another women turn out to be victims of epistolary intrigues, and have to look for happiness not on earth but in heaven. Their spectacular deaths leave an indelible imprint not only on the reading public but also on the fiction to come. This imprint provoked a number of responses. One was an attempt to salvage the epistolary form but alter the content, leaving the heroine alive and kicking. Such, for instance, is the rebellion of Jane Austen's heroine, Lady Susan, who not only escapes earthly punishment but manages to turn epistolary intrigues to her advantage, securing for herself a life of luxury with her meek husband. But Jane Austen mocked the model of a female victim manipulated by letters only in the privacy of her own room, since neither *Love and Freindship* nor *Lady Susan* was intended for publication, and both reached the reading public only after her death.

The other response came in an attempt to resurrect the novel with plotting letters through the politicization of sentimental discourse. Nicola Watson's brilliant study of the political significance of the sentimental epistolary novel covers the period between 1790 and 1820. Assuming that Roussau'e *La Nouvelle Héloïse* provided a plot which "came to inform much of the discourse stimulated by the Revolution," Watson traces the means employed to intercept, redirect, and eventually totally eliminate uncensored letters, viewed as a disruptive power, a threat not only to the domestic order but to the nation. She examines

5: Deconstructing the Definition of Female Letters 141

a series of novels by such radical novelists as Helen Maria Williams, Eliza Fenwick, Mary Hays, Mary Wollstonecraft, and Charlotte Smith, and traces the itinerary of letters which express "the heroine's self-legitimating revolutionary desire."[6] The response to that rampant, politically dangerous epistolarity, came almost instantaneously in the novels of Jane West, Maria Edgeworth and Jane Austen. Watson argues that the authors "interested in establishing a post-Revolutionary consensus" use respectively three major strategies: "to shut down the letter into the decorous silence of the private," to "return it to the authoritative reading of public consensus," and to "redirect it into the bosom of the patriarchal family" (72). Walter Scott's novels, claims Watson, concluded the mission to successfully neutralize and domesticate the power of uncensored correspondence, and by implication, the rebellious heroine. The comment on Aphra Behn supposedly made by Scott's great-aunt, a certain Mrs Keith, put a final seal of disapproval and rejection on the fiction that for a century exploited the thrill of indecent conduct:

> 'But is it not', she said, 'a very odd thing that I, an old woman of eighty and upwards, sitting alone, feel myself ashamed to read a book which, sixty years ago, I have heard read aloud for the amusement of large circles, consisting of the first and most credible society in London?' This, of course, was owing to the gradual improvement of the national taste and delicacy.[7]

Decorum reigns supreme and, with it, a total ban on uncensored correspondence. "The epistolary," concludes Watson "would remain a surreptitious but troubling ghost in the fiction of the nineteenth century and beyond" (193).[8]

Yet another form of response to face that troubling ghost came in the domestic fiction of the early nineteenth century in England and America. This fiction discarded both the epistolary format and the image of a female victim associated with it. Nina Baym rejects the view that women's fiction in the nineteenth century was a historical continuation of the works of Richardson and his early American imitator Susanna Rowson. "In fact," says Baym, "women who wrote after 1820 detested Richardson's fiction and planned their own as an alternative to it."[9] The most important reason for this hatred was the representation of the heroine "who lived entirely in her feelings," thus setting "a pernicious example to young women starting out to battle with life" (25). According to Baym, women writers

> objected to the sexual center of these novels of sensibility and not merely on prudish grounds. They were unwilling to accept a concept of woman as inevitable sexual prey. They refused to agree that women had to be

victims. They insisted that male-female relations could be conducted on a plane that allowed for feelings other than lust. Scarcely any of these novels is a novel of seduction. The disappearance of the novel of seduction is a crucial event in women's fiction. (26)

The disappearance of the novel of seduction necessarily affected the epistolary form, since the shift from an almost exclusive focus on the power-laden sexual relations between men and women to that of friendship or purely professional relations called for changes in epistolary communication.

Although there were very few epistolary novels in the early nineteenth century, letters were still used as a narrative device, and often constituted a substantial part of novels. They ceased, however, to function as a battleground of the sexes and as a plot-moving device in the novel of seduction, and they now had new roles to play. Epistolary exchange became an arena for sincere and genuine communication between men and women, the "correspondence" according to the meaning of the word in Lovelace's comment. But this time it was the mind, not the heart that, "employed the vassal fingers." A letter's role was to explain, comment, and clarify rather than to deceive and dazzle—in other words, to communicate rather than manipulate. An example of this development is Jane Austen's use of letters, for instance, those of Darcy to Elizabeth in *Pride and Prejudice*.

If the role of letters called for a redefinition, so did the categories established by the law of genre which stamped letters by women as sentimental, nonliterary, and private. In this chapter I will show how three women writers deconstruct these categories. I have selected Fanny Fern's *Ruth Hall* (1855), Dacia Maraini's *Lettere a Marina* (1980) and Oriana Fallaci's *Lettera a un bambino mai nato* (1975). Despite the difference in time, over a hundred years separating Maraini from Fern, and in culture, the three novels share the goal of liberating women's letters from the constraining clichés. The three novels complement one other because each of them deals primarily with one element of the infamous trio. Thus *Ruth Hall* probes the notion of sentiment and the ways in which it excluded women's writing from the literary scene, as well as hampered women's professional lives. *Lettere a Marina* questions the nonliterary label attached to female epistolary production. *Lettera a un bambino mai nato* exposes the strategies that underlie the social division into the private and public spheres. However, despite the focus on one element, each novel provides a forum for addressing the remaining issues, and exposes their mutual interdependence. Thus, they engage in a dialogue not only with each other but also with the preceding epistolary tradition.

5: Deconstructing the Definition of Female Letters

Ruth Hall and the Deconstruction of the Heart/Mind Opposition

Ruth Hall, a novel by Fanny Fern published in 1855, illustrates the shift from manipulation to communication in letters. It explores the possible ways in which correspondence between men and women may be redeemed as a territory of mutual respect and trust, redefining the notion of mind and heart in the process. Ruth Hall is a young woman who is forced to earn her living in order to support herself and her two little daughters after the sudden death of her husband. Ruth appeals for help to her own father and the parents of her late husband, only to find out that no one will come to her assistance. After failing to find employment first as a seamstress, later as a teacher, Ruth, on the brink of despair, tries her hand at writing for a newspaper. She quickly becomes an enormous success, manages to establish herself as a columnist for a prestigious magazine, and signs a contract for a novel. At the end of the novel Ruth acquires the status of a well-known figure among the reading public, and a wealthy woman, capable of providing a comfortable home for her two daughters.

Apart from a few details, the novel reflects faithfully the events in the life of Sarah Parton, the author of *Ruth Hall*, writing under the pseudonym of Fanny Fern. Ruth's successful "entrance into the world" as a professional journalist and writer paves the path for a new heroine, "a heroine before her desk."[10] Like her literary predecessor, Burney's Evelina, Ruth has to discover the values that operate in the hostile world she needs to enter, and learn the rules of a game called survival. *Ruth Hall* thus functions similarly to *Evelina*, providing a sort of guide for female readers. Moreover, as in *Evelina*, the act of writing and reading letters becomes a vital part of her education.

What lesson on letters does Fanny Fern provide for her readers in *Ruth Hall*? First of all, she eliminates completely love letters, or any other forms of sentimental communication (sentimental meaning expressing excessive emotion). This becomes apparent in a scene in which a letter addressed to Ruth arrives at the editor's office:

'A letter for 'Floy!' said Mr Lescom, smiling. 'Another lover, I suppose. Ah! When you get to be my age,' continued the old man, stroking his silver hair, 'you will treat communications with more attention.' As he finished his remark, he held the letter playfully for a moment, and then tossed it into Ruth's lap. Ruth thrust it unread into her apron pocket. She was thinking of her book, and many other things of far more interest to her than lovers, if lover the writer were.[11]

Two elements in the above scene expose the difference between the role of letters in the novel of seduction and in domestic fiction. Mr. Lescom, a representative of the older generation, assumes automatically that a young attractive woman can receive only one kind of letter, a love letter, and expects Ruth to behave in a manner suitable to the occasion. But Ruth's reaction to the arrival of that letter contradicts the tenets of the sentimental novel. Ruth receives it without any signs of emotion or excitement, revealing her complete lack of interest in love letters or any sentimental communication. How different is her behavior from that of Charlotte Temple on a similar occasion: "But, said [the earlier heroine] pausing, and drawing the letter from her pocket while a gentle suffusion of vermillion tinged her neck and face, he gave me this letter; what shall I do with it?"[12] Ruth does not blush with pleasant anticipation, she does not tear it open; she "thrusts" it into her apron pocket unopened, and reads it only after her return home.

Contrary to Mr. Lescom's assumption, it is not a love letter, but a business letter from John Walter, the editor of the prestigious journal *Household Messenger*. That letter marks the beginning of a long and important relationship between Ruth and John, a relationship that is "partly business and partly friendly," as John states in his first letter (142). Ruth's reaction on its first reading is tinged with apprehension and suspicion about the intentions of the writer, a reaction which would be deemed praiseworthy by Fanny Burney, and advocated by cautious Evelina:

> Ruth sat with the letter in her hand. The time *had* been when not a doubt would have arisen in her mind as to the sincerity of the writer; but, alas! adversity so rough a teacher! ever laying the cold finger of caution on the warm heart of trust. Ruth sighed, and tossed the letter on the table, half-ashamed of herself for her cowardice, and wishing that she *could* have faith in the writer. Then she picked up the letter again. She examined the hand-writing; it was bold and manly. She thought it would be treating it too shabbily to throw it aside among the love-sick trash she was in the habit of receiving. She would read it again. The tone was respectful; *that won her*. (143, Fern's emphasis)

Ruth's decision to answer John's letter comes as a result of a probing analysis of every element in the letter, the content, the tone, the style. What ultimately tips the balance in his favor is his respectful tone and the appeal to friendship and brotherly interest, which is decidedly not an attempt "to awaken new emotions in her youthful bosom."[13] Ruth, in reply, writes him "a long, sisterly" letter, accepting his offer to work exclusively for his magazine (144). When the new contract

5: Deconstructing the Definition of Female Letters 145

drawn by John Walter arrives, Ruth examines it carefully, and her comment subtly ridicules the social division between men's and women's abilities to deal with business: "Then she took up the contract and examined it; it was brief, plain and easily understood *even by a woman,* as the men say. 'It is a good offer,' said Ruth, 'he is in earnest, so am I; it's a bargain.' Ruth signed the document" (147, Fern's emphasis).

The tenor of their relationship is professional, built on mutual respect and admiration for talent and journalistic skills that mark their achievements. Letters reflect that relationship. Walter praises Ruth's articles in a letter to Mr Lescom:" 'Floy' is a genius; her writings wherever published, would have attracted attention, and stamped the writer as a person of extraordinary talent" (152). Ruth admires Walter "as a most energetic young man, who had wrung success from an unwilling world, and fought his way, single-handed, from obscurity to an honorable position in society, against, what would have been to many, overwhelming odds" (144). Ruth welcomes him as a brother she never had, and a companion whose disinterested friendship provides her with support and assists her in achieving financial and professional stability. Throughout their correspondence and during rare personal contacts the author continually emphasizes the asexual stamp of their relationship. John Walter is happily married, and the existence of his wife, even though she never actually appears in the novel, is a constant reminder that Ruth is nothing more to him than a friend. Ruth herself has no intention of remarrying, and the final scene in the novel takes place at the cemetery, where Ruth, accompanied by John and her two daughters, visits the grave of her beloved husband, a rather unconventional ending for a man-meets-woman story.

Thus, *Ruth Hall* performs the operation of substituting a friend for a lover, shifting male-female relations from the plane of uncontrolled emotion to that of mind which serves as a filter for sentiment. But in order to effect this shift Fanny Fern needs to address the mind-heart dichotomy as representative of the opposition between male and female modes of writing and reading, discussed ad nauseam in literary speculations and illustrated abundantly in conduct material and epistolary novels. Fern, obviously aware of the tenacity of this cliché, tries to subvert it. She lives in a world that limits women's access to language and views their literary aspirations as the invasion of a foreign territory. In John Richetti's words,

> when they do speak, women must always use language in a marked or self-conscious way that indicates they have been granted temporary or

unusual access to its resources. As writers or speakers, they are recognized as awkward or extraordinarily good, like foreigners.[14]

Fanny Fern opens up a polemic on the division of writing into masculine and feminine modes of expression, and challenges the validity of such division. Does a woman's writing always have to be a product unrhetorical, unliterary, and devoid of common sense? Once again Fern resorts to letters to show that this view is still very much alive. Ruth Hall receives a letter from one of her readers, William Stearns, "Professor of Greek, Hebrew, and Mathematics, in Hopetown College, and author of 'History of Dark Ages'" (166). Professor Stearns considers himself an expert on writing, and feels entitled to instruct Ruth on the matter:

> You have written tolerably, all things considered, but you violate all established rules of composition, and are as lawless and erratic as a comet. You may startle and dazzle, but you are fit only to throw people out of their orbits. Now and then there's a gleam of something like reason in your writings, but for the most part they are unmitigated trash—false in sentiment—unrhetorical in expression; in short were you my daughter, which I thank Providence you are not, I should box your ears, and keep you on a bread and water diet till you improved. (166)

Professor Stearns's "fatherly" comment, which echoes La Bruyère's comments on the differences between male and female modes of writing, is to put Ruth in her place, and remind her that her gender is a factor that will forever doom her writing to a category well below literary standards set by and for men. According to Professor Stearns Ruth "is no genius." He seriously doubts whether she will ever contribute anything worth reading to the existing bulk of literature, since "the *female* mind is incapable of producing anything which may be strictly termed *literature*" (166, Fern's emphasis). Although Ruth's immediate reaction to that letter is only an exclamation of exasperation: "Oh vanity! thy name is William Stearns" (166), she challenges that critique on various occasions.

Ruth addresses the controversy of mind versus heart on two levels: on the level of life values, and on the level of writing and reading. She makes it clear that she sets mind before heart not only in the domain of literature but also in life. In a scene which immediately follows Professor Stearns's letter with its doubts as to Ruth's common sense, Ruth undergoes a phrenological exam performed by a celebrity in his field, Professor Finman. His explanation of "the bumps" on Ruth's head, which supposedly contain a key to her personality, focuses on the abilities of her mind. He maintains that her "love is a

5: Deconstructing the Definition of Female Letters 147

mental love—a regard for the mind, rather than the person of the individual" (169). In his opinion, Ruth displays a number of characteristics usually considered masculine: she "can plan well; can lay out work for others to advantage," she exhibits "a predominance of the reflective intellect over the perceptive," which is "characterized for thought, judgment, and the power to comprehend ideas," she "remembers and understands what [she] reads, better than what [she] sees or hears" (170). Prof. Finman concludes his exam by remarking to Ruth that "very much might be said with reference to the operations of your mind, for we seldom find the faculties so fully developed, or the powers so versatile as in your case" (171). Ruth is not the only woman in her family who proves to have "a versatile mind." Her precocious daughter, Nettie, demonstrates unusual verbal skills: her quick repartees and witty puns astonish John and Ruth. To Mr. Walter's question: "Will you have some soup?," Nettie replies: "Ask my mother, she's the *soup*-intendent" (186, Fern's emphasis). John sees in her "Ruth 2nd," "another genius" in the family (186).

The phrenological exam serves as a scientific proof that Ruth is fully capable of using her mind to the same extent as men do and possesses the abilities hitherto considered masculine. She cannot simply proclaim it herself, however, but has to hide behind the authority of Prof. Finman. She uses a similar strategy to denounce the clichés regarding feminine writing. Having written a letter of acceptance to the publisher of her book, Ruth shows it to John Walter. His reply silences any doubts or reservations Ruth might have about the style and the tone of her letter. To her question "You don't approve it?," John answers,

> But I do though. I was only thinking how excellent a substitute strong common-sense may be for experience. Your answer is brief, concise, sagacious, and business-like; I endorse it unhesitatingly. It is just what I should have advised you to write. (163)

The emphasis in John's remark falls on brevity and commonsense, two features usually attributed to masculine style. Thus the adjectives John uses to describe Ruth's style belie the stereotype of the feminine letter as an endless outpouring of unrelated thoughts, lacking organization and conciseness (cf. Godfrey Singer's comment to that effect: "There are few of us who have not, at one time or another, suffered from the lengthy outpourings that only a feminine correspondent may send us").[15] Fern employs John's praise of Ruth's letter in the same way as Professor Finman's verdict: John's being no ordinary reader but an editor and a writer himself gives credibility to his judgment.

In other words, if two male specialists renowned in their fields proclaim openly that women not only have minds but are capable of using them, it must be true.

If the presence of Prof. Finman and John Walter in the novel is meant to convince readers of Ruth's choice of mind over heart with respect to thinking and writing, letters from her readers fulfill that function with respect to reading. Ruth, as an extremely popular columnist, receives an inordinate number of letters, and her job is to sort through them, discarding trash, and selecting letters of importance or value. She discards all the letters that treat of love such as the offer of marriage from a rich widower who promises her eternal love should she consent to "a union" with him: "Oh, pshaw!. said Ruth, throwing the letter to Nettie, "make anything you like of it pussy; it is of no value to me" (181). She treats equally mercilessly all the attempts to exploit her, appealing to her "feminine" heart susceptible to human suffering and poverty; such as the following:

Dear Madam:

I am a poor devil, and worse editor; nevertheless, I have started a paper. If you will but allow me to put your name on it as Assistant Editress, I am sure it will go like a locomotive. If, in addition to this little favor, you could also advance me the sum of one hundred dollars, it would be an immense relief to your admirer,

John Staples. (182)

Ruth's only reaction is a sigh of contempt directed at human arrogance and egoism.

The "trash-pile" constitutes only a small portion of the letters she receives from her readers. The bulk of her correspondence expresses deep admiration for her talent as a writer, her ability to probe human conduct, her acute awareness of social problems, and her involvement in search of remedies. Ruth's articles make the readers question their own behavior and suggest ways to deal and communicate better with others. A reader, known only by his initials, claims that, owing to Ruth's articles, he is "a better son, a better brother, a better husband, and a better father" (183). John Stokes, "a rough old man, not used to writing or talking to ladies," professes that Ruth's "pieces have got the real stuff in 'em, and so I told my son John the other night; and *he* says, and I say, and neighbor Smith, who comes in to hear 'em, says, that you ought to make a book of them, so that your readers may keep them" (135, Fern's emphasis). Unlike Clarissa's letters, which attested to the failure of her writing endeavors, the readers' letters are tangible proofs of Ruth's success as a journalist. And unlike

5: Deconstructing the Definition of Female Letters   149

Clarissa, who needs letters as documents to decipher Lovelace's games underlying her tragic fate, Ruth values them as documents that might be useful in business transactions, as for instance when she deliberates the question of selling her copyrights: "No, gentlemen, I will *not* sell you my copyright; these autograph letters, and all other letters of friendship, love, and business, I am constantly receiving from strangers, are so many proofs that I have won the public ear" (153, Fern's emphasis). Ruth needs the support of her readers to convince herself and her superiors that the quality of her journalistic work equals that of a male journalist, and that she deserves to be treated on an equal footing.

Ruth Hall presents, then, a new heroine, a heroine, who not only sits behind a desk, but makes a success of her life as a writer. The new heroine rejects the virtues that "Samuel Richardson had taught reading women on both sides of the Atlantic," namely, "sentiment, submission, sacrifice, and long-suffering."[16] This rejection enables her to achieve emotional and financial independence from men. With the ban of love letters, Ruth bans any sentimental ties in her life, and hails fame and money as a key to happiness. Of course, as Nina Baym observes, "Ruth loves her children but this is the love of a benefactor toward dependents; Fanny Fern has rejected entirely the idea that women need a love they must lean on. She does not even accept the ideal of a love between peers" (253). The exclusion of the sexual domain "was a radical step, meant to force men to approach women as human beings with minds and hearts rather than objects of lust."[17] Thus *Ruth Hall* offers an alternative to the tale of seduction and betrayal, an alternative that cancels out the victim/aggressor pair and fosters a model of male-female relations based on mutual respect and equality. Letters, the notorious battleground, are used to offer a reconciliatory image: Ruth's daughter, Nettie, playing with letters, constructs a house of them. Ruth's house of letters, however, stands on sound common sense.

LETTERE A MARINA AND THE DECONSTRUCTION OF THE LITERARY AND NONLITERARY CATEGORIES

Just as *Ruth Hall* demonstrates that a woman's act of writing a letter needs to constantly address the clichés that inscribe it, a choice of epistolary format entails coming to grips with the preceding epistolary tradition. Thus Dacia Maraini's decision to adopt the epistolary format in her 1981 novel, *Lettere a Marina,* cannot be innocent. It implies a desire to take a stand, to continue the dialogue with the past. Maraini is very conscious of stereotypes pervading comments on feminine writing,

> Di solito per scrittura al femminile si intende o si intendeva qualcosa di sentimentale, di delicato, di fumoso e di crepuscolare. Una trama fatta di 'sensibleries' fragranti e leziose, un vorticare di lucciole e di spore che il vento della critica avrebbe pensato di spazzare via dal mondo della letteratura.[18]

> [Usually feminine writing means or meant something sentimental, delicate, smoky, crepuscular. A plot made of 'sentimentalities' sweet-smelling and affected, a swirl of glowing dust that the wind of criticism would sweep away from the world of literature.]

She is also conscious of the inferior position that feminine writing occupies in the literary hierarchy. Writing has been divided into two voices; one that carries the tone of authority, "basso e forte," [low and loud]—the male voice. And the other one: "quella leggera, acuta, saltellante, la voce che sa di cucina, di camera da letto, non convince neanche le donne stesse, per la sua totale mancanza di prestigio e di autorità" (xiv) [that light, shrill, hopping, the voice that smells of a kitchen, of a bedroom, and does not even sound convincing to women themselves because of its total lack of prestige and authority]. Maraini's awareness of the distinction between the feminine and the masculine voices, and the repercussions of that distinction, extend to the division into typically masculine or typically feminine genres.

In *Lettere a Marina,* Chantal, a friend of the protagonist, and a professed feminist, says, "Scrivere vuol dire isolarsi separarsi dalle altre assumere un membro mentale,"[19] [To write is to isolate and separate oneself from other women and to adopt the mental attitudes of a man's prick][20] to which the protagonist, Bianca, replies: "Non lo dici anche tu che le donne hanno sempre scritto memorie confessioni diari lettere?" [But Chantal you must admit that women have always written memoirs confessions diaries and letters, 40]. Unlike Chantal, Bianca does not want to write in isolation. Her words relate letters to a feminine tradition, the tradition that needs to be revoked, remembered, and resurrected. Maraini ponders the question why many women writers, famous during their lifetime, pass into oblivion as soon as they are dead: "Così è successo da noi con Sibilla Aleramo, con Cristina Belgioso, con Veronica Franco. E perfino Grazia Deledda che ha avuto il premio Nobel in vita, sta scivolando fuori del quadro"[21] [This has happened to our Sibilla Aleramo, Cristina Belgioso, and Veronica Franco. And even Grazia Deledda, who won the Nobel Prize is slipping into oblivion] Why and how does it happen? The

5: Deconstructing the Definition of Female Letters

discrimination does not actually happen at the moment of writing; after all, no one prohibits women from writing, explains Maraini. Nor does it happen at the moment of direct contact with the market; we know well that women constitute the majority of readers and the publishers look only for profit. "The crucial moment of selection comes afterwards, when "the big sifter starts separating the wheat from the tares" (xviii). It is in that transition that each generation loses

> le sue intellettuali, le sue poetesse, le sue romanziere. Libere in un mercato libero sono sopportate finché sono in vista, ma è difficile che siano ammesse, una volta morte, fra i grandi da onorare, da studiare, da prendere a modello. (xix)

> [its women intellectuals, its female poets and writers. Free in a free market, they are visible as long as they live; after their death they do not find place among the great ones that are honored, studied, and taken as a models.]

What is lacking in the case of women writers is the prestige that accompanies any great writer, the prestige that "provoca imitatori, scuole, tendenze e sopratutto un corpo critico con cui ogni studente dovrà poi fare i conti" [provokes imitators, schools, tendencies, and above all a body of criticism which every student has to consider]. In order to reclaim female literature, we need to provide it with critical studies that establish links between the past and the present.

Responding to Maraini's appeal, my reading of *Lettere a Marina* will focus on her own reaction to the epistolary tradition, in particular, on the ways in which Maraini addresses the stereotype of a feminine love letter and its association with the—by now familiar—heart/nonliterary/private category. *Lettere a Marina* is a series of letters, written by the protagonist, Bianca, to Marina, her former lover. Bianca arrives in a small seaside town to escape the aftermath of a love affair with Marina, and to dedicate her time and energy to writing a novel. The letters, without dates or signature, constitute a serialized account of her daily occupations, meetings with people, progress of the novel, and reflections on the past. The last letter coincides with the completion of the novel and the decision to leave the quiet little port for Sicily.

Bianca's letters manifest a double breach with the traditional love letter category. They are addressed to a female, not a male, lover, and they insist on adopting the plane of friendship, not love. Bianca sets out to reconstruct in writing the course of their love affair: "Bisogna che io ti racconti come è nato e cresciuto questo spinoso amore" (6) [Just now I want to tell how this painful love was born, 7]. In the very first letter, she declares her wish to maintain contact with Marina, but to alter the nature of their relationship—to substitute friendship for love: "Quando torneremo amiche se mai lo vorrai ci parleremo lasciando il sesso dentro un paniere appeso fuori dalla finestra" (5) [If you ever want us to become friends again we'll hang our sex outside the window like cherries in a basket, 7]. Bianca wants to escape the emotional tensions and absorption in a love affair that, like all passionate love affairs, resembles a war—"Il nostro incontrarci e scontrarci," (5) [all those comings and goings, 8], with subterfuges and cunning strategies to outwit and dominate the enemy-lover. She portrays herself as "un san Giorgio sul suo cavallo alato e sono partita con elmo corazza spada bandiera per entrare nel mondo degli amori femminili" (33) [St George on his winged horse and I set out with helmet breast plate sword and banner to enter the world of women's love, 34]. She realizes that cruelty and the desire for domination are parts of any love affair, and are also parts of her affair with Marina: "Ho avuto delle tentazioni di crudeltà ... Volevo cambiarti odore sapore volevo farti a pezzi" (22) [I've been tempted to retaliate ... I was trying to change your smell and taste]. Her own streak of cruelty is reflected in Marina's look: "Mi fissi come fossi il tuo peggior nemico" (14) [you stare at me as if I were your worst enemy, 16]. She senses the mutual fear of inflicting pain, of wounding each other. "Tu dici che vuoi ferirmi perché io ti rifiuto," she writes to Marina, "ma forse io ti rifiuto perché tu vuoi ferirmi" (6) [You say you want to hurt me because I've rejected you but perhaps it's I who reject you because you want to hurt me, 8].

She is afraid of Marina's possessiveness: "Sono qui per sfuggire a una figlia che mi vuole mangiare" (21) [I'm here to escape from a girl who wants to gobble me up, 22]. But she is well aware of her own desire to strengthen the invisible ties linking Marina to her. In her own words, "Ero già entrata nella costellazione magnetica dei tuoi pensieri. O forse no sbaglio forse ero io che ti giravo intorno tenendo lacci e reti per acciuffarti" (12) [I was already trapped in the magnetic constellation of your thoughts. Or was I mistaken? Was it I who circled around you holding out enticements like a net to ensnare you? 14]. She sees every gesture as an attempt to draw her closer to total dependence and submission to her lover. Even gifts can become an effective weapon used to ensnare and entice the lover-enemy:

> L'ultima volta che mi sono tolta l'anello che mi avevi regalato mi hai soffiato nell'orecchio come un drago furibondo e ho sentito la fiamma che arrivava fino in gola. Tu non vuoi farmi dei regali tu vuoi chiudermi con piccoli segni magici dentro il cerchio della tua volontà. La goccia nera sul

petto la piccola corona di spine insanguinate sul dito il serpentello di smalto verde al polso. (19)

[The last time I picked up the ring you gave me I could feel your breath in my ears like a ferocious dragon. I felt the flames reaching right down my throat. It isn't presents you are giving me but little magic signs to imprison me inside the charmed circle of your will. The black glass teardrop on my throat the small crown of bleeding thorns on my finger the green enamel serpent encircling my wrist.] (21)

Those gifts, symbolizing the pain of submission and martyrdom—like the "corona di spine insanguinate" for ring—imply Marina's willingness to make the lover-enemy participate in the cruel game ("gioco crudele e morboso," 12) of seduction and betrayal. But the search for a complete, not partial, truth prompts Bianca to admit her own desire to initiate the seduction game: "E un pensiero vagante come un serpentello voglioso mi girava nelle viscere il pensiero di sedurti di cominciare io il gioco" (30) [an idea wandered like a willful serpent twisting inside my head—the idea of starting the game myself and seducing you, 33].

Bianca does not hesitate to confront the manipulative schemes that form a part of her relationship with Marina. Her behavior towards Marina tends to become more guarded and less spontaneous, in a constant anticipation of a sudden attack. "Volevo abbracciarti," she admits recollecting one of their encounters, "sarei stata felice di abbracciarti ma nello stesso tempo avevo paura di ricominciare il gioco del rifiuto e della seduzione" (14) [I wanted to put my arms around you but at the same time I am wary of repeating this old game of seduction and rejection, 16]. Her reservations and fears remind her of another period in her life when she was experiencing similar sentiments in her relationship with Marco. Like "tutti gli uomini che fanno della seduzione il loro mestiere" (29) [all the men for whom womanising is a way of life, 31], Marco also resorted to subterfuges to dominate their affair. Part of what Bianca calls his "amorous technique" was "l'attesa l'incertezza che fa agonizzare l'amore appassionato e poi il tradimento la sincerità mista alle menzogne" (30) [the expectation the titillation the uncertainty that make a death agony out of every love affair and finally the betrayal the lies the sincerity all mixed up together, 32].

But Bianca does not want to "mix sincerity with lies"; she wants to reconstruct the past with absolute frankness. Questioning Marina's motives and actions, Bianca includes her own reactions and desires under that scrutinizing gaze. Each comment or reflection on Marina is immediately counterbalanced by a comment or reflection on her

5: Deconstructing the Definition of Female Letters

reflections: "È assurdo che io sia venuta qui per scappare da te e poi senta il bisogno di scriverti tutti i giorni. Mi ero abituata a parlarti di quello che penso che sogno che scrivo. Mi riesce difficile smettere" (35) [It seems absurd to think that I came here to escape from you and then feel the need to write to you every day. I've got into the habit of talking to you about what I've been thinking or dreaming or writing and it's not easy to stop, 36]. The end of their love affair does not mean the end of any contact but the passage from the plane of love to that of friendship. And to continue existence on that plane, Bianca feels the urge to disclose to Marina the most intimate details from her past, to present to Marina the complete person she never knew before. "Ti parlo di me," she writes to Marina, "perché tu hai amato una statua senza passato" (55) [I want to tell you about myself because the person you were in love with was a lifeless statue without a past, 56]. Her desire to tell it all makes her discover herself and uncover the past she never dared to confront before,

> Nello sforzo di farmi conoscere da te ritrovo cose lontane che credevo morte per sempre. Vengono su piccoli oggetti misteriosi perfettamente conservati in qualche parte dei miei sensi e mi danno un senso di ubriachezza. (60)

> [In my attempts to reveal myself to you I'm finding all sorts of far-away things which I thought were dead forever. I come upon small mysterious objects perfectly preserved in some part of my emotions.] (61)

Thus, letter writing becomes for Bianca also a process of self-analysis leading to a better understanding of her own self.

Bianca uses her letters to Marina not as a means of manipulating or controlling their relationship, but as a means of preserving it. Letters do not act as a weapon used on the battleground of seduction to destroy the adversary, but rather function as a bridge that connects that battleground to the territory of mutual understanding and respect. "Credo di amarti di un amore simile a quella marina del sogno," she writes to Marina, "qualcosa di fermo e assoluto lontano dal sesso e dalle terribili trasformazioni della vita quotidiana qualcosa di delicato e inquietante senza tempo" (189) [I think my love for you is like that seascape in my dream—something delicate and timeless something enclosed and entirely remote from sex and the drudgery of daily existence, 192]. Marina, the lover and adversary, turns into Marina, the friend and confidante, "una sorella che cammina col mio stesso passo" (35) [a sister who has marched in step with with me, 36]. Merging the two, heretofore antagonistic, roles of lover and confidante, Maraini dissolves the tension existing in the epistolary novel of seduction and betrayal. Moreover, with the double image of Bianca/san Giorgio, she undercuts two stereotypes with regard to love letters: the cliché of a feminine love letter as an uncontrolled flow of sentiment (letter of a seduced and abandoned woman), and that of a seducer's love letter as a tool of manipulation and destruction.

Although the story of Marina and Bianca occupies the central position in the letters, Bianca manages to escape total self-absorption in her feelings, memories, and recollections, an absorption typical of love letters. She also brings into her epistolary relationship with Marina the life stories of other people who have crossed her path. Her insatiable curiosity and capacity for compassion and solidarity with anyone who is suffering and needs a sympathetic ear or a helping hand, do not allow her to stand aloof but prompt her to become actively involved in other people's lives. Bianca paints a vivid portrait of her neighbor, Basilia, a downtrodden and dowdy mother of two little boys, who, thanks to Bianca's caring interest, finds a welcome respite from her monotonous existence. An evening passed in an elegant restaurant transports Basilia into another world, a world of luxury and beauty that Basilia could only dream of: "In un momento di euforia Basilia mi ha confessato che è proprio come nell'ultimo fumetto con Fabio Tesi. E come in un fumetto abbiamo recitato le nostre parti. Abbiamo mangiato bevuto riso e giocato a fare le signore (201) [In a moment of euphoria Basilia confessed that it reminded her of the latest photo-comic with Fabio Testi. And just like the people in the comic we were playing our parts—eating and drinking and behaving like ladies, 206]. Bianca restores Basilia's youth, at least for a moment. She helps Massimo, her friend's brother, and hides him in her apartment from the police who are investigating his political activities. She listens to the story of the ill-fated love of Damiano, a waiter from a nearby bar, and his stepmother.

Bianca weaves all these stories into the letters in order to transform reality into a narrative, the ephemeral into the permanent, to save seemingly insignificant existences, like Basilia's, from oblivion. By populating her letters with other faces, other voices, other perspectives than her own, Bianca manages to escape the egoistical "I" looming over them. As a writer, she is still the organizing and the uniting force of the narrative, but she does not claim the right to dominate it constantly and ostentatiously. Her writing strategy reflects the aversion to the domineering voice of the author, the voice that knows all and overshadows any other voices trying to speak. In *A Room of One's Own*, Virginia Woolf ponders the question of what was amiss in the new novel of a famous writer, Mr. A, and comes to the conclusion that

5: Deconstructing the Definition of Female Letters 157

it was a straight dark bar, a shadow shaped something like the letter 'I'. One began dodging this way and that to catch a glimpse of the landscape behind it. Whether that was indeed a tree or a woman walking I was not quite sure. Back one was always hailed to the letter 'I'. One began to be tired of 'I'. But why was I bored? Partly because of the dominance of the letter 'I' and the aridity, which, like the giant beech tree, it casts within its shade. Nothing will grow there.[22]

By letting in multiple voices, Bianca erases that shadow, and attenuates the author's authority.

This multiplicity of voices reflects Bianca's desire to show that her relationship with Marina constitutes a part of her life, significant, but by no means the only one. Mariane from *Lettres portugaises* complains that

les miens [yeux] sont privés de la seule lumière qui les animait, il ne leur reste que des larmes, et je ne les ai employés à aucun usage qu'à pleurer sans cesse, depuis que j'appris que vous étiez enfin résolu à éloignement qui m'est si insupportable qu'il me fera mourir en peu de temps.[23]

[mine are deprived of the only light that made them shine, all they have left now are tears, and I have been using them for incessant weeping since the moment I learned about your departure: I do not know how I can endure it, it makes me die a little each time I think about it.]

Bianca by contrast does not intend to die of a broken heart. Although she feels the pain of separation from Marina, she is able to enjoy the tranquility of her new life divided between her book and her newly-made friends. She is perfectly capable of living alone and writes with disdain of commonly accepted assumptions about women who do so:

Se sono sola cioè senza uomo e senza famiglia lui mi proteggerà. Così mi pare di capire. Anche la vicina di casa la prima volta che è entrata da me con la scusa dei bambini che dormono mi ha chiesto: è sola? e da allora la sua curiosità cresce ogni giorno. Una donna che sta in vacanza da sola nasconde qualcosa: una pena un amore non corrisposto una malattia chissà. (21)

[If I am here without a man and without a family he will protect me—at least that's how I interpret it. The first time my neighbour came to see me on the excuse that her children were asleep she asked me 'Are you all by yourself?' and from then on her curiosity has grown daily. A woman on holiday alone must hide something: some sort of grief or unrequited love or illness. Who knows what secret sorrow it might be?] (22)

Her isolation is a matter of choice, not of necessity, and so is her decision to write to Marina. Letters to Marina are not an outlet for Bianca's pent-up creativity brought to life by her emotional upheavals (a commonly accepted view on women writing letters), since her letters are only a diversion from her real writing, that is the writing of her novel.

Bianca the writer is equally important in the letters as Bianca, Marina's correspondent. In the very first letter, she identifies herself as a writer: "Perché sono qui? per scappare da te per finire il romanzo a cui lavoro ormai da due anni senza molta convinzione" (5) [Why am I here? To escape from you to finish the novel I've been working on halfheartedly for more than eighteen months, 7]. The references to her novel are scattered throughout the letters. The tone of Bianca's letters corresponds to her creative moods. She complains to Marina of a writer's block and the frustration of not being able to write: "Col romanzo non riesco ad andare né avanti né indietro" (169) [As for my novel I am completely stuck with it, 172]. Nonetheless she does not get discouraged, knowing that writing requires patience and total dedication: "Devo mettermi a sedere e scrivere perché questo è il desiderio più sensato e più profondo che ho. Non un dovere il dovere è sterile ha il colore delle banane ma un piacere che va coltivato" (174) [I must get down to writing because that is the sanest and most profound aim of my life. It's not a duty—duty is as sterile as the colour of a banana—it's a sense of fulfilment that grows with use, 176]. Her life revolves around her novel, and the act of writing dominates it completely. "Non ho voglia di uscire," she confesses to Marina, "ogni minuto che non dedico al romanzo mi sembra perduto. Sono inchiodata alla macchina da scrivere. Ho paura allontanandomi di perdere questo stato di pienezza" (189) [I don't feel like going out—every minute I don't give to the novel seems wasted. I am nailed to my typewriter and I daren't leave it for fear that this fecundity will slip away from me, 192]. The urge to write absorbs her to the point of intoxication, blotting out everything else: "Mi sono immersa nel mio romanzo fino a rimanere intossicata. Per dodici giorni ho scritto dieci ore al giorno. Poi ho finito" (191) [For twelve days I wrote for ten hours a day until I ended up in a state of intoxication. Then I stopped, 194].

Along with the frustrations and absorptions of a writer, Bianca experiences the additional tension of being a woman writer. Reading the poems of Emily Dickinson, and admiring their poignant beauty, she cannot help but recollect the condescending critical voices that disparaged Dickinson's poetry:

5: Deconstructing the Definition of Female Letters 159

Il vecchio e pomposo signor Higgins trovava che le poesie della giovane Emily erano 'senza forma' anche se le riconosceva un 'potere lirico senza confronti, nonché audacia di associazioni ideologiche e coraggio verbale'. Insomma queste donne hanno idee passioni ma non sanno scrivere le forme sono le loro nemiche. Quando Emily chiese al vecchio Higgins che lei idolatrava se le consigliava di pubblicare qualche verso lui rispose ottusamente di no non valeva la pena. (100)

[That pompous old Mr Higgins thought the poems of young Emily 'lacked structure' even though he did recognise her as having 'an incomparable lyrical gift of audacity of ideological associations and verbal assurance.' In other words women have passionate ideas but don't know how to write. Form and structure are beyond them. When Emily asked old Mr Higgins (whom she idolized) whether he advised her to publish a few verses he told her bluntly that it was not worth the trouble.] (99)

In view of Dickinson's struggle for recognition, Bianca anticipates with anxiety the reception and the scrutiny of her own novel, should it be published.[24] That anxiety is reflected in a double-voiced comment on her novel. One voice criticizes it severely: "Sono convinta di avere fatto una cosa brutta e ridicola" (194) [I'm convinced that what I've done is bad and ridiculous, 197]. But having said that she hastens to assume the other one that considers it a "cosa preziosa" (194) [a precious thing].

Bianca's response to being a woman writer is a mixture of defiance and conformism in an effort to reconcile her idiosyncrasies (as a writer and a woman) with the norm set by male critics. She defies Higgins's opinion about the lack of form in feminine writing by rejecting an obvious formal requirement, the rules of punctuation. She uses only periods and question marks, disregarding commas, colons, and semicolons—in fact the only comma in the whole novel is the one used in the quotation from Higgins's comment. In consequence, the sentences have the breathless quality that make the reader rush from one period to the next, and then reread the sentence to find the right moments to pause, and decide on the meaning.

The aspect of writing that absorbs her most is precisely the form she should adopt for her novel. "È insensato questo mio scriverti di me chiusa in questo brutto appartamento anonimo," begins one of the letters,

mentre mi sforzo di costruire un romanzo che si rifiuta a ogni costruzione. Mi sfugge da ogni parte. Metto su mattoni su dei mattoni o quello che io credo siano mattoni e me li trovo sgregolati mangiati da una malattia che divora la pietra. (101)

[It doesn't make much sense writing to you about myself while I'm shut away inside this ugly anonymous flat trying to force myself to construct a novel which refuses to have a structure. I escape in every possible way. I build up bricks or what I think are bricks and I find them crumbling away eaten by some disease that devours stone.] (101)

Bianca, like an architect, has to design and plan every single detail of her novel, to make it a solid and accommodating structure with a sense of harmony and organization. She perceives her novel as "l'immagine che le mie dita pazienti hanno tirato fuori dal disordine" (191) [the puzzle you watch emerging out of chaos, 193]. The persistence with which she talks about "construction" and "order," as the essential elements in the act of writing, demonstrates her preoccupation with its literary quality. Writing is not a spontaneous, effortless activity in which she, a woman writer, engages to pass the time. It is hard work, a process that requires caution, concentration, and, to use La Bruyère's expression, "pénible recherche."[25] Bianca, then, undermines the non-literary nature of feminine writing postulated in eighteenth-century literary theories.

Throughout the letters to Marina, Bianca claims that they run parallel to the writing of the novel, that the letters and the novel are two entities, united only by having the same author. But in fact the letters might also acquire the status of a novel. We find out that Bianca never sends them to Marina. In her last letter, she writes: "Mi sono messa a scrivere a te l'ultima lettera prima di partire. Poi in treno le rileggerò tutte" (203) [I sat down to write this last letter to you before leaving. Then I shall read them all on the train, 207]. Her last gesture is that of a critic who scrutinizes a literary piece that happened to fall into her hands. By virtue of this gesture Bianca turns her private love story into a story recorded in letters, a piece of writing that presupposes the possibility of publication. If published, Bianca's collection would join a long list of letter collections by women. Hailed by the eighteenth-century critics as the mode of feminine expression, and thus allowed to enter the public scene, those collections of letters are often the only documents that preserved traces of a culture otherwise condemned to oblivion. We can get acquainted with Mme. de Sévigné, Dorothy Osborne, and others whose private correspondence acted as a back door to the public stage. Ultimately it does not really matter how they managed to get there; the important thing is that their voices are still audible, loud and clear.

Maraini's *Lettere a Marina* constitutes, then, an attempt to reclaim the female epistolary tradition, to use letters as a way of preserving women's lives and their stories.[26] By acknowledging the debt of grati-

5: Deconstructing the Definition of Female Letters

tude to her predecessors, Maraini tries to dispel the myths and clichés pervading that tradition, in particular the sentimental and nonliterary category to which it had been assigned. Hers is not an open attack on the stereotypical images, but rather a methodical and cautious confrontation that eventually proves them fallacious, and establishes new ways of approaching them. *Lettere a Marina* seeks to widen the vision, make room for novel approaches, and find new solutions to what seemed petrified models:

> È buffo accorgersi dopo quarant'anni che si portano le stesse scarpe con la noncuranza imbecille di chi è nato dentro che ci stanno strette. Sono un numero più corto e non lo sapevamo. Ti guardi i piedi e li trovi rattrappiti pieni di calli nati dalla costrizione. Ti accorgi che il tuo camminare è sempre stato doloroso anche se spedito. Provi a toglierti le scarpe e non riesci più a camminare perché quella costrizione era diventata parte del tuo modo di incedere parte del tuo stile della tua visione del mondo. Così le donne con una cultura che è stata fatta senza di loro contro di loro ma che pure amano crudelmente come si amano i propri amanti. (38)

> [How strange that after forty years one is still wearing the same shoes one was born with. How stupid that without one even being aware of it or concerned about it they've always been a size too narrow. Look at your own feet and you'll see: they're covered with corns because of the way your shoes pinch you and restrict your circulation. Haven't you ever noticed that walking has always been painful even when it seemed quick and easy. But then—take off your shoes and you'll find you can't walk because the way you walk has become part of your whole life-style and perception of the world. So we women live our lives in a world that has been created without us and acts against us. But we also have a sadistic love-hate attitude towards this culture as we always have towards those who tyrannize over us.] (40)

Maraini's aim in adopting the epistolary format in *Lettere a Marina* is not, to use her own metaphor, to discard the uncomfortable shoes allotted her by tradition, but to adapt them to fit modern female realities.

Lettera a un bambino mai nato and the Deconstruction of the Bourgeois Concept of the Private Sphere

If *Ruth Hall* and *Lettere a Marina* took aim at sentimental and nonliterary labels applied to female letters, Oriana Fallaci in *Lettera a un bambino mai nato,* confronts the third element of the infamous trio, the private versus public category. Her brief novel begins with a poem that illuminates her intention:

> A chi non teme il dubbio
> a chi si chiede i perché
> senza stancarsi e a costo
> di soffrire di morire
> A chi si pone il dilemma
> di dare la vita o negarla
> questo libro è dedicato
> da una donna
> per tutte le donne.²⁷
>
> [To those who do not fear doubt—
> To those who wonder why
> Without growing tired and at the cost
> of suffering and dying—
> To those who pose themselves the dilemma
> of giving life or denying it—
> this book is dedicated
> by a woman
> for all women.]²⁸

Fallaci's protagonist proposes to use her own personal experience as a starting point for a public discussion on a question concerning all the women, the question of giving birth to a child. The novel is a monologue of a mother directed to her unborn child, a monologue which addresses her doubts, fears, and hopes connected with its birth. Its closes with a scene in the hospital where the mother is taken after having had a miscarriage.

Oriana Fallaci sets out to expose the hypocrisy underlying the rigid separation between the domains of the private (for women) and public (for men), and the ways in which they are constructed. As I have shown in the first chapter, the conduct material published in the last three centuries advocated the separation of these domains in an attempt to impose on women socially desirable and acceptable roles of mothers and wives. Although the word "society" appeared occasionally, the rhetoric of conduct material concentrated primarily on the universal laws of God and nature, thus excluding any possible doubt as to their validity, and requiring complete obedience. Conduct material was one of the public channels that camouflaged the demand for supervising the family as a socially indispensable unit, by appealing to its private character. The expression "private sphere" thus found its way to a public discourse which, in the disguise of friendly "counsel" and "advice," became a mode of controlling familial life.²⁹

Michel Foucault presents a drastic example of the transformation of a supposedly private matter into a public discourse in offering his readers the story of Herculine Barbin, a nineteenth-century French

5: Deconstructing the Definition of Female Letters 163

hermaphrodite. In his introduction to Barbin's memoirs, Foucault gives a brief sketch of the treatment of hermaphrodites in France. Prior to the eighteenth century, hermaphroditism was considered a matter of personal choice. At the birth of a child, his or her godfather "was advised to choose the sex that seemed to have the better of the other, being 'the most vigorous' or 'the warmest.'"[30] At the age of eighteen hermaphrodites "were free to decide for themselves if they wished to go on being of the sex which had been assigned them or if they preferred the other" (viii). The eighteenth century, however, no longer respects an individual's right to a free choice of gender. It becomes a matter of law and medicine. Thus, a decision concerning the private life of a person enters into the public scene, channeled into medical, legal, and religious discourses. The whole case of Herculine is shrouded in silence; she cannot discuss it with her friends or family, but only with selected representatives of institutions, a doctor, a lawyer, and a curé. It is their verdict that declares Herculine Barbin a man. Shortly afterwards he commits suicide, unable to live with a new identity.

In his *History of Sexuality,* Foucault explains the increasing preoccupation in the eighteenth century with the problems of population and the state's needs to regulate it according to its demands. "At the heart of this economic and political problem of population," notes Foucault,

> was sex: it was necessary to analyze the birthrate, the age of marriage, the legitimate and illegitimate births, the precocity and frequency of sexual relations, the ways of making them fertile or sterile, the effects of unmarried life or of the prohibitions, the impact of contraceptive practices—of those notorious 'deadly secrets' which demographers on the eve of the Revolution knew were already familiar to the inhabitants of the countryside.[31]

Thus, concludes Foucault, "the sexual conduct was taken both as object of analysis and as target of intervention" (26). Such intervention did not assume the form of crude prohibitions, but was administered in small doses, diluted in multiple discourses. Still considered a private matter, the question of birth control, for instance, was a taboo subject for conversation in public, but became a topic of legal, medical, and religious discourses. This created the impression that such matters were placed outside society; that only the body of a woman and her baby were of importance, seen from biological, medical, and, moral perspective, not the possible consequences of birth control in a society.

Oriana Fallaci attacks the hypocrisy of these practices, relating them to the question of giving birth to a child. Her novel participates in the feminist debate of the 1970s about the "privatizzazione" of the feminine role. As Carol Lazzaro-Weiss points out,

> Despite the many political and juridical victories of the feminist movement, women were still viewed as the affective center of the household when affective values were undergoing constant devaluation in a capitalist economy. The popular slogan of neofeminists, 'the personal is political,' stressed the inseparability of the political and personal realms: the exclusion of women from public to private domains that society considered unproductive was a political action, the roots and ramifications of which feminist writers strove to define, examine, and expose.[32]

Although Fallaci's protagonist refers to her own experience as a pregnant woman, she is convinced that all women ask themselves the same questions and have the same doubts as she does. So her hesitant voice "Come faccio a sapere che non sarebbe giusto buttarti via?" is immediately echoed by :"Molte donne si chiedono: mettere al mondo un figlio, perché?" (8) [How can I know that it wouldn't be better to throw you away. A lot of women ask themselves why they should bring a child into the world?, 10–11]. In juxtaposing "figlio" and "mondo," Fallaci links the public repercussions of a supposedly private act—giving birth to a child. The immediate connection takes place on legal grounds—the stamp of illegitimacy for children born out of wedlock. "Nel mondo in cui ti accingi ad entrare, e malgrado i discorsi sui tempi che mutano", explains the protagonist to her unborn baby: "una donna che aspetta un figlio senza esser sposata è vista il più delle volte come una irresponsabile. Nel migliore dei casi, come una stravagante, una provocatrice. O un'eroina. Mai come una mamma uguale alle altre" (21) [In the world you are about to enter, and despite all the talk about changing times, an unmarried woman expecting a child is most often looked on as irresponsible. At best, as an eccentric, a troublemaker. Or a heroine. Never as a mother like the others, 24]. That division is reflected in the reaction of the people who learn that she is an unwed expectant mother. There is no verbal response to the announcement, but their disapproval mixed with embarrassment (after all it is considered a private matter) is mirrored in the tone of voice, gestures, or silence. The protagonist describes the scene in the clinic, and the doctor's behavior:

> Con un tono che oscillava tra il solenne e l'allegro, ha alzato un foglietto ed ha detto: 'Congratulazioni, signora'. Automaticamente ho corretto: 'Signorina'. È stato come tirargli uno schiaffo. Solennità ed allegria sono scomparse, e fissandomi con voluta indifferenza, ha risposto: 'Ah.' (19)

5: Deconstructing the Definition of Female Letters   165

[In a tone wavering between the solemn and the cheerful, he lifted a sheet of paper and said: 'Congratulations, Madam.' Automatically I corrected him: 'Miss.' It was as though I'd given him a slap. Solemnity and cheerfulness disappeared, and staring at me with calculated indifference, he replied, 'Ah!'] (23)

She encounters a similar reaction on a number of occasions. The pharmacist to whom she gives the prescription "mi ha fissato con sgomento" (21) [stared at me with dismay, 24]. When she asks the tailor taking her measurements to make her coat loose enough to fit her for the whole period of pregnancy, he blushes violently and "ha spalancato la bocca e ho temuto che inghiottisse gli spilli. Non li ha inghiottiti, grazieaddio, ma gli son caduti per terra" (21) [his jaw dropped and I was afraid he'd swallowed the pins. He hadn't, they had fallen on the floor, 24]. That tacit reaction, manifested only in a look, a blush, a gesture of embarrassment exposes the façade of privacy that covers up society's fear with regard to the break-up of a family, and its possible consequences in terms of population control.

This silence on a personal level dissolves in the loquacity of public discourses that define that supposedly private bond between a mother and the baby she is carrying in her womb. The unborn baby becomes an object of scientific research and a subject of controversy.

Perfino il feto, dichiara costui [il dottor H. B. Munson], è materia pressoché inerte, quasi un vegetale estirpabile con un cucchiaio. Al massimo lo si può considerare un 'sistema coerente di capacità irrealizzate.' Secondo alcuni biologi, invece, l'essere umano incomincia col concepimento perché l'uovo fertilizzato contiene DNA. (29)

[Even the fetus, this man declares, is practically inert matter, little more than a vegetable that can be extirpated with a spoon. At most it can be considered a 'coherent system of unrealized capacity.' According to some biologists, on the other hand, the human being begins at the time of conception since the fertilized egg contains DNA.] (33)

The unborn baby becomes in turn the object of preoccupation in the discourses of religion and law. The voice of a priest accuses: "lei ha ucciso una creatura" (28) [You've killed a human being, 32]; the voice of law warns: "L'importante è che non mi proponga soluzioni criminali! La legge lo proibisce" (20) [It was important not to consider criminal decisions. The law forbids it, 24]. The baby, viewed as the property of God, society, science, loses its private status as a creature born of and dependent solely on its mother, and becomes a public issue.[33]

own behavior or wishes. Almost every reference to their love story is symmetrical, and consists of a statement and a counterstatement: "Non so cosa nasca prima se la tua voglia di mangiarmi e quindi la mia fuga oppure la mia fuga e quindi la tua voglia di mangiarmi" (7) [Which comes first? Your wish to swallow me up followed by my flight or my flight followed by your determination to swallow me, 8]? That double-sided, mirror-like description finds its expression in the act of making love between two women, when one experiences a shock of the familiar, confronted with a mirror-image of oneself: "Solo quando mi sono trovata davanti al tuo sesso sciolto dall'emozione e dal desiderio ho avuto un momento di panico. Ecco l'ultima resistenza è caduta e mi trovo davanti cosa? me stessa" (32) [Only when I find myself face to face with your sex melted by sensation and by desire do I have a moment of panic. Now the last resistance has given way and what do I find myself confronting? My own self, 34]. Unlike Lovelace, who boasted of his complete control in the seduction game in his long list of comparisons where he was the pursuer and Clarissa a helpless victim, Bianca does not play the role of either victim or victor. She is both Bianca and "san Giorgio," doubling as seducer and seduced. And so is Marina. They both accept a part of each role, they hurt and are hurt, suffer and cause suffering, seduce and are seduced. The symmetry of their actions and feelings establishes an equilibrium, an equality that cancels out the roles of the dominated and the domineering. The word "gioco" repeated over and over again with regard to their love affair may refer to the combat-like nature of that affair, seen as a game of wills and skills. But it may also refer to the partnership such a game requires, alternating winning with losing, knowing with loving: "Da quel momento sono entrata in un mare pieno di correnti contrarie: dovevo amare per conoscerti ma dovevo conoscerti per amare e tutte due le cose erano fatte con diligenza e allegria" (33) [From that moment I entered an ocean filled with opposite currents. I had to know you in order to love you but I had to love you in order to know you. I experienced both freely and happily, 43]. The acceptance of these rules results in the joy of discovery, not the bitterness of defeat.

The letters to Marina, "lettere a puntate," as Bianca calls them, are then not love letters but letters about love, an attempt to confront and account for both sides of a love story. Bianca does not write down the dictates of her heart; rather she uses her mind to probe and dissect the heart with an amazing honesty. Marina, her partner in the love story, remains her partner also in its account. The fact that Bianca writes letters, not a diary or a third-person narrative, attests to her need to include Marina as a presence that shares her thoughts and

Under the burden of these various discourses, the mother has no authority. Indeed, her voice is the one that counts the least when it comes to the decision of bringing the baby into the world. When she realizes that she has probably miscarried, she has a dream in which she stands accused of killing her unborn baby by negligence. She remains speechless throughout the whole trial while the voices representative of public discourses debate her case. Each speaker provides indisputable evidence to support his view. The male doctor offers medical proofs that demonstrate her guilt beyond reasonable doubt. The female doctor offers equally convincing evidence that proves her innocent of carelessness. Her lover and her feminist friend argue over the role of the baby in a marriage, and the ways in which both a husband and a wife need the baby to construct around themselves comfortable images that assure them of the significance of their existence in society. In all these discussions, both mother and baby are only objects that others use to advance their cause, whether it be religion, society, or feminism. But, asks the mother, should it be so? She should be the one to take "la responsabilità della scelta," since "essere mamma non è un mestiere. Non è nemmeno un dovere. È solo diritto fra tanti diritti" (13) [To be a mother is not a trade. It's not even a duty. It's only one right among many, 16]. Society has denied women this right, and has placed the power of making decisions in the hands of politicians, doctors, lawyers, and priests.

Fallaci's protagonist does not offer facile answers to the doubts she expresses at the beginning of the novel, "il dilemma di dare la vita o negarla" (1) [the dilemma of giving life or denying, 7] She only probes and questions her own motives, her fears and hopes, and her attitude remains ambivalent until the end:

> Non sei un bambino: sei un uovo . . . Creatura della mia fantasia, riuscisti appena a realizzare il desiderio di due mani e due piedi, qualcosa che assomigliava ad un corpo. In fondo amai un pesciolino. E per amore di un pesciolino mi inventai un calvario in seguito a cui rischio di finire anch'io. È inaccettabile. Ma perché non ti ho fatto togliere prima? Perché ho perso tanto tempo prezioso lasciando che tu mi avvelenassi? (98).

> [You're not a child: you're an egg . . . Creature of my imagination, you barely succeeded in realizing the wish for two hands and two feet, something that resembled a body. It was a little fish, I loved after all. And for the love of a little fish, I invented a calvary that has cost me the risk of dying myself. I won't accept it. Why didn't I get you removed before? Why did I waste so much time letting you poison me?] (111)

5: Deconstructing the Definition of Female Letters

But although she cannot resolve the dilemma of whether or not to give birth to a child, she manages to uncover the hypocrisy that pervades the so-called private sphere. She calls the family

> una menzogna costruita da chi organizzò questo mondo per controllare meglio la gente, sfruttarne meglio l'obbedienza alle regole e alle leggende. La famiglia non è che il portavoce di un sistema che non può lasciarti a disubbidire, la sua santità non esiste. (36–37)

> [a lie constructed the better to control people, the better to exploit their obedience to rules and legends. The family is nothing but a mouthpiece for a system that cannot let you disobey, and its sanctity is nonexistent.] (42)

Referring to the family as a lie, and a system of control, Fallaci challenges the validity of the concept of the private sphere—home. It is not a universal truth, but rather a social construct invented to help produce law-abiding, submissive citizens.

And it is the blind submission to the laws of society, religion, science, any laws imposed on one's life by the outside world, that becomes the target of the mother's concern. She discusses a set of values that play an important part in her own life and that, she hopes, will provide a guide for her child's life. The keywords in that guide are to question and to challenge general truths, concepts, and rules handed down to us by tradition, history, religion, or customs, not to accept their existence in silent obedience. "Non immagini quanto siano soffocanti le loro abitudini da imitare, le loro leggi da rispettare. Non fare questo, non fare quello, fai questo, e fai quello" (37) [You have no idea how suffocating it is to imitate their habits, to respect their laws. Don't do this, don't do that, do this and do that, 42]—warns the mother her unborn child. It is relatively easy to spot what she calls "le leggi dei prepotenti" (37) [the laws of the arrogant, 42] and rebel against them; any totalitarian system has always provoked a strong reaction on the part of the oppressed. It is much harder, however, to question "le leggi della brava gente" which "non t'offrono scampo perché ti si convince che è nobile accettarle" (37) [the laws of decent people offer no escape since you've been persuaded that it's noble to accept them, 42]. But if we seek a certain degree of liberty, only the courage to constantly probe and analyse ourselves and the world around us will open for us the road to freedom—the freedom of formulating our own doubts and thoughts.

One of the notions that usually remain undisputed is the authority of science. Science controls life and regulates its functions on the basis of empirical knowledge. It measures, tests, and examines physical reality to establish facts and provide solutions to problems. Its laws defy doubts since they derive from the results which can be proved and measured. The mother challenges its authority by resorting to intuition as another source of knowledge.[34] She senses the baby's existence through an intuitive revelation, not through a physical manifestation: "Stanotte ho saputo che c'eri: una goccia di vita scappata dal nulla. Me ne stavo con gli occhi spalancati nel buio e d'un tratto, in quel buio, s'è acceso un lampo di certezza: sì, c'eri. Esistevi. È stato come sentirsi colpire in petto da una fucilata" (7) [Last night I knew you existed: a drop of life escaped from nothingness. I was lying, my eyes wide open in the darkness, and all at once I was certain you were there, 9]. However, when she visits the doctor to ask his advice, he cannot prove that she is pregnant because it is too early to detect the baby's presence by use of scientific methods: "Per risposta ha scosso la testa dicendo che sono impaziente, non può ancora pronunciarsi, ripassi tra quindici giorni, pronta a scoprire che eri un prodotto della mia fantasia" (12) [His answer was to shake his head and tell me I'm impatient, he still can't say, and I should come back in two weeks prepared to discover that you're a product of my imagination, 14]. His arrogant self-confidence upsets and offends her: "Tornerò solo per dimostrargli che è un ignorante. Tutta la sua scienza non vale il mio intuito" (12) [I'll go back just to show him he's an ignoramus. All his science is not worth my intuition, 14]. She visits the doctor for the second time to confirm her pregnancy, to hear him say what she has already known for weeks: "Così in una stanza gelidamente bianca, attraverso la voce di un uomo gelidamente vestito di bianco, la Scienza mi ha dato l'annuncio ufficiale che c'eri. Non mi ha impressionato per niente, visto che lo sapevo già e molto prima di lei" (19) [Thus, in a cold white room, through the voice of a man coldly dressed in white, Science gave me its official announcement that you existed. It made no impression on me, since I'd already known long before it did, 23]. With that slightly ironical tone, perceptible in the "cold whiteness" of the room and of the doctor's clothes, she creates a critical distance between her own intuitive knowledge and the tangible knowledge of strangers.

Even the seemingly most noble concepts such as work or love become objects of the mother's scrutiny. "Ti racconteranno un mucchio di storie sulla necessità del lavoro, la gioia del lavoro, la dignità del lavoro. Non ci credere, mai. Si tratta di un'altra menzogna inventata per la convenienza di chi organizzò questo mondo" (37) [They'll tell you a lot of stories about the necessity of work, the joy of work, the dignity of work. Don't ever believe it. It's just one more lie invented for the convenience of whoever organized this world, 43]. The notion of work as a liberating experience is nothing but an illusion, a myth

5: Deconstructing the Definition of Female Letters 169

propagated over the ages, to better control people. "Lavori sempre per qualcuno, mai per te stesso"—explains the mother to the child—"Lavori sempre con fatica, mai con gioia. E mai nel momento in cui ne avresti voglia" (37) [You always work for someone, never for yourself. You always work with effort, never with joy. And never in the moment you would have liked, 43]. Even jobs considered the least dependent on others, such as agriculture or art, in reality depend on a number of outside factors which shape and condition what we do, and how and when we do it.

What is love, she muses, if you project its image against the background constructed over the ages to enhance its propensity for manipulation:

> il mio sospetto è che si tratti di un imbroglio gigantesco, inventato per tener buona la gente e distrarla. Di amore parlano i preti, i cartelloni pubblicitari, i letterati, i politici, coloro che fanno all'amore, e parlando di amore, presentandolo come toccasana di ogni tragedia, feriscono e tradiscono e ammazzano l'anima e il corpo (17).

> [My guess is that it's just a gigantic hoax, invented to keep people quiet and diverted. Everyone talks about love: the priests, the advertising posters, the literati, and the politicians. And in speaking of love and offering it as a panacea for every tragedy, they wound and betray and kill both body and soul.] (20)

And yet despite the fear of love which "serve solo a dimenticare te stesso, i tuoi diritti, la tua dignità e cioè la tua libertà" (18) [it only means forgetting yourself, your rights, your dignity, and thus your freedom, 21] she recognizes the need for love and the power of emotion as she is desperately seeking to unravel its mystery: "Deve pur esserci qualcosa in grado di farmi scoprire cos'è, e che c'è. Ne ho tanto bisogno e tanta fame" (18) [And yet, there must still be a way to find out what it is and that it exists. I have such a hunger and need for it, 21]. Her search for the meaning of love does not conclude with an answer but with a question mark.

Questions become the hallmarks of the fairy tales ("le fiabe") which the mother tells her unborn child. A traditional fairy tale presents a world where hero/ines can achieve happiness only after having successfully removed the obstacles placed by fate or evil forces on their life-path. The hero/ines are aided in their search of a happy ending by a system of values at their disposal. If they choose correctly, they will live happily ever after in a world of order and peace. The doubts raised at the beginning of a fairy tale (how will Cinderella escape the drudgery of her stepmother's house?) find a resolution at the end of the story (her beauty and goodness will earn her the prince). The tales told by the mother offer no such comfort. "Si concludevano sempre con una domanda, le tue fiabe tristi"—says the child to the mother (90) [Your sad fairy tales always ended with a question, 101]. And indeed, the three stories present a world of disappointment, pain, and death.

In the first story a little girl fell in love with a magnolia tree growing by her house. She spent hours watching the flowers grow and fall until one day she noticed a woman who appeared on a balcony to hang clothes to dry. She was followed by a man who embraced her and the two "caddero insieme per terra dove insieme sussultarono a lungo, e infine giacquero addormentati" (39) [they fell down on the terrace together and lay gasping together for a long time and finally went to sleep, 45]. Soon another man appeared and started to chase them: the first man managed to escape but the woman did not. He picked her up and threw her down on the magnolia tree:

> La donna impiegò tanto tempo per giungere alla magnolia. Ma poi vi giunse, e si posò sui rami con un tonfo più sordo dei fiori che cadevano gialli per terra. Un ramo si ruppe. E nello stesso momento in cui il ramo si ruppe, la donna si aggrappò ad un fiore. E lo colse. E rimase lì ferma col suo fiore in mano. (38)

> [It seemed a long time for the woman to reach the magnolia, but when she did, she landed on the branches with a loud crack as if a branch was broken. At that moment the woman grabbed at a flower and plucked it. She stayed there motionless with her flower in her hand.] (45)

The little girl then came to the conclusion that "per cogliere un fiore una donna dovesse morire" (40) [that if a woman picked a flower she must die, 45]. The moral of the story is the unsettling truth that "la vita dipende da un rapporto di forza basato sulla violenza. La sopravvivenza è violenza" (40) [It depends on a relation of forces based on violence. And survival is violence, 46]. To survive does not mean to choose between right or wrong but to be stronger than the others. The question which the mother asks at the end of the story is: "Ed è proprio il caso che tu venga a conoscere simili orrori, tu che vivi e ti nutri e ti scaldi senza ammazzare nessuno?" (41) [But is now the time for you to know these horrors, you who live and nourish and warm yourself without killing anybody ?, 47].

The second tale is about a little girl who loved chocolate but since her family lived in poverty she could only dream of it. In the house of a rich lady for whom her mother worked there was a candy-box full of exquisite chocolates. The girl would watch it, craving the taste

5: Deconstructing the Definition of Female Letters 171

remembered from the remote past of prosperity. One day the woman noticed two children of her rich neighbors and showered them with chocolates, laughing; "Gianduiotti per i miei piccioncini" (43) [Chocolates for my little pigeons, 50]. Then she took one chocolate and ate it slowly in front of the little girl whose hungry eyes watched her every movement. Generosity is reserved for the rich, for those who do not need it, while the needy experience only humiliation and a sense of injustice. And again the story ends with a question that echoes the one from the first tale: "ma è proprio il caso che tu venga a conoscere tali ingiustizie, tu che lì vivi senza servire nessuno?" (45) [Is it really time for you to come to know of these injustices, you who live there and serve no one?, 51].

The third story is not a fairy-tale, claims the mother, although it begins with a typical opening line: "C'era una volta una ragazzina che credeva nel domani" (45) [Once upon a time there was a girl who believed in tomorrow, 51]. The war was raging in the world and life was full of misery and fear. But the little girl believed in a better tomorrow since her father assured her of this and she trusted his words. And yet when the "tomorrow" came she witnessed a scene when a man was about to be executed for stealing a piece of bread. His executioner was one of the "friends" who were supposed to bring the better tomorrow: "La ragazzina non seppe mai se il ladro era stato giustiziato, ma da quel giorno diffidò sempre della parola domani. E poiché la sua mente aveva associato la parola domani alla parola amici, da quel giorno diffidò anche degli amici" (48) [The girl never found out if the thief had been executed, but from that day on she was always suspicious of the word "tomorrow". And since her mind had connected the word "tomorrow" with the word "friends" she was also suspicious of friends, 55]. The promise of a better life to come was never to be fulfilled and the little girl learned to distrust promises.

The three stories form a sort of a triptych of life, each part representing a different aspect of that "rosario di delusioni" (49), [rosary of disappointments, 56] in the mother's words. Although she introduces them as fairy tales, she admits that they are stories taken from her own life. In each story the mother is the little girl and it is her own experience that she wants to share with her unborn child. The fourth tale recounts a story that happened to the mother when she was an adult. All her life she had been fascinated by the moon and dreamed of possessing even the tiniest bit of it. Her dream was not irrational or impossible to realize since she knew personally the astronauts who participated in expeditions to the moon. One of them she even considered her friend and it was this friend who promised to bring her some moon dust. When he came back, however, he seemed to avoid meeting her. Eventually, one evening he invited her to dinner at his house and she was sure that she would get her life-long dream—a speck of moon dust to keep. After dinner the man opened a closet which contained a number of objects: a hoe, a spade, a tube, covered with moon dust. With awe and reverence, the woman touched the spade and let the dust cover her hand. When she reminded the man of his promise to give her some of it, he answered that that was it: he allowed her to touch the dusty objects and that she could keep the dust resting on her hand. Her disappointment was as bitter as it was unexpected: would a friend, a human being refuse to share with her a tiny bit of the magical dust? How could he have been so cruel, knowing how much it meant to her? Is it human to shatter someone's dream on a whim of base greed or to feel a sense of power? This tale sums up the series of the fairy tales with a powerful final note: the humiliation and pain experienced by the little girl form a constant of life: promises are not to be kept, dreams are there to be shattered, and friends may betray. Even though the girl learned that truth about life very early, the lesson does not in any way eliminate the pain of suffering or the bitterness of betrayal in her adult life. Life experience or wisdom does not make one less vulnerable and or less sensible to the cruelty or thoughtlessness of others.

In bringing the real life examples under the guise of fairy tales, O. Fallaci reverses the role played by such stories in conduct books. One might call them anti-examples, since the traditionally accepted values undergo a careful scrutiny and ideals are measured against reality. In her novel the world is not a place where order prevails, where virtue is rewarded, where hope brightens the monotony of everyday life. The ordered universe of conduct material with its neatly segregated categories of good versus bad, legal versus illegal, legitimate versus illegitimate collapses; in its place stands a world of doubts and questions impossible to answer. Only immense courage may induce one to enter it. And the unborn child does not have it and refuses to be born explaining to the mother that

> se la vita è un tormento, approdarci perché? Non mi avevi mai detto perché si nasce. Ed eri stata abbastanza onesta da non imbrogliarmi con le leggende che avete inventato per consolarvi: il Dio onnipotente che crea a sua immagine e somiglianza, la ricerca del bene, la corsa al paradiso. (91)

> [if life is a torment, what's the use of it? You had never told me why one is born. And you had been honest enough not to deceive me with the legends you who are born have invented to console yourselves: the omnipotent God who creates in his image and likeness, the search for good, the race to paradise.] (102)

5: Deconstructing the Definition of Female Letters   173

Lettera a un bambino mai nato is thus an anti-conduct book. It voices questions and doubts rather than resolving them; it challenges accepted ideals rather than upholds them; it presents a disconcerting vision of reality rather than a reassuring one. Its epistolary format revives the tradition of conduct books for women written by women, when letters were an accepted medium for giving advice.[35] They were allowed to become a public medium for two reasons. First, the private nature of a letter—and most of these epistolary conduct books purported to be written by family members, usually mothers to daughters, or aunts to nieces—created the impression of intimacy and friendliness conducive to giving and accepting advice. Readers had the impression of eavesdropping on a private conversation between two members of a family. The rhetoric of intimacy also successfully masked the social significance of those conversations, and guaranteed the invisibility of the controlling grid. The second reason for their acceptance as a public medium was that their intimate nature excluded any interference in what was considered public matters, such as politics, education, art, and other topics reserved for men. Fallaci employs a title that suggests the continuation of the tradition but then deconstructs it by exposing the strategies underlying it.

Incidentally, intuition played a mysterious role in the choice of the title for Oriana Fallaci's novel. As she told me in a telephone conversation on 29 April 1996, she had thought about writing it ten years earlier but it was only an attempt ("un aborto," in her words). Then during the heated debate on abortion in Italy in the 1970's, she decided to accept her publisher's offer to make her own contribution to that debate and the book "exploded" (to quote her word). She was not at all aware that some three hundred years before, in 1625, a little book had come out in England bearing a title *Mother's Legacie to her Unborn Childe*. Its writer, an expectant mother, Elizabeth Joceline decided to write a letter to her unborn child, a letter of advice and lessons for the future. The mother died in childbirth, but a baby girl survived. I came across it in the series "Women's History on Microfilm" while doing research on conduct material. The similarity of titles and form was too bizzare to ignore and I decided to look for links between the two novels. Oriana Fallaci's reaction to that coincidence was unbound astonishment. Only a writer's intuition could have prompted her to pick up a title which lay forgotten among a pile of conduct books and revive it through creating a contemporary work of art.

Each of the three novels I have discussed in this chapter confronts the clichés that were handed down together with the body of eighteenth-century epistolary fiction. The denunciation of stereotypes is one of the ways that can help establish real equality of sexes. As Dacia Maraini claims, it may happen only when stereotypes cease to affect our perception of reality.

> A questo punto si direbbe che non si tratta più di acquisire nuove leggi e nuovi diritti sulla carta, ma di lavorare su quella parte dell'immaginazione, del costume, del linguaggio e della morale che costituiscono la vita di un popolo perché cambino le abitudini mentali, i modi di dire, le ottiche sociali, la coscienza storica della convivenza fra i sessi.[36]

> [At that point one could say that it is no longer a question of obtaining new laws and new rights on paper, but a question of redefining that part of imagination, customs, language, and morals which constitute the life of a people. Such a redefinition will in turn effect a change in people's mentality, sayings, social viewpoints, and the historical awareness of the coexistence of the sexes.]

In the process of redefining the female epistolarity, each writer not only unmasks the clichés but also offers alternative solutions, new ways of approaching reality. Fanny Fern shows that it is possible to correspond with a man without being immediately drawn into a web of intrigue that leads to disaster. Dacia Maraini merges adversary and confidante into one and succeeds in transforming a love affair into friendship and a collection of letters into a novel. Oriana Fallaci demonstrates that the value of life lies in constant questioning, not in providing putative answers. As she puts it, "Battersi è molto più bello che vincere, viaggiare è molto più divertente che arrivare" (13) [To fight is much better than to win, to travel much more beautiful than to arrive, 16]. In each novel letters function not only as means of communicating with the addressees/readers but also as comments on the epistolary mode of writing. Each letter is a concrete letter and a comment on a particular aspect of letter writing. In fulfilling that double role these novels challenge the censors who established the categories of private and public, of literary and nonliterary, of sentiment and reason, and erase the dividing lines.

Conclusion

ONE OF THE ESSAYS INCLUDED IN STANISLAW BARANCZAK'S BOOK ON Eastern Europe, *Breathing under Water,* offers a reflection on a new literary genre born in the twentieth century, namely, a prison letter. Taking as an example the prison correspondence of the Czech playwright Václav Havel, Baranczak compiles a long list of restrictions imposed on prison letters: restrictions of frequency, space, addressee, subject matter, tone, vocabulary, etc. "The prison letter in countries ruled by oppressive regimes," concludes Baranczak,

> is governed by a detailed set of strict prohibitions and injunctions regulating its size, structure, tone, and content. The author's mastery lies precisely in how he handles these rules, complying with them yet managing to slip his message through, remaining within the standardized model of utterance yet imbuing it with the urgency of his individual voice.[1]

Because of the internal conflict between the desire for individual expression and the limits set to curb it, prison letters merit a reading of their own; a reading that highlights and isolates the points where a written word performs amazing acrobatics in order to survive and surpass the prison walls. "It might seem a miracle," says Baranczak that "a prison letter gets written, sent, and delivered. It might seem a miracle of the second degree that a letter's message makes sense. But then, as we know, the chief wonder of art is that it thrives on overcoming difficulties" (50).

The uncanny resemblance between Baranczak's definition of a prison letter and the definition of female corespondence produced in the eighteenth century justifies the application of the prison metaphor to the rereading of that correspondence. The prison that contained it took a long time and effort to build. In its initial stage it was a clumsy structure with heavy bars (installed by the law of genre) and visible guards of decorum posted outside. And yet although oppressive, the bars were sparse enough, and the guards careless enough, to let some letters slip through. *Lettres portugaises* and the early epistolary novels of Behn, Haywood, and Hearne demonstrate that with a certain degree of cunning and planning such slips were easily executed. Clandestine communication, allowed women closed in convents, houses and harems, some measure of independence despite constraints imposed on their movements and contacts with the outside world. The epistolary heroines were able to challenge and defy the authoritarian character of their families and claimed the right to choose their own course of life. Their transgression of social conventions, the acts of illicit communication, relied on the letter's suitability for such schemes and the choice of the right tactics to deal with the guards. As a mere slip of paper a letter offered innumerable possibilities of being slipped in and out of enclosures, and into people's hands under the noses of their guardians. In *Les Liaisons dangereuses*, Cécile Volanges writes to her friend Sophie: "I left the room, and there and then wrote with pencil on a slip of paper . . . I slipped the piece of paper between the strings of my harp."[2]

The relative ease of executing physical slips did not escape the attention of censors who focused on more effiecient ways of controlling women's letters. The guards posted outside vanished almost completely, as did the external bars. What replaced them were invisible bars of self-control and discipline. The goal was to make women internalize the laws of decorum and make them responsible for controlling potential dangers and risks of clandestine correspondence. This new censoring strategy imposed less obvious but far more significant restraints on women letter writers, and on women writers, in general:

> Redefining the feminine form of the novel, making it newly respectable, was also an act of redefinition that severely limited Behn's, Manley's, and Haywood's female successors in the genre. Women may have entered the field of novelistic genre in far greater numbers than they had done in the late seventeenth and eighteenth century, but they did so on more confined terms.[3]

The shift from external to internal control provoked a shift from physical to verbal transgression. If early epistolary production focused on acts of physical slipping of innocuously looking paper slips, the later novels illustrated a letter's potential for other kinds of slips. These other slips brought chaos into a well-ordered world because they were capable of rupturing the neat categories established by the laws of genre and decorum. And so Evelina slipped from spontaneity to caution, Lady Susan from truth to deception, Ruth Hall from the realm of the heart to that of the mind, Piovene's Rita from fact to fiction. Maraini mixed the literary and nonliterary elements, and Fallaci undermined the rigid separation of the private and public spheres. The fact that a letter lies at the intersection of all these categories accounts for its power to shatter "the totalitarian censor's dream," that is, tailoring reality to preconceived and preapproved shapes (Baranczak, 66).

If an act of letter writing may deconstruct and destabilize the literary and social categories, an act of reading in accord with these categories will prove inadequate. The frustration of censors unable to read "correctly" other people's texts demonstrates the pitfalls of interpretation. The novels of male authors which I have included in my analysis are crucial not only because they illustrate the censors' strategems but also because they reveal the frustrations of censorship. The novels of Montesquieu and Piovene are of particular value in this regard. Usbek is a failed censor who loses Roxana through his own inability to see through her deceptive words. What he accepts as truth is only a skilfully contrived lie. The physical control he exercises over her will not guarantee a success in taming her. Neither of the protagonists in *Lettere di una novizia* has ever met Rita in person; their perception of her is based solely on her texts/letters. Their failure to decode them will bring disastrous consequences. Both failures result from accepting letters at face value, assigning meaning to signs that reflect back to other signs, not reality. Piovene's reflections on vicissitudes of texts may have been motivated by his own frustrations experienced in his career as a censor, with don Conti acting as an emblem of a failed censor. In his novel *Ziele na kraterze (A Blade of Grass on a Crater)* Melchior Wankowicz quotes a supposedly true story about a German censor in charge of private letters in the Nazi-occupied Poland during World War II.[4] Since no political allusions were allowed, people developed a system of coded messages to share information. One of such messages was a sentence about the poor health of auntie Gerda who would probably pass away before long. Everybody knew that "auntie Gerda" referred to Germany and her death to the victory of the Allied Forces—everybody, including the censor who wrote on one of the letters: "Don't worry! Your auntie is in perfect health and won't die for a long time yet!" Both the letter writer and the censor who acts in this story as a reader/interpreter step over the boundary of literal meaning, since the words no longer mean what they are supposedly saying. Language shifts from being a transparent object to an opaque one, a semiotic context to be decoded. The word "perusal," when it refers to an act of reading based on mimesis, so dear to Clarissa, seems to be inadequate—reading letters requires a slip into interpretation. An autonomous reader must resist the impulse of credulity and adopt interpretative distance. Thus, letter writing and letter reading function as allegories of textual cunning and interpretative resistance. The promise of truth, spontaneity, and naturalness may deceive readers luring them instead into the realm of fiction, artifice, and calculated design.

Notes

INTRODUCTION

1. Fanny Burney, *Evelina* (New York: W. W. Norton, 1965), 337.
2. Montesquieu, *Persian Letters*, trans. C. J. Betts (New York: Penguin Books, 1981), 277.
3. Nancy Armstrong, *Desire and Domestic Fiction* (New York and Oxford: Oxford University Press, 1987), 7. In the case of works cited more than once, page references to the edition first noted will be thereafter given parenthetically in the text.
4. *Writing the Female Voice*, ed. Elizabeth Goldsmith (Boston: Northeastern University Press, 1989), xii.
5. Terry Eagleton, *The Rape of Clarissa* (Oxford: Basil Blackwell, 1982), 48.
6. E. A. Poe's story "The Purloined Letter" demonstrates what an effective weapon a letter could become in the hands of an adversary. Edgar Allen Poe, "The Purloined Letter" in *The Purloined Poe: Lacan, Derrida, and Psychoanalytic Reading*, ed. J. P. Muller and William J. Richardson (Baltimore: John Hopkins University Press, 1988).
7. Poe, "The Purloined Letter," Poe's emphasis, 11.
8. *The Purloined Poe*, 40.
9. In the "Seminar on *The Purloined Letter*" Jacques Lacan, alluding to the nature of femininity, considers the letter the sign of woman, precisely because femininity and letters belong to the "foreign chain" of the illegitimate. "It is significant," he claims "that the letter which the Minister, in point of fact, addresses to himself is a letter from a woman: as though this were the phase he had to pass through out of natural affinity of the signifier. Thus the aura of apathy, verging at times on an affectation of effeminacy: the display of an ennui bordering on disgust in his conversation; the mood the author of the philosophy of furniture can elicit from virtually impalpable details (like that of the musical instrument on the table), everything seems intended for a character, all of whose utterances have revealed the most virile traits, to exude the oddest *odor di femina* when he appears" (Lacan's emphasis, 48).
10. Anonymous, *The Lady's New Year's Gift; or, Advice to a Daughter*, 3d edition (London: printed for Matt Gillyflower in Westminster Hall and James Partridge at Charing Cross, 1688), the chapter "On Censure," 125.
11. Nicola J. Watson, *Revolution and the Form of the British Novel 1790–1825* (Oxford: Clarendon Press, 1994), 1.
12. Thomas Gisborne, *An Inquiry into the Duties of the Female Sex* (London: T. Caldell and W. Davies, 1797), 111.
13. "It is not surprising," says Linda C. Hunt, "to find that many of these conduct book writers, especially the women, also write novels. It is not surprising because the line between conduct books and the female novels of the period is often quite thin; the two genres at times virtually shade into one another. Because both were usually epistolary in form, it was easy for an author to make the shift from one to

another" (Linda C. Hunt, "A Woman's Portion, Jane Austen and the Female Character" in *Fetter'd or Free? British Women Novelists 1670–1815*, ed. Mary Anne Schofield and Cecilia Macheski [Athens, Ohio: Ohio University Press, 1986], 9).

14. Michel Foucault, *Discipline and Punish*, trans. Alan Sheridan (New York: Vintage Books, 1979), 141.

15. Samuel Richardson, *Familiar Letters on Important Occasions* (London: George Routledge and Sons, Ltd., 1928), 129.

16. The spectacular deaths I am referring to include those of Mme de Tourvel in *Les Liaisons dangereuses* and Charlotte Temple in Susanna Rowson's novel *Charlotte Temple*. I discuss them in more detail in chapter V.

17. *A New Letter Writer for the Use of Ladies* (Philadelphia: Porter and Coates, 1860), 134.

18. The rhetoric of a statement which justified censorship of literary works in Australia, in the 1930s, bears an uncanny resemblance to Richardson's rhetoric of protection: "Prohibiting indecent works did not mean the suppression of lawful political opinion, but merely the protection of innocence against blatantly corrupt work, and the prevention of exploitation by those who sought to make money by trafficking in filth." The people assigned to "protect innocence" were not professional censors but educated people "with the time for thankless and unpaid job, and who would possess the confidence of the general public as to their qualifications." The censor, like Richardson's editor, hides behind the façade of a respectable and trusted citizen. (Robert Darby, "The Censor as Literary Critic", *Westerly: A Quarterly Review*, 4 [1986]: 30–40).

19. Foucault regards the shift from "the spectacle of the scaffold" to "the gentle way of punishment" as a further refinement in the development of disciplinary practices. He also points to the importance of texts: "The publicity of punishment must not have the physical effect of terror; it must open up a book to read" (*Discipline and Punish*, 69, 111).

20. *The Black Book of Polish Censorship*, trans. and ed. by Jane Leftwich Curry (New York: Vintage Books, 1984), 47.

21. Antonio Gramsci, *Lettere dal carcere* (Turin: Einaudi, 1965).

22. In her essay "Female Resources: Epistles, Plot, and Power," Patricia Meyer Spacks explains briefly why she considers early epistolary fiction by women of little interest to feminist critics: "The only example of the genre [epistolary fiction] people know is Fanny Burney's *Evelina*—a work different from the others in virtually all respects, and far less disturbing than fictions that openly question the benignity of families and the possibility of carefree marriage. Their troubling message of despair and their demonstration of female ineffectuality may have ensured the disappearance of other epistolary works . . . However disturbing the female epistolary tradition, though, however angry and despairing its fictional arrangements, its novels reinforced the status quo by assuming it. Declaring in their reliance on epistolary form their concern only with 'private' matters women novelists apparently accepted the necessity of the system from which they suffered" (Patricia Meyer Spacks, "Female Resources: Epistles, Plot, and Power" in *Writing the Female Voice*, 75).

The reluctance to discuss these works stems from a false assumption that only fiction that openly and loudly challenged the patriarchal system is worth considering. Patricia Meyer Spacks regards Jane Austen's *Lady Susan* as such a "unique and bold experiment in the real, subversive possibilities of the letter novel form" (Introduction to *Writing the Female Voice*, ix). Thus, she opposes Austen's subversive attempts to the inertia and passivity of earlier women writers of epistolary fiction. However, what she overlooks in her analysis is the fact that Jane Austen never intended to publish that novel, and it appeared only much later, after her death. That fact is significant because it points to the caution female writers had to exercise in order to remain within socially acceptable boundaries.

23. Introduction to *Writing the Female Voice*, xii.

24. The revisions and rewritings include correspondence between specific texts—for instance, Oriana Fallaci's *Lettera a un bambino mai nato* and the seventeenth-century text by Elizabeth Joceline *Mother's Legacie to an Unborn Childe* or seventeenth-century text *Portuguese Letters* and its twentieth century counterpart *New Portuguese Letters*—or confrontation of broader categories—for instance, the category of public and private domains.

25. The Introduction to *Refiguring Woman: Perspectives on Gender and the Italian Renaissance*, ed. Marilyn Migiel and Juliana Schiesari (Ithaca and London: Cornell University Press, 1991), 15. Kelly's concept of the double vision is discussed in the chapter "The Double Vision of Feminist Theory," in *Women, History and Theory: The Essays of Joan Kelly* (Chicago: University of Chicago Press, 1984).

26. *The Comparative Perspectives on Literature: Approaches to Theory and Practice*, ed. by Clayton Koelb and Susan Noakes (Ithaca and London: Cornell University Press, 1988).

27. Linda S. Kaufman, *Special Delivery: Epistolary Modes in Modern Fiction* (Chicago and London: University of Chicago Press, 1992), xiv.

CHAPTER 1. FEMALE LETTERS IN CONDUCT MATERIAL

1. Eliza Leslie, *Behavior Book; A Guide and Manual for Ladies as Regards Their Conversation, Manners, Dress . . . etc.* (Philadelphia: T. B. Peterson and Brothers, 1859), 162.

2. Among the numerous historical studies on that subject the works that focus on changes within the family structure and the role a family plays in the new bourgeois society are: Jacques Donzelot's *The Policing of Families*, Michel Foucault's *Discipline and Punish* and *Madness and Civilization*, Leonore Davidoff and Catherine Hall's *Family Fortunes* and the studies of Lawrence Stone and Jurgen Habermas.

3. The most representative text is Baldassar Castiglione's *Il Cortigiano* (*The Book of the Courtier*, trans. Charles S. Singleton [New York: Anchor Books, 1959]). First published in Venice in 1528, it gained widespread fame and was translated into Spanish in 1534, French in 1537, English and Latin in 1561, and German in 1566. *Il Cortigiano* is divided into four parts: the first and the longest one describes the characteristics of the ideal courtier, the second discusses the application of these characteristics in practice, the third is dedicated to the female partner of the ideal courtier—la donna di palazzo—and the fourth treats of politics and love. How does Castiglione envision the ideal court lady? Since her task is to play the role of a perfect partner for a model courtier, Castiglione dwells only on those characteristics which would have a particular bearing on that role. A number of traits would then be equally important either for the courtier or for the court lady. They both must be of noble origin, and must abide by the same set of moral values:

> For I hold that many virtues of the mind are as necessary to a woman as to a man; also, gentle birth; to avoid affectation, to be naturally graceful in all her actions, to be mannerly, clever, prudent, not arrogant, not envious, not slanderous, not vain, not contentious, not inept, to know how to gain and hold favor of her mistress and of all others, to perform well and gracefully the exercises that are suitable for women. (206)

The ability to fulfill well the duties of a wife and a mother is taken for granted, and Castiglione mentions it only in passing: "ability to manage her husband's property and house and children, if she is married, and all qualities that are requisite in a good mother" (207). Much more important is the ability to please the court company and to make the court a lively and enjoyable place. A court lady must, therefore, be beautiful, know how to dress, how to move, and which gestures to use to enhance her charms

> But since women are not only permitted but bound to care more about beauty than men—and there are several sorts of beauty—this Lady must have the good judgment to see which are the garments that enhance her grace and are most appropriate to the exercises in which she intends to engage at a given time. (211)

Besides she must have a number of accomplishments required by the courtly life:

> And so, in her talk, her laughter, her play, her jesting, in short in everything, she will be most graceful and will converse appropriately with every person in whose company she may happen to be, using witticisms and pleasantries that are becoming to her. (212)

While the appearance and accomplishments of a court lady seem fairly easy to determine, her behavior in the court company poses some problems. Castiglione, like his contemporaries, struggles with the double-bind situation that demands that a court lady be visible, affable, endearing to men, and that she display the modesty and emotional reticence befitting a woman. With his typical gift for avoiding problematic issues, Castiglione leaves it to the court lady to strike the right balance between eloquence and silence, wittiness and vapidity, modesty and licentiousness:

> I say that, in my opinion, in a Lady who lives at court a certain pleasing affability is becoming above all else . . . a quick vivacity of spirit whereby she will show herself a stranger to all boorishness; but with such a kind manner as to cause her to be thought no less chaste, prudent, and gentle than she is agreeable, witty and discreet: thus she must observe a certain boundary (difficult to achieve and, as it were, composed of contraries) and must strictly observe certain limits and not exceed them. (207)

Castiglione is clearly aware of the difficulty (if not impossibility) of reaching the ideal, since even he cannot define the boundaries that should not be crossed.

Also, like most of his contemporaries, Castiglione places the notion of "a woman" within his own historical and social reality, perceiving it as a product of culture rather than nature. The world of the courtier consists of women admirers and misogynists, and the opinion one hears depends on which group it comes from. Thus, as il signor Ottaviano claims, women are "imperfect creatures, and consequently have less dignity than men, and that they are not capable of virtues that men are capable of" (213). But, can his judgment be taken at its face value when it is immediately disproved by il Magnifico Giuliano who observes that "men have always been very chary in writing praise of women" (215)? If women would willingly trade places with men, it is not because men are more perfect than women, but because in the world governed by men, women have always been treated as inferior and have had to live under the male rule: "the poor creatures do not desire to be men in order to become more perfect, but in order to gain freedom and to escape that rule over them which man has arrogated to himself by his own authority" (217).

In the dialogue "Della Virtú Femminile e Donnesca," Torquato Tasso discusses the female virtues and vices in the historical context, presenting the opinions of the "wise men," from Plato and Aristotle to Petrarch. Thus his treatise is a compilation of what has been said rather than a description of a solid and stable model:

> I thought, therefore, that if I present to your Highness a brief comment on the virtue of women, or various opinions about it expressed by learned men, I shall be presenting you with a mirror or a portrait in which each part of your inner beauty will find its reflection (Torquato Tasso, *Discorso Della Virtù Femminile e Donnesca* [Venezia: Appresso Bernardo Giunti e Fratelli, 1582], 2. All translations are mine, unless otherwise indicted).

Castiglione, by using a discussion format, and Tasso, by quoting famous philosophers and writers, provide their readers with a female model which lacks rigid and stable contours. It oscillates between the various bits and pieces of information that are supposed to produce it. It is thus a reader's task to extract the instructive elements and apply them in practice.

For detailed discussion of domestic books in Renaissance England, see Chilton Latham Powell's *English Domestic Relations 1488–1653* (New York: Columbia University Press, 1917). Powell argues that "Although a great deal of attention was given in the domestic books to woman and her duties, practically no books were written for the instruction of women alone before the first part of the seventeenth century, except such as deal with specific subjects, like cookery, dairying, housekeeping, etc" (154). Powell's well documented study supports my view that women became both the main subjects and objects of conduct material only in the latter half of the seventeenth century and shifted to the center of attention dominating the conduct literature in the eigtheenth century.

4. *The Ideology of Conduct*, eds. Nancy Armstrong and Leonard Tennenhouse (New York and London: Methuen, 1987), 15. Armstrong returns to that issue in her later book *Desire and Domestic Fiction* (New York, Oxford: Oxford University Press, 1987).

5. Janet Todd, *The Sign of Angellica. Women, Writing and Fiction, 1660–1800* (New York: Columbia University Press, 1989), 11.

6. Michel Foucault, *Discipline and Punish*, trans. Alan Sheridan (New York: Vintage Books, 1979), 77.

7. Jacques Donzelot, *The Policing of Families*, trans. Robert Hurley (New York: Pantheon Books, 1979), xvii.

8. Nicola Watson, *Revolution and the Form of the British Novel 1790–1825* (Oxford: Clarendon Press, 1994), 13.

9. Cited in the Preface to Samuel Richardson's, *A Collection of the Moral and Instructive Sentiments*, A Facsimile Reproduction with an Introduction by James Evans, Scholars' Facsimiles and Reprints (New York: Delmar, 1980), vi.

10. D. A. Miller, *The Novel and the Police* (Berkeley, Los Angeles, London: University of California Press, 1988), 17.

11. Foucault, *Discipline and Punish*, 173.

12. The full title of Jane Aston's conduct book reads as follows: *The young woman's guide and instructor, in grammar, writing, arithmetic, geography, drawing, bookkeeping, chronology, history, letter-writing, cooking, carving, pickling, brewing, winemaking* (Manchester, n.p., 1806).

13. I have chosen three examples of that rhetoric from texts published in Italy, America, and England to show how identical, despite cultural, political, religious, and economic differences, were the strategies used to create the ideal of a perfect domestic woman.

14. Quoted in Fiorella D'Alia, *La donna del settecento* (Rome: Fratelli Palombo Editori, 1990), 27.

15. Hubbard Winslow, *Woman as She Should Be* (Boston: T. M. Carter, 1838), 52.
16. Charles Dole, *Noble Womanhood* (Boston: L. C. Company, 1900), 16.
17. Richard Allestree, *The Ladies Calling* (London: printed by Edward Jones for Edward Powlett, the seventh impression, 1696), 262.
18. Cf. Angeline Goreau's discussion of hostility and open misogyny evident in the majority of treatises on women published in the seventeenth century (*The Whole Duty of a Woman*, [New York: Dial Press, 1985]).
19. *Noble Womanhood*, 12, my emphasis.
20. The goal of conduct books was to provide models for female readers, "models for acceptable behavior, legitimate values, and even permissible thoughts" (Mary Poovey, *The Proper Lady and the Woman Writer* [Chicago: University of Chicago Press, 1984], xii). By defining the ideals to which female readers should aspire, the conduct material reproduced the ideology of the society it was intended for. I do not consider it necessary to present here the debate pertaining to the term "ideology." However, since that term may have various connotations (cf. the two definitions of ideology in Marx where it means "false consciousness" and in Althusser where it is "the imaginary relationship of individuals to their real conditions of life"), let me clarify its use here. I propose to adopt Mary Poovey's "working definition of ideology" because it articulates most clearly all those aspects and functions of ideology that illuminate my argument. According to that definition,

> ideology is a set of values which governs not just political and economic relations but social relations and even psychological stresses as well. Ideology is virtually inescapable, for simply by living together, men and women establish priorities among their needs and desires, and generate explanations that ratify these priorities by making them seem natural . . . By its very nature, ideology always contains contradictions precisely because it "explains" or "naturalizes" the discrepancies that inevitably characterize lived experience. (xiv)

Every individual narrative participates in the makings of ideology, since, in Fredric Jameson's words, "it is to be grasped as the imaginary resolution of a real contradiction" (Fredric Jameson, *Political Unconscious* [Ithaca, New York: Cornell University Press, 1981], 77).

21. Janet Todd, *Sign of Angellica*, 34.
22. Michel Foucault, *Discipline and Punish*, 175.
23. *Advice to Young Ladies* from "The London Journal" of 1855 and 1862, selected by R. D. (London: Methuen, 1933).
24. The conduct material I reviewed for that purpose (about forty-five books) spans the period of roughly 180 years (from 1680 till 1860). The books I selected were widely read (most of them went through several editions), and constituted an essential part of education for young girls and women in England, America, and France. The majority of the conduct material I read was circulated in these countries almost immediately after publication in their country of origin. Frequent references to the already existing conduct books, attacks or praises on them, numerous quotations, or even borrowings of particularly handy examples almost verbatim, show how tight was the network of conduct material and how closely these societies collaborated to produce an identical model of female perfection.
25. John Dunton, *The Challenge, Sent by a Young Lady to Sir Thomas & C. or, the Female War* (London: Printed & Sold by E. Whitlock, 1697), v. I, 104.
26. Hannah Wooley, *The Gentlewoman's Companion; or A Guide to the Female Sex* (London: Printed by A. Maxwell for D. Newman, 1673), 234. In *Virtue of Necessity. English Women's Writing 1649–88*, Elaine Hobby questions Wooley's authorship of *The Gentlewoman's Companion* and argues convincingly that it was prob-

ably a compilation of extracts from Wooley's previous, extremely popular books put together by Dorman Newman who used Wooley's name and her counterfeit portrait to benefit from her fame (Elaine Hobby, *Virtue of Necessity. English Women's Writing 1649–88*, [London: Virago Press, 1988], 172–75.

27. Hannah Wooley, *The Gentlewoman's Companion*, 219.

28. Although Wooley includes both daughters and sons in talking about filial disobedience, only a daughter's vow is invalid, when not sanctioned by the parents' consent.

29. Bernard Mandeville, *The Virgin Unmask'd*, (London: G. Strahan, 1724), 38; my emphasis.

30. Ruth Perry tells Lady Montague's story in *Women, Letter, and the Novel* (New York: AMS Press Inc., 1980), 80.

31. Samuel Richardson, *Familiar Letters on Important Occasions*, 125, my emphasis.

32. Fanny Burney, *Evelina* (New York: W. W. Norton, 1965).

33. Jane Aston, *The Young Woman's Guide and Instructor*, (Manchester: n.p., 1806), 32.

34. Other conduct books that repeat that model include Emily Thornwell's *The Young Lady's Guide to Perfect Gentility in Manners, Dress, and Conversation* (New York; Derby and Jackson,1858), and *The Young Lady's Book of Classical Letters*, published in 1836).

35. Hannah More "On the Danger of Sentimental or Romantic Connections" in *The Works of Hannah More* (New York; Harper and brothers, 1855), vol. II, 357.

36. Michel Foucault, *Discipline and Punish*, 66.

37. In *The Virgin Unmask'd*, Bernard Mandeville observes: "What disorders young women so much at the Sight of Man is the conflict between their natural Wishes and the Inborn Modesty of Virgins" (25).

38. Richard Allestree, *The Ladies Calling*, 164.

39. For the discussion of More's didactic fiction see Mitzi Meyer's essay "Hannah More's Tracts for the Times. Social Fiction and Female Ideology" in *Fetter'd or Free? British Women Novelists, 1670–1815*, ed. Mary Anne Schofield and Cecilia Macheski, (Athens, Ohio: Ohio University Press), 264–84.

40. Hannah More, *Coelebs in Search of a Wife* in *The Works of Hannah More*, vol. II, 325.

41. *The Young Lady's Friend* by a Lady (Boston: American Stationers' Company, 1837), 279.

42. William Alcott in *The Young Woman's Guide to Excellence*, published in 1847, also advises letter writing as a valuable practice in writing, better than diary or journal.

43. Jane Aston, *The Young Woman's Guide and Instructor*, 32.

44. The epistolary communication between women was often the only outlet through which they could voice their hopes, dreams, and problems, and share the details of their uneventful lives with someone who sympathized with them. Often friendships made at boarding schools or convents survived years of separation owing to epistolary communication. In her essay "The Female World of Love and Ritual," Carroll Smith-Rosenberg (*Disorderly Conduct* [New York; A. A. Knopf, 1983]) discusses the importance of such bonds, and the role played by letters in keeping them alive:

> Virtually every collection of letters and diaries in my sample contained evidence of women turning to one another for comfort when facing the frequent and unavoidable deaths of the eighteenth and nineteenth centuries ... Women thus lived in emotional proximity to one another. Friendships and intimacies followed the biological ebb and flow of women's lives. (71)

45. The undeniable need for such a correspondence was often dampened by the fear of public exposure. Examples of such exposure, and the violent public attacks which that exposure incited, abound in the eighteenth and nineteenth centuries. Mary Wollstonecraft's correspondence, in particular her letters to her sister and to Gilbert Imlay, edited and published after her death by her husband, William Godwin, revealed the details about her sister's marriage and Mary's love affair with Imlay, and unleashed a wave of attacks on her corrupt morals and loose conduct (cf. Rev. Wise, and J. Aston).

46. Charles Dole, *Noble Womanhood*, 35.

47. Rev. Daniel Wise, *The Young Lady's Counsellor; or Outlines and Illustrations of the Sphere, the Duties, and the Dangers of Young Women* (New York: Carlton and Phillips, 1854), 89, my emphasis.

48. It is worth noting how generations of critics have insisted on classifying Mme. de Sévigné's letters as a nonliterary creation, although it is clear form her correspondence that she knew they were read in public and was fully aware of their impact on that public cf. Frances Mossiker, *Madame de Sévigné: A Life and Letters* (New York: Columbia University Press, 1985).

49. Rev. George Sumner Weaver, *Hopes and Helps for the Young of Both Sexes* (New York: Fowler and Wells, 1857), 106–107.

50. Leonore Davidoff and Catherine Hall, *Family Fortunes: Men and Women of the English Middle Class, 1780–1850*, (Chicago: University of Chicago Press, 1987), 13. Subsequent references are given parenthetically in the text.

51. Barbara Corrado Pope, "Angels in the Devil's Workshop: Leisured and Charitable Women in Nineteenth-Century England and France" in *Becoming Visible: Women in European History*, ed. Renate Bridenthal and Claudia Koontz (Boston: Houghton Mifflin, 1977), 305.

52. Davidoff and Hall, *Family Fortunes*, 27.

53. Janet Todd, *The Sign of Angellica*, 212–13.

54. In *Married Women's Separate Property in England, 1660–1883* (Cambridge, Massachusetts: Harvard University Press, 1990), Susan Staves points out that it is not only a bourgeois ideal but is embraced also by the aristocracy, 225.

55. Davidoff and Hall, *Family Fortunes*, 273.

56. Ruth Perry, *Women, Letters, and the Novel* (New York: AMS Press Inc., 1980), 37.

57. Davidoff and Hall, *Family Fortunes*, 304.

58. Davidoff and Hall note that "there was a growing feeling that genteel women, particularly the young and unmarried should be removed from contact with such a workforce [farm labourers] both by physical and psychological barriers" (*Family Fortunes*, 274).

59. The question of transport is one of the recurring issues in the novels of Jane Austen, whose heroines worry constantly about the propriety of their traveling arrangements as well as the cost and access to the means of transport (cf. *Pride and Prejudice, Northanger Abbey*, or *Mansfield Park*).

60. Quoted in *Family Fortunes*, Davidoff's emphasis, 273.

61. In "Leisured Women in the Nineteenth Century," Barbara Corrado Pope, following "women's careers from their teens to their marriages" in England and France, shows how "one ideal of women fit into two cultural patterns," that ideal being, of course, the guardian angel of hearth and home (299).

62. Carolyn Lougee, *Le Paradis des Femmes: Women, Salons, and Social Stratification in Seventeenth Century France* (New Jersey: Princeton University Press, 1976), 7. Subsequent references are given parenthetically in the text.

63. Quoted in Lougee, 30.

64. As Lougee notes,"The idea of the housewife was old-fashioned; one of Pure's ladies bewailed 'these tiresome maxims of our forefathers, who approve of women only in the home, and have esteem for beauty only insofar as it is useful, and prefer rags of the housekeeper to the ornaments and proprieties of a coquette'" (21).

65. Women should be invisible in their homes. "The oft-repeated admonition that women should again wear veils expressed less the desire for a change in headgear than the insistence that women be cut off from public roles" (Lougee, 85).

66. Quoted in Lougee, 86.

67. Barbara Corrado Pope, 302.

68. Pierre Darmon, *Mythologie de la femme dans l'Ancienne France: XVIe–XVIIIe siècle*, (Paris: Editions du Seuil, 1983), 195.

69. Jean Stockard and Miriam M. Johnson, *Sex Roles: Sex Inequality and Sex Role Development*, (New Jersey: Prentice-Hall, Inc., 1980), 48. The authors discuss the views of Talcott Parsons, who regards the separation of spheres as "highly functional for the industrial society," so much so that it underlies our notion of "the specialized family that is removed from the world of work" (49).

70. Quoted in Davidoff and Hall's *Family Fortunes*, 328.

Chapter 2. Letters as a Means of Liberation for Female Correspondents

1. "By mid-eighteenth century," notes Janet Todd "review after review stated what women should write and how they did write, ringing the changes on the abstract terms denoting female authorship: elegance, modesty, spontaneity and artlessness" (*The Sign of Angellica* [New York: Columbia University Press, 1989], 126).

2. Fritz Nies, "Un genre féminin?", *Revue d'Histoire Litteraire de la France* 78: (1978); 995.

3. Michèle Longino Farrell, *Performing Motherhood: The Sévigné Correspondence* (Hanover and London: University Press of New England, 1991), 29.

4. Jean de La Bruyére, *Les Caractères* (Paris; Garnier Frères, 1962), 79.

5. Translation by Michèle Longino Farrell in *Performing Motherhood*, 30.

6. The chapter "Women and the Epistolary Domain," in Michèle Longino Farrell's *Performing Motherhood*, provides an interesting discussion of the linguistic aspects of La Bruyére's comment on women and writing, the choice of words, pronouns, and adjectives. His rhetoric then is part of a strategy that tends to marginalize women as writers (27–33).

7. John Dunton, *The Female War* (London: Printed and Sold by E. Whitlock, 1697), vol. I, 217.

8. Quoted in Jean-Michel Pelous, "Une héroïne romanesque entre le naturel et la rhétorique: le langage des passions dans les *Lettres portugaises*", *Revue d'histoire littéraire de la France* 77 (1977): 554–63.

9. The equation of emotion and a female letter reappears time and again in literary criticism with reference not only to epistolary fiction but also to real correspondence. Two hundred years after La Bruyére, the letters of Madame de Sévigné are praised by an American scholar in the following way: "The advantages of a letter as an exponent of a woman's nature is that, it is, after all, only written conversation, the artless play of her mind, the candid utterance of her sentiment, designed to be interpreted by one she loves" (qtd. in *Writing the Female Voice*, 53).

10. James Cochrane, *Woman as She Is and as She Should Be* (London: J. Cochrane and Co., 1835), 73.

11. Pietro Chiari, *Le memorie di Madama Tolot ovvero la giocatrice di lotto* (Rome: Edizioni Moderne Canesi, 1960), 280.

12. Even today that view still seems to hold true. In *Rhetoric, Romance, and Technology*, Walter Ong (Ithaca: Cornell University Press, 1971) ponders the question of a classical education for women, and comes to the conclusion that "even in its present attenuated form Latin has never been assimilated in the curriculum for girls' schools as it has been for boys. One suspects that something of what it stood for, and in a certain degree still stands for, cannot be assimilated. It is a matter of record that women students who today matriculate at Oxford or Cambridge Universities, where some classical tradition remains fairly strong, are almost invariably less well prepared in Latin than the men matriculating from the English public schools. Curricula are the product of complex and fugitive forces, but the forces are real and cannot be gainsaid" (123).

13. Quoted in Angeline Goreau, *The Whole Duty of a Woman* (New York: Dial Press, 1985), 24.

14. In her essay "Male Models of Feminine Epistolarity," Katharine Jensen (*Writing the Female Voice*, ed. Elizabeth Goldsmith [Boston: Northeastern University Press, 1989]) notes that the real object of the literary theory was to neutralize the power women exercised in the salons "as arbiters of language and social interaction":

> Male theories and models of feminine epistolarity reveal an anxiety about women's power. By presenting women's letter models and offering through them a social or sexual thematics for imitation, male publishers may have been addressing this anxiety by *attempting to limit women's access to the literary.* (28, my emphasis)

15. Thomas Gisborne, *An Inquiry into the Duties of the Female Sex* (London: T. Caldell, and W. Davies, 1797), 110, my emphasis.

16. Quoted in *Readings in Classical Rhetoric*, ed. Thomas W. Benson, Michael H. Prosser (Davis, California: Hermagoras Press, 1988), 112.

17. Katharine Jensen, "Male Models of Female Epistolarity" in *Writing the Female Voice*, 32.

18. Gabrielle Verdier, "Gender and Rhetoric in Some Seventeenth-Century Love Letters", *Esprit Createúr* 23 (Summer 1983): 45–57.

19. Verdier notes that "the association [between women and passion] was made immediately by one of the two male writers who composed 'answers' to the *Portugaises*. His task was difficult, he maintains, because in women passion is 'more ardent' than in men" (47).

20. Robert Adams Day, *Told in Letters* (Ann Arbor: University of Michigan Press, 1966), 33.

21. Charles Kany, *The Beginnings of Epistolary Novel in France, Italy, and Spain* (University of California Publications in Modern Philology, vol. 21, no. I. Berkeley: University of California, 1939), 112.

22. Introduction to *Lettres portugaises* in *Lettres portugaises, Lettres d'une peruvienne, et autre romans d'amour par lettres*. Textes établis, présentés et annotés par Bernard Bray and Isabelle Landy-Houillon, (Paris: Garnier Flammarion, 1983), 25.

23. Introduction to *Lettres portugaises*, 23.

24. Introduction to *Lettres portugaises*, 29, 30.

25. Gabriel de Lavergne Guilleragues, *Lettres portugaises. Lettres portugaises, Lettres d'une peruvienne, et autres romans d'amour par lettres*, 79.

26. This novel consists of three parts, but since they were added to the first part

later on and are not written in the epistolary form, I am going to focus my analysis only on the first part. Natascha Würzbach included only the first part in her *The Novel in Letters*, regarding it as a complete whole in itself (*The Novel in Letters: Epistolary Fiction in the Early English Novel 1678–1740*, ed. Natascha Würzbach [Florida: University of Miami Press, 1969]).

27. Aphra Behn, *Love-Letters between a Noble-Man and his Sister* in *The Novel in Letters*, 22.

28. Mary Hearne, *The Lover's Week*, in *The Novel in Letters*, 69.

29. Mary Hearne makes an allusion to Behn's novels: "There was a Book lying on the Table which, taking up on examination, I found to be the famous Mrs. Behn's novel" (*The Lovers' Week*, 74).

30. In fact, Robert Day considers Behn's novel "the original piece of English fiction to adopt the method of *Portuguese Letters*" (*Told in Letters*, 159). For a discussion of French influence on Behn, see also Ros Ballaster's *Women's Amatory Fiction from 1684–1740* (Oxford: Clarendon Press, 1992), 69–113.

31. Janet Todd, *The Sign of Angellica*, 41.

32. In "Aphra Behn and the Works of the Intellect," Robert Adams Day also points to that paradox: "the denial of 'higher' literary forms to a woman writer who wanted to earn money by her work operated paradoxically to free her natural talents and enable them to flourish in the literary limbo of vernacular prose fiction" (in *Fetter'd or Free? British Women Novelists, 1670–1815*, eds. Mary Anne Schofield and Cecilia Macheski [Athens, Ohio and London: Ohio University Press, 1986], 372–82).

33. Virginia Woolf, *A Room of One's Own*, (San Diego, New York, London: A Harevst/HBJ Book), 1957, 63–64.

34. Isabelle Landy-Houillon arrives at the same conclusion with regard to women writers in France, in the late seventeenth and early eighteenth century: "ainsi, dans une société qui lui refuse la condition d'écrivain, l'élite intellectuelle féminine trouve dans la pratique épistolaire un compromis entre l'effacement propre à son sexe et la disposition qu'il a à dire 'les plus tendres' sentiments de coeur" [thus in a society which denied women the status of writers, the female intellectual élite found in the epistolary mode a compromise between a complete effacement of its sex and the restriction of its voice to the expression of sentiment] (Introduction to *Lettres portugaises*, 19).

35. Montesquieu, *Lettres persanes* (Genève: Librairie Droz, 1954), L 7.

36. Montesquieu, *Persian Letters*, trans. C. J. Betts (New York: Penguin Books, 1981), 47.

37. The famous school of Saint-Cyr based its curriculum on the notion that "in spite of the decreed dependence of women on men, nevertheless, men are less opposed to obedience than women are" (cited in Carolyn Lougee, *Le Paradis des Femmes* [New Jersey: Princeton University Press, 1976], 193).

38. Susanne Rodin Pucci, "Letters from the Harem" in *Writing the Female Voice*, ed. Elizabeth Goldsmith (Boston: Northeastern University Press, 1989), 129.

39. This letter collection was originally published by Edmé Boursalt under the title *Lettres nouvelle, avec treize lettres amoureses d'une Dame à un cavalier* (Paris, 1699) and translated by Eliza Haywood as *Letters from a Lady of Quality to a Chevalier* (London: William Chetwood, 1721).

40. Fiorella D'Alia, *La donna nel romanzo del settecento* (Rome: Fratelli Palombi Editori, 1990), 30.

41. The title of Jane Austen's first published novel *Sense and Sensiblity*, with its two heroines who personify "sense" (reason) and "sensibility" (heart), reflects the importance of that debate and Austen's condemnation of blind passion.

42. Carol Lazzaro-Weiss, *From Margins to Mainstream. Feminism and Fictional Modes in Italian Women's Writing, 1968–1990* (Philadelphia: University of Pennsylvania Press, 1993), 44.

43. For a discussion of Haywood's works, see the chapter "Preparatives to Love: Fiction as Seduction in Eliza Haywood's Amatory Prose, in Ros Ballaster's *Women's Amatory Fiction from 1684–1740* (Oxford: Clarendon Press, 1992), 153–95.

44. Janet Todd, *The Sign of Angellica*, 146.

CHAPTER 3. *CLARISSA*—WOMAN WRITER AND READER IN AN EPISTOLARY WEB

1. Godfrey Singer, *The Epistolary Novel* (Philadelphia: University of Pennsylvania Press, 1933), 51.

2. Janet Todd, *The Sign of Angellica*, 131.

3. Carol Houlihan Flynn, *Samuel Richardson A Man of Letters* (Princeton, New Jersey: Princeton University Press, 1982), 53, 65.

4. Preface to *The History of Clarissa Harlowe* in 5 vols, in *The Works of Samuel Richardson*, in 12 volumes, ed. Leslie Stephen (London: Henry Sotheran and Cooperation, 1883), I, xi.

5. Samuel Richardson, *Familiar Letters on Important Occasions* (London: George Routledge and Sons Ltd., reprinted from the 1741 edition in 1928), 59.

6. La Bruyère, *Les Caractères* (Paris: Gallimard, 1965).

7. The dichotomy between the masculine and the feminine in *Clarissa* has been discussed by a number of critics. Ian Watt perceives it as the dichotomy between masculine and feminine codes of behavior. Lovelace is "a representative of the masculine stereotype against which the feminine code is a defense" (*The Rise of the Novel* [London: Chatto and Windus, 1957], 225–38). In *The Rape of Clarissa*, Terry Eagleton (Oxford: Basil Blackwell, 1982) discusses that dichotomy in psychoanalytic terms. He begins by saying that Clarissa's writing is masculine because her letters "are signs of a unified self," while Lovelace "lives on the interior of his prose, generating a provisional identity from the folds of his text" (53). I would argue that despite attempts to retain the control over her self and her letters Clarissa fails and Lovelace is in control of both Clarissa's and his own writing. Eagleton concludes his discussion with an extremely confused argument based on psychoanalytic images, claiming that Clarissa ultimatelty represents the penis Lovelace is looking for. It seems a rather strained interpretation. Whereas Eagleton's psychoanalytic analysis does not offer convincing solutions, his Marxist approach offers a very persuasive interpretation of the function of letters. Eagleton views a feminine letter as a symbol of female sexuality and thus "a commodity" for sale in the bourgeios society. I support his view and show how the domination over letters reflects the desire to dominate women and their sexuality.

8. Sylvia Kasey Marks's article "Clarissa as Conduct Book," dicusses the obvious links of the novel with the current conduct material and emphasizes the validity and necessity of rereading Richardson's novel from that viewpoint. Her analysis focuses mainly on the definition of nobility and the questions of female education (Sylvia Kasey Marks, "Clarissa as Conduct Book" *South Atlantic Review* 51:4 [1986], 3–16).

9. An almost identical situation is described in *Les Liaisons dangereuses* where Cecile' s desk becomes the object of close supervision. (Choderlos de Laclos, *Les Liaisons dangereuses*, L 61).

10. Terry Eagleton opposes idealistic Clarissa to "astringently critical" Anna, per-

ceiving her as a "militant feminist." Although I agree that Anna does criticize overtly the familial order, she is, nonetheless, as susceptible to Lovelace's rhetorical skills as Clarissa, and her critical faculties fail her when dealing with a male cunning of Lovelace's order. As Lovelace's reader, then, Anna is as much at fault as Clarissa, and her failure to unmask Lovelace's plots underlines Richardson's moral that women cannot be trusted as readers (*The Rape of Clarissa*, 78).

11. William J. Farrell links Lovelace's ornate rhetoric in his letters to Belford with the eloquent missives found in Richardson's predecessors, Aphra Behn and Eliza Haywood. But he also points out that Lovelace "is much more sophisticated stylistically than the seducers in conventional romances" because he is capable of adopting a variety of styles. I agree that Richardson endows him with the whole arsenal of rhetoric precisely to make him a much more dangerous and real figure than an average hero of romance. (William J. Farrell, "The Style and the Action in *Clarissa*" in *Samuel Richardson—A Collection of Critical Essays*, ed. John Carroll [New Jersey: Prentice Hall Inc., 1969], 95.)

12. Lovelace has much more confidence in the power of his writing than of his words. When Clarissa refuses to become his wife, he hopes that persuasive letters will make her change her mind: "I will press her with letters for the Thursday. She shall yet be mine" (IV, 163). Writing unlike speech precludes any possibility of a spontaneous gesture, of an uncontrollable impulse that may inadvertently betray his real intentions. Writing allows him time and space to plan and plot whereas speech requires instantaneous response.

13. That distinction follows J. L. Austin's (*How to Do Things with Words* [Cambridge, Massachusetts: Harvard University Press, 1975]) classification of speech acts—Lovelace's letters belong to the performative category, Clarissa's to the constative one. As Shoshana Felman points out in *The Literary Speech Act* (trans. Catherine Porter [Ithaca, New York: Cornell University Press, 1983]), "irresistible seduction dramatizes nothing other than the success of language, the felicity of speech act. To seduce is to produce felicitous language" (28). Lovelace produces "felicitous" letters and his control over Clarissa consists in his manipulation of the written language.

14. Marijke Rudnik-Smalbraak offers a very interesting and persuasive analysis of the image of the "ensnared volatile" as a "living emblem of everything which his heroine's fate shared with the common life of his world and time, and, possibly, our own." That image reflects also the aim of conduct material—to domesticate women; or, to continue Smalbraak's imagery to turn a free-flying bird into a caged one. (Marijke Rudnik-Smalbraak, *Samuel Richardson: Minute Particulars within the Large Design* [Leiden: Leiden University Press 1983], 87.)

15. Keiko Izubuchi in the essay "Subversive or Not? Anna Howe's Function in *Clarissa*" argues that although not a feminist in "the twentieth-century sense," Richardson presents in Anna "the enlightened thought of women, not yet accepted by society." Although I agree that Anna seems to represent the subversive element in *Clarissa*, there is a gap between what she says and what she achieves. After all, her attempts to help Clarissa are unsuccessful and her letters miss the target. (Keiko Izubuchi, "Subversive or Not? Anna Howe's Function in *Clarissa* ," in *Samuel Richardson: Passion and Prudence*, ed. Valerie Grosvenor Myer [London: Vision Press, 1986], 78–93).

16. Clarissa's sermon on filial duties and the absolute necessity of constant parental supervision sounds painfully ironic in view of the Harlows's cruel and inhuman treatment of Clarissa and their implacable insistence on marrying her to Solmes against her wishes. That incongruity reveals Richardson's dilemma in confronting a no-win situation. Clarissa does not have any other choice but to run away from

home, if she does not want to marry Solmes. On the other hand, once she leaves her parents, there can be no happy resolution to her problems.

17. Preface to *Clarissa*, I, xii.

18. Both Flynn and Eagleton overlook these possibilities in their analysis focusing only on the Clarissa-Lovelace relationship. That omission distorts Richardson's presentation of Clarissa's case since in that particular moment Clarissa realizes that she cannot possibly atone for her sins on earth and no earthly solution exists for her.

19. That division resurrects the Ovidian tradition of letters, the tradition established not by the well-known model "of an abandoned woman" (cf. Christina Marsden, *The Paradox of Privacy—Epistolary Form in Clarissa* [Gainesville, Florida: University of Florida Press, 1984], 126) present in the first part of *Heroides*, but by the contrast between active and passive letters found in the second, less famous, part of *Heroides*. In that part Ovid presents three letters written by men to persuade the women of their love and the women's replies. The letters of Paris, Accontius, and Leander, like the letters of Lovelace, achieve their goal, and the replies of women to whom they are written, attest to the men's efficiency as letter writers. Thus it is not so much the return to a single female voice as the return to the contrast between female and male epistolary voices. (Ovid, *Heroides and Amores*, trans. Grant Showerman [Cambridge, Massachusetts: Harvard University Press, 1971]).

20. Samuel Richardson, *The History of Sir Charles Grandison* (London: George Rutledge and Sons, n.d.), 39.

21. Michel Foucault, *Discipline and Punish*, 93.

Chapter 4. Female Epistolary Strategies in *Evelina*, *Lady Susan*, and *Lettere di Una Novizia*: The Tactics of Caution, Convention, and Cliché

1. Extreme popularity of all Richardson's novels, but in particular, the popularity gained by *Clarissa* not only in England and America but also in France and Italy, establishes Richardson as the most prominent figure of epistolary fiction in the eighteenth century. Pietro Chiari, Carlo Goldoni, and the first major Italian novelist, Alessandro Manzoni, acknowledged the impact of his novels on their own literary production. The intertextual echoes that link the Italian novel to the Richardsonian fiction have been recognized by a number of critics but no systematic studies have been done (cf. the article of Maria Ines Bonatti "L'educazione femminile nel pensiero degli Illuministi e nei romanzi di Chiari," *Annali d'Italianistica*, 7 [1987]: 226–41).

2. Frank Gees Black, *The Epistolary Novel in the Late Eighteenth Century* (Eugene: University of Oregon Press, 1949), 1. Although Black's study was published more than half a century ago, it provides a detailed inventory and a perceptive analysis of the minor epistolary fiction after Richardson in England. Other, more recent books that focus on that period include chapters 7–14 in Janet Todd's *The Sign of Angellica* (New York: Columbia University Press, 1989), Elenor Ty's *Unsex'd Revolutionaries: Five Women Novelists of the 1790s* (Toronto, Buffalo, London: University of Toronto Press, 1993), and Nicola Watson's *Revolution and the Form of the British Novel 1790–1825*, which I discuss in more detail in chapter 5.

3. The literary misfortunes of Laetitia Pilkington, illustrate the disastrous consequences of nonconformism. Pilkington, who invaded the male territory of satire paid dearly for her intrusion, earning the name of "the most profligate whore in either kingdom" (Todd, *The Sign of Angellica*, 128–30).

4. Janet Todd, *The Sign of Angellica*, 154.

5. François Jost, "Le roman épistolaire et la technique narrative au XVIII siècle" in *Comparative Literature: Matter and Method*, ed. O. Aldridge (Chicago: University of Illinois Press, 1969), 189.

6. Jean Rousset, *Forme et signification: essais sur les structures littéraires de Corneille à Claudel* (Paris: J. Corti, 1964), 70. After the enormous success of Wolfgang Goethe's *Sorrows of Young Werther*, that type of epistolary fiction gained popularity at the end of the eighteenth century, and continued to appear in the nineteenth and twentieth centuries, either in faithful imitation of Goethe's model (Foscolo's *Ultime lettere di Jacopo Ortis* or Saul Bellow's *Herzog*), or as a variation on a theme, as in Verga's *Storia di una capinera* or Alice Walker's *The Color Purple* (the protagonist is female, not male). It is worth mentioning that a number of epistolary novels that appear in the nineteenth century are experiments with the narrative form, as an alternative to an all-pervasive third person narration. Both Dostoyevsky in *Poor Folk* and Verga in *Storia di una capinera*, by using the epistolary format, seek to discard the authority of the omniscient narrator. Thus, they create a work of art in which the writer is invisible, and the readers become directly involved in the narrated events without any apparent interference of the author.

7. Quoted in Julia Epstein, *The Iron Pen: Frances Burney and the Politics of Women's Writing* (Madison: University of Wisconsin Press, 1989), 197.

8. Fanny Burney, Preface to *Evelina or The History of a Young Lady's Entrance into the World* (New York: Norton Library, 1965).

9. Marjorie Dobbin, "The Novel, Women's Awareness, and Fanny Burney," in *English Languages Notes* 22 (March 1985): 42–52.

10. In fact most critics consider *Evelina* to be a journal in letters. Marjorie Dobbin notes that the novel is "a compilation of episodes recounted in letters" (47). According to John Richetti ("Voice and Gender in Eighteenth-Century Fiction: Haywood to Burney," in *Studies in the Novel* 19, [Fall 1987]: 263–72), "Nominally, an epistolary novel, the book is in fact the heroine's journal in which she records the events—mostly conversations—that make up 'the history of the young lady's entrance into the world.'"

11. Julia Epstein, "Evelina's Deceptions: The Letter and the Spirit," in *Fanny Burney's Evelina*, ed. Harold Bloom (New York, New Haven, Philadelphia: Chelsea House, 1988), 113.

12. Julia Epstein, *The Iron Pen*, 99.

13. Samuel Richardson, *Familiar Letters on Important Occasions* (London: George Routledge, 1928), 129.

14. Julia Epstein, *The Iron Pen*, 117.

15. Kristina Straub, *Divided Fictions—Fanny Burney and Feminine Strategy* (Lexington: Kentucky University Press, 1987), 72.

16. Julia Epstein, *The Iron Pen*, 95.

17. Preface to *Clarissa*, xi.

18. Reginald Brimley Johnson, Preface to *Evelina* (London: J. M. Dent, 1893), xvii.

19. Julia Epstein, *The Iron Pen*, 118.

20. Annette B. Hopkins, "Jane Austen's *Love and Freindship*: A Study in Literary Relations" in *South Atlantic Quarterly* 34 (1925): 34–39.

21. John Halperin, "Unengaged Laughter: Jane Austen's Juvenilia" in *Jane Austen's Beginnings, The Juvenilia and Lady Susan*, ed. J. David Grey (London, Ann Arbor: U.M.I. Research Press, 1989), 30–44.

22. Juliet McMasters, "Teaching *Love and Friendship*" in *Jane Austen's Beginnings*, 135–51.

23. Patricia Meyer Spacks, "Plots and Possibilities: Jane Austen's Juvenilia" in *Jane Austen's Beginnings*, 124–34.

24. Julia Epstein, "Jane Austen's Juvenilia and the Female Epistolary Tradition," in *Papers on Language and Literature: A Journal for Scholars and Critics of Language and Literature* 21 (4), (Fall 1985): 399–416.

25. Jane Austen, *Love and Freindship and Other Early Works* (New York: Frederick A. Stokes, 1922), 1.

26. Brian Southem, "Publisher's Preface" to *Lady Susan* (London: Athlone Press, 1984), xii.

27. Jane Austen, *Lady Susan* (London: The Athlone Press, 1984), 63.

28. Barbara Horwitz, "The Wicked Mother in Jane Austen's Work," in *Jane Austen's Beginnings*, 183.

29. Deborah Kaplan, "Female Friendship and Epistolary Form: *Lady Susan* and the Development of Jane Austen's Fiction" in *Criticism* 29, (Spring 1987):163–78.

30. Jane Austen, *Pride and Prejudice* (New York: Holt, Rinehart and Winston, 1961), 87.

31. Samuel Richardson, Postscript to *Clarissa*, V, 538.

32. Samuel Richardson, *A Collection of Moral and Instructive Sentiments*, preface, vi.

33. Julia Epstein, "Jane Austen's Juvenilia and the Female Epistolary Tradition," 415.

34. The author of *Evelina*," notes Black, "though active in fiction, turns aside from the epistolary method" (5). Jane Austen wrote the early draft of *Sense and Sensibility* in the epistolary form, but the final published version was changed to third person narration. Her two epistolary novels, *Love and Freindship* and *Lady Susan*, were never published during her lifetime. Black claims that "the fact that she withheld all these early epistolary pieces from publication and abstained from epistolary method in her six published novels, indicates a dissatisfaction with the form" (*The Epistolary Novel in the Late Eighteenth Century*, 108).

35. Tibor Wlassics, "Guido Piovene," in *Novecento. I contemporanei*, (Milan: Marzorati, 1979), 5110–45.

36. Tibor Wlassics, *Da Verga a Sanguineti, microcosmi critici* (Biblioteca Siciliana di cultura: Niccolò Giannotta Editore, 1976), 162.

37. Guido Piovene, *Lettere di una novizia* (Milan: Bompiani, 1941), 10.

38. Guido Piovene, *Confessions of a Novice,* trans. Eithne Wilkins (London: William Kimber, 1950), x.

39. Carlo de Matteis claims that "l'assenza di una demarcazione etica nei comportamenti coscienziali dà luogo ad una sorta di elogio della ambiguità, all'impossibilità cioè di cogliere i contorni della verità: il libro appare così come una lucida esplosione dei meandri del male nelle sue forme più autentiche e disperanti, in quanto qualità costitutive della natura umana" [the absence of an ethical boundary in the conduct of the characters hails ambiguity, that is, the impossibility of drawing the contours of truth; the novel appears as a bright explosion of the meandering of evil in its most authentic and desperate forms that constitute nonetheless human nature] (*Il romanzo italiano del novecento*, [Florence: Scandicci, 1984], 206).

40. Wolfgang Iser, *The Act of Reading—A Theory of Aesthetic Response* (Baltimore: Johns Hopkins University Press, 1978), ix.

41. Umberto Eco, *Lector in fabula* (Milan: Bompiani, 1979), 53.

42. Ruth Amossy, "The Cliché in the Reading Process" in *Sub-stance* 35, no. 2 (1982): 34–45.

43. Pierre Maranda, "The Dialectic of Metaphor," in *The Reader in the Text,*

eds. Susan R. Suleiman and Inge Crosman (Princeton: Princeton University Press, 1980), 183–204.

44. Ruth Amossy, "The Cliché in the Reading Process," 36–37.

45. Ruth Amossy, Elisheva Rosen, *Les discours du cliché* (Paris: Société d'Edition d'Enseignement Supérieur, 1982), 16.

46. Eco, *Lector in fabula*, 83.

47. Alessandro Manzoni, *I Promessi Sposi* (Florence: Zanichelli, 1987), 188.

48. Alessandro Manzoni, *The Betrothed*, trans. Bruce Penman (New York: Penguin Books, 1983), 170.

49. Ruth Amossy, "Cliché in the Reading Process," 43.

50. Naomi Schor, "Fiction as Interpretation/Interpretation as Fiction" in *The Reader in the Text*, 165–82.

51. If Piovene's literary works invite a reflection on certain aspects of his life, as numerous critics suggest, one wonders to what extent Piovene's career as a literary censor during the fascist regime might have provoked his fascination with the deciphering of texts and the "correctness" of their interpretation. Cf. Gabriele Catalano's essay on "Guido Piovene" in *Letteratura italiana. I contemporanei* (Milan: Marzorati, 1963, v.II), 1429–52. Giorgio Barberi Squarotti sees in Piovene's works "un'autodifesa del proprio atteggiamento pubblico sotto il fascismo" [a self-defense against his public conduct during the fascist regime] (*La narrativa italiana del dopoguerra*, [Rocca San Casciano: Capelli, 1979], 79–84). It is puzzling, however, that none of the critics actually mentions Piovene's career as a censor; they only allude vaguely to his dubious political reputation in the fascist period. A more direct approach to that aspect of his biography can be found in Giovanni Falaschi, "Interventi redazionali negli anni trenta" in *Belfagor: Rassegna di Varia Umanità* 40 (1985): 497–528.

Chapter 5. Deconstructing the Definition of Female Letters as Sentimental, Nonliterary, and Private

1. Samuel Richardson, *Clarissa* (Boston: Houghton Mifflin Company, 1962), 477.

2. Choderlos de Laclos, *Les Liaisons dangereuses* (Paris: Editions Jean-Jaques Pauvert, 1968), L 165, 512.

3. Choderlos de Laclos, *Les Liaisons dangereuses*, trans. P. W. K. Stone (New York: Penguin Books, 1961), L 165.

4. Susanna Rowson, *Charlotte Temple* (New York, Oxford: Oxford University Press, 1986), 115.

5. Frank Black (*The Epistolary Novel in the Late Eighteenth Century*, [Eugene: University of Oregon, 1940]) cites a long list of such tales, published in the last decade of the eighteenth century, where "the descendants of Lovelace continue to stalk through the pages of fiction" (73).

6. Nicola J. Watson, *Revolution and the Form of the British Novel 1790–1825* (Oxford: Clarendon Press, 1994), 19.

7. John Gibson Lockhart in *Memoirs of Sir Walter Scott* (London: MacMillan and Co., Limited, 1900, v. 3) maintains that Scott told this story to Lady Luisa Stuart commenting on his Lives of the Novelists and "the curious question concerning change of taste" (512–13). Scott attributes that change to fashion that "is very powerful in literary composition." However, the question of decorum crops up in the *Memoirs* over and over again; for instance, in Mr. John Leycester Adolphus's letters to Richard Heber with eulogy of Scott's novels, we find the following passage which demonstrates the preoccupation with propriety of behavior: "The sins against propri-

ety in manners are as frequent and as glaring. I do not speak of the hoyden vivacity, harlot tenderness, and dancing-school affability, with which vulgar novel-writers always deck out their countesses and principessas, chevaliers and dukes, and marquises; but it would be easy to produce, from authors of a better class, abundant instances of bookish and laborious pleasantry, of pert and insipid gossip or mere slang, the wrecks perhaps of an obsolete fashionable dialect . . . incredible outrages on the common decorum of life" (493). Ros Ballaster also quotes the anectode on Behn to show why the writers of amatory fiction, Behn, Haywood and Manley, in particular, disappeared from the reading lists. (*Seductive Forms; Women's Amatory Fiction from 1684–1740* [Oxford: Clarendon Press, 1992], 205).

8. In a chapter devoted to the novels in letters after 1800 in England, France, and Italy, Godfrey Singer notes that" the graph [of epistolary novels] may be seen to enter upon a sharp and distinct decline. "If we investigate the spread of English literature from 1800 to the present day," Singer continues, "we are able to find that there exists, sporadically scattered throughout its vastness, a considerable number of novels and stories in letters" (156). Epistolary fiction, then, does not vanish completely but moves from the mainstream to the margins of the literary scene, with only "the occasional author" resorting to it "from time to time" (156). Godfrey Frank Singer, *The Epistolary Novel* (Philadelphia: University of Pennsylvania Press, 1933), 156. I refer to Singer's study because it is the only study to date that gives a chronological overview of the epistolary fiction in England, France, Italy and America from the seventeenth century until the beginning of the twentieth century.

9. Nina Baym, *Woman's Fiction* (Ithaca and London: Cornell University Press, 1978), 25.

10. Linda Huf, *A Portrait of the Artist as a Young Woman* (New York: Frederick Ungar Publishing Co., 1983), 20.

11. Fanny Fern, *Ruth Hall & Other Writings* (New Brunswick and London: Rutgers University Press, 1988), 142. All further references are given parenthetically in the text.

12. Susanna Rowson, *Charlotte Temple*, 31.

13. Susanna Rowson, *Charlotte Temple*, 32.

14. John Richetti, "Voice and Gender in Eighteenth-Century Fiction: Haywood to Burney," *Studies in the Novel* 19 (1987): 267.

15. Godfrey Singer, *The Epistolary Novel*, 86.

16. Linda Huf, *The Portrait of the Artist as a Young Woman*, 20.

17. Nina Baym, *Woman's Fiction*, 254.

18. Dacia Maraini, *La bionda, la bruna e l'asino* (Milan: Rizzoli, 1987), x.

19. Dacia Maraini, *Lettere a Marina* (Milan: Bompiani, 1981), 39.

20. Dacia Maraini, *Letters to Marina*, trans. Dick Kitto and Elspeth Spottiswood (Freedom, California: Crossing Press, 1988), 40.

21. Dacia Maraini, *La bionda, la bruna e l'asino*, xix.

22. Virginia Woolf, *A Room of One's Own* (San Diego, New York, London: A Harvest/HBJ Book, 1957), 103–4.

23. Gabriel Guilleragues, *Lettres portugaises* in *Lettres portugaises, Lettres d'une peruvienne, et autres romans d'amour par lettres*. Textes établis, présentés et annotés par Bernard Bray et Isabelle Landy-Houillon. (Paris: Garnier Flammarion, 1983), 71.

24. Apparently Bianca's fears of reception appear to be well-grounded. In his article "Dacia Maraini: From Alienation to Feminism" Augustus Palotta (*World Literature Today* 58, No. 3 [1984]: 359–63) discusses briefly the development of Maraini as a writer from her very first novel (*La vacanza*, 1962) until *Donna in guerra* (1975). While Palotta assigns a certain literary value to her earlier works (in particular *La*

vacanza and *L'età del malessere*, which he considers as belonging to the prefeminist period—he calls Maraini "a writer with a proven ability"), her later works present for him mere political manifestoes, where the social and political agenda of a militant feminist obscures her vision of "the natural complexities inherent in human relationships." Thus, if Maraini continues to "nurture the belief" that "for a woman, every literary discourse becomes immediately a social and political discourse," concludes Palotta, "we can continue to expect what is essentially a simplified, sexually stratified view of the human condition that ultimately will prove of limited value even to the selected audience it is meant to serve." Maraini's professed feminism affects Palotta's judgment and demonstrates his unwillingness to look for a writer behind a woman (361).

25. Bianca constructs a whole series of images around the name of Marina. Playing with its homophone "marina," Bianca writes: "ecco io ho l'impressione di essere scappata da te per venire da te. Da Marina alla marina con un ostile cuore marinaro e una gran voglia di non esserci" (71) [Here I am and I can't help feeling that I escaped from you only so as to come back to you. With my hostile mariner's heart I escaped from Marina to the marine-blue sea and a desperate longing to be anywhere but here, 70]. Marina, the object of her desire, becomes "la marina splendente che mi trovavo davanti nel momento giusto per fare un bagno purificatore" (33) [you were the resplendent sea in which I could bathe and be purified, 34].

26. Like Maraini, Alice Walker tries to record and preserve women's stories. She wrote *The Color Purple* as a historical novel in the epistolary form. Walker rejects the concept of history as an account of battles, wars, the births and deaths of heroes. She substitutes for it "a search for our mothers' gardens," a search for women's culture that was never allowed to cross the public boundary line. This culture needs to be rediscovered, reread and reinterpreted. In *The Color Purple,* Albert hides Nettie's letters in the trunk: "Now that I know Albert hiding Nettie's letters, I know exactly where they is. They is in his trunk. Everything that mean something to Albert go to his trunk. He keep it locked tight, but Shug can git the key" (Alice Walker, *The Color Purple* [New York: Pocket Books, 1985], 129). This metaphorical trunk contains the treasures of a female culture—both the women writers of the epistolary novels in England, and the black women writers who were never allowed a place in the literary history. These absences need to be refilled. "Because for her," says Walker, "there is not simply a new world to be gained, there is an old world that must be reclaimed. There are countless vanished and forgotten women who are nonetheless eager to speak to her . . . But she must work to find them, to free them from neglect and the oppression of silence forced upon them because they were black and they were women." (Alice Walker, *In Search of Our Mothers' Gardens* [San Diego New York London: J. B. Harcourt, 1983], 36.)

27. Oriana Fallaci, *Lettera a un bambino mai nato* (Milan: Rizzoli, 1977), 5. In 1993 Oriana Fallaci recorded the reading of her novel on four cassettes for the Publisher Rizzoli in Milan. She not only read the text herself but also selected the musical pieces.

28. Oriana Fallaci, *Letter to a Child Never Born,* trans. John Shepley (New York: Simon and Schuster, 1976), 7.

29. In fact, a number of conduct books contain the word "friend" or "counsellor" in the title. Cf. *The Young Lady's Friend,* by a lady, published in 1837 or Rev. Wise's *The Young Lady's Counsellor,* published in 1854.

30. *Herculine Barbin, Being the Recently Discovered Memoirs of a Nineteenth-Century French Hermaphrodite,* intr. Michel Foucault, trans. Richard McDougal, (New York: Pantheon Books, 1980), viii.

31. Michel Foucault, *History of Sexuality*, v. I, trans. Robert Hurley (New York: Vintage Books, Random House, 1980), 26.

32. Carol Lazzaro-Weiss, *From Margins to Mainstream. Feminism and Fictional Modes in Italian Women's Writing 1968–1990* (Philadelphia: University of Pennsylvania Press, 1993), 65.

33. Three hundred years before Fallaci, Elizabeth Joceline makes a similar comment: "who would not condemn me if I should be careless of thy body when it is within me" (Elizabeth Joceline, *Mother's Legacie to her Unborn Childe*, reprint from the edition of 1625 [Edinburgh, London: W. Black and Sons, 1852], 9).

34. The reliance on intuition as an alternative source of knowledge goes back to the Presocratics who used it to explain the process of cosmogony. I do not intend to reproduce here the whole argument of their philosophical tradition but that connection should be explored in more detail.

35. There are a number of conduct books in the form of letters. Elizabeth Joceline's *Legacie to an Unborn Childe* (1625), Jane West's *Letters to a Young Lady in which the Duties and Character of Women Are Considered Chiefly with a Reference to Prevailing Opinions* (1806), *Advice from a Lady of Quality to her Children in the Last Stage of a Lingering Illness* (1789). There were also similar collections by men; e.g., Lord Chesterfield's letters to his son. Besides collections of letters containing advice, the sections on letters in conduct books acted as conduct material. They were to serve not only as models of correspondence but also as models of comportment.

36. Dacia Maraini, *La bionda, la bruna e l'asino*, 65.

Conclusion

1. Stanislaw Baranczak, *Breathing under Water and Other East European Essays* (Cambridge, Massachussetts, and London: Harvard University Press, 1990), 48.

2. Choderlos de Laclos, *Les Liaisons dangereuses*, trans. P. W. K. Stone (New York: Penguin Books, 1961), L 18.

3. Ros Ballaster, *Seductive Forms. Women's Amatory Fiction from 1684–1740* (Oxford: Clarendon Presss, 1992), 210.

4. Melchior Wankowicz, *Ziele na kraterze* (Warszawa: Pax, 1957), 347.

Bibliography

Primary Sources

Advice to Young Ladies from 'The London Journal' of 1855 and 1862, selected by R. D. London: Methuen, 1933.

Allestree, Richard. *The Ladies Calling*. London: printed by Edward Jones for Edward Powlett, 1696.

Aston, Jane. *The Young Woman's Guide and Instructor*. Manchester, n. p., 1806.

Austen, Jane. *Love and Freindship*. New York: Frederick A. Stokes Company Publishers, 1922.

———. *Lady Susan*. London: The Athlone Press, 1984.

———. *Pride and Prejudice*. New York: Holt, Reinhart and Winston, 1961.

Behn, Aphra. *The Love—Letters Between a Nobleman and His Sister*. *The Novel in Letters: Epistolary Fiction in the Early English Novel 1678–1740*. Ed. Natasha Würzbach. Coral Gables, Florida: Univ. of Miami Press: 1969.

Burney, Fanny. *Evelina*. New York: W. W. Norton, 1965.

Castiglione, Baldassar. *The Book of the Courtier*. Trans. Charles S. Singleton. Garden City, New York: Anchor Books, Doubleday and Company, Inc., 1959.

———. *Il Cortigiano*. Milan: Rizzoli, 1973.

Chiari, Pietro. *Le memorie di Madama Tolot ovvero la giocatrice di lotto*. Rome: Edizioni Moderne Canesi, 1960.

Cochrane, James. *Woman as She Is and as She Should Be*. London: J. Cochrane and Co., 1835.

Dole, Charles. *Noble Womanhood*. Boston: L. C. Company, 1900.

Dunton, John. *The Challenge, Sent by a Young Lady to Sir Thomas & C. or The Female War*. London: Printed and Sold by E. Whitlock, 1697.

Fallaci, Oriana. *Lettera a un bambino mai nato*. Milan: Rizzoli, 1977.

———. *Letter to a Child Never Born*. Trans. John Shepley. New York: Simon and Schuster, 1976.

Fern, Fanny. *Ruth Hall and Other Writings*. New Brunswick and London: Rutgers University Press, 1988.

Gisborne, Thomas. *An Inquiry into the Duties of the Female Sex*. London: T. Caldell and W. Davies, 1797.

Gramsci, Antonio. *Lettere dal carcere*. Turin: Einaudi, 1965.

Guilleragues, Gabriel de Lavergne, sieur de. *Lettres portugaises*. *Lettres portugaises, Lettres d'une péruvienne, et autre romans d'amour par lettres*. Textes établis, présentés et annotés par Bernard Bray et Isabelle Landy-Houillon. Paris: Garnier Flammarion, 1983.

Haywood, Eliza. *Epistles for Ladies*. London: T. Gardner, 1765.

———. *Letters from a Lady of Quality to a Chevalier.* Trans. from the French. London: Printed for William Chetwood, 1721.

Hearne, Mary. *The Lovers' Week. The Novel In Letters.* Ed. Natascha Würzbach. Coral Gables, Florida: Univ. of Miami Press, 1969.

Joceline, Elizabeth. *Mother's Legacie to her Unborn Childe.* Reprint from the edition of 1625. Edinburgh, London: W. Black and Sons, 1852.

La Bruyère, Jean de. *Les Caractères ou les moeurs de ce siècle.* Paris: Garnier Frères, 1962.

Laclos, Choderlos de. *Les Liaisons dangereuses.* Paris: Editions Jean Jacques Pauvert, 1968.

———. *Les Liaisons dangereuses.* Trans. P. W. K. Stone. London: Penguin Books, 1961.

The Lady's New Year's Gift: or, Advice to a Daughter, Anonymous. London: printed for Matt Gillyflower in Westminster Hall and James Partridge at Charing Cross, 1688.

Mandeville Bernard. *The Virgin Unmask'd: or Female Dialogues Betwixt and Elderly Maiden and her niece, on Several Diverting Discourses on Love, Marriage, Memoirs and Morals, & c. of the Times.* London: Printed and sold by G. Strahan, 1724.

Manzoni, Alessandro. *The Betrothed.* Trans. Bruce Penman. New York: Penguin Books, 1972.

———. *I Promessi Sposi.* Florence: Zanichelli, 1987.

Maraini, Dacia. *Lettere a Marina.* Milan: Bompiani, 1981.

———. *Letters to Marina.* Trans. Dick Kitto and Elspeth Spottiswood. Freedom, California: Crossing Press, 1988.

Montesquieu, Charles Louis de Secondat. *Lettres persanes.* Genève: Librairies Droz, 1954.

———. *Persian Letters.* Trans. C. J. Betts. New York: Penguin Books, 1981.

More, Hannah. *Coelebs in Search of a Wife. The Works of Hannah More,* v. II. New York: Harper and brothers, 1855.

———. "On the Danger of Sentimental or Romantic Connections." *The Works of Hannah More,* v.II. New York: Harper and brothers, 1855.

———. *The Works of Hannah More.* 5 vols. New York: Harper and brothers, 1855.

A New Letter Writer for the Use of Ladies, Anonymous. Philadelphia: Porter and Coates, 1860.

Piovene, Guido. *Confessions of a Novice.* Trans. Eithne Wilkins. London: William Kimber, 1950.

———. *Lettere di una novizia.* Milan: Bompiani, 1941.

Poe, Edgar Allen. "The Purloined Letter." *The Purloined Poe: Lacan, Derrida, and Psychoanalytic Reading.* Eds. J. P. Muller and William J. Richardson. Baltimore: Johns Hopkins University Press, 1988.

Richardson, Samuel. *A Collection of the Moral and Instructive Sentiments.* Scholars Facsimiles and Reprints. New York: Delmar, 1980.

———. *Familiar Letters on Important Occasions.* London: George Routledge and Sons, Ltd., 1928.

———. *The History of Clarissa Harlowe.* 5 vols. London: Henry Sothran and Cooperation, 1883.

———. *The History of Sir Charles Grandison*. London: George Routledge and Sons, Ltd., n.d.

Rowson, Susanna. *Charlotte Temple*. New York, Oxford: Oxford University Press, 1986.

Tabucchi, Antonio. *Il gioco del rovescio*. Milan: Il Saggiatore, 1981.

Tasso, Torquato. *Discorso Della Virtù Femminile e Donnesca*. Venezia: Appresso Bernardo Giunti e Fratelli, 1582.

The Young Lady's Friend. Anonymous. Boston: American Stationers' Company, 1837.

Thornwell, Emily. *The Young Lady's Guide to Perfect Gentility in Manners, Dress, and Conversation*. New York: Derby and Jackson, 1836.

Verga, Giovanni. *Storia di una capinera*. Pordenone: Studio tesi, 1985.

Walker, Alice. *The Color Purple*. New York: Pocket Books, 1985.

Wankowicz, Melchior. *Ziele na kraterze*. Warszawa: Pax, 1957.

Weaver, Rev. George Sumner. *Hopes and Helps for the Young of Both Sexes*. New York; A. S. Barnes, 1857.

Winslow, Hubbard. *Woman as She Should Be*. Boston: T. M. Carter, 1838.

Wise, Rev. Daniel. *The Young Lady's Counsellor; or Outlines and Ilustrations of the Sphere, the Duties, and the Dangers of Young Women. . . .* New York: Carlton and Phillips, 1854.

Wooley, Hannah. *The Gentlewoman's Companion; or A Guide to the Female Sex*. London: Printed by A. Maxwell for D. Newman, 1673.

Secondary Sources

D'Alia, Fiorella. *La donna nel romanzo del settecento*. Rome: Fratelli Palombi Editori, 1990.

Altman, Janet Gurkin. *Epistolarity: Approaches to a Form*. Columbus: Ohio University Press, 1982.

Amossy, Ruth. "The Cliché in the Reading Process." *Sub-stance* 35 (1982); 34–45.

———. and Rosen, Elisheva. *Les discours du cliché*. Paris: Société d'Edition d'Enseignement Supérieur, 1982.

Armstrong, Nancy and Tennenhouse Leonard, eds. *The Ideology of Conduct*. New York and London: Methuen, 1987.

Austin, J. L. *How to Do Things with Words*. Cambridge: Harvard University Press, 1975.

Bakhtin, M. M. *The Dialogic Imagination*. Ed. Michael Holquist. Austin: University of Texas Press, 1981.

Ballaster, Ros. *Women's Amatory Fiction from 1684–1740*. Oxford: Clarendon Presss, 1992.

Baranczak, Stanislaw. *Breathing under Water and Other East European Essays*. Cambridge, Massachussetts, and London: Harvard University Press, 1990.

Baym, Nina. *Woman's Fiction*. Ithaca and London: Cornell University Press, 1978.

Benson, Thomas W. and Prosser Micheal H. eds. *Readings in Classical Rhetoric*. Davis, California: Hermagoras Press, 1988.

Black, Frank Gees. *The Epistolary Novel in the Late Eighteenth Century*. Eugene: University of Oregon Press, 1949.

Bibliography 201

Bloom, Harold ed. *Fanny Burney's Evelina*. New York, New Haven, Philadelphia: Chelsea House, 1988.

Bonatti, Maria, Ines. "L'educazione femminile nel pensiero degli Illuministi e nei romanzi di Chiari." *Annali d'Italianistica* 7 (1987): 226–41.

Carroll, John, ed. *Samuel Richardson—A Collection of Critical Essays*. New Jersey: Prentice-Hall Inc., 1969.

Cogan, Frances B. *All-American Girl. The Ideal of Real Womanhood in Mid-Nineteenth-Century America*. Athens and London: University of Georgia Press, 1989.

Curry, Jane Leftwich ed. *The Black Book of Polish Censorship*. New York: Vintage Books, 1984.

Darby, Robert. "The Censor as Literary Critic." *Westerly: A Quarterly Review*, 4 (1986): 30–40.

Darmon, Pierre. *Mythologie de la femme dans l'Ancienne France: XVIe–XVIIIe siècle*. Paris: Editions du Seuil, 1983.

Davidoff, Leonore and Hall, Catherine. *Family Fortunes: Men and Women of the English Middle Class, 1780–1850*. Chicago: University of Chicago Press, 1987.

Day, Robert Adams. "Aphra Behn and the Works of the Intellect." *Fetter'd or Free? British Women Novelists 1670–1815*. Eds. Mary Ann Schofield and Cecilia Macheski. Athens, Ohio: Ohio University Press, 1986.

———. *Told in Letters*. Ann Arbor: University of Michigan Press, 1966.

Derrida, Jacques. *The Post Card*. Trans. Alan Bass. Chicago and London: University of Chicago Press, 1987.

Dobbin, Marjorie. "The Novel, Women's Awareness and Fanny Burney." *English Language Notes* 22 (March 1985): 42–52.

Donzelot, Jacques. *The Policing of Families*. Trans. Robert Hurley. New York: Pantheon Books, 1979.

Eagleton, Terry. *The Rape of Clarissa*. Oxford: Basil Blackwell, 1982.

Eco, Umberto. *Lector in fabula*. Milan: Bompiani, 1979.

Epstein, Julia. "Evelina's Deceptions: The Letter and the Spirit." *Fanny Burney's Evelina*. Ed. Harold Bloom. New York, New Haven, Philadelphia: Chelsea House, 1988.

———. *The Iron Pen : Frances Burney and the Politics of Women's Writing*. Madison: University of Wisconsin Press, 1989.

———. "Jane Austen's Juvenilia and the Female Epistolary Tradition." *Papers on Language and Literature: A Journal for Scholars and Critics of Language and Literature* 21 (Fall 1985): 399–416.

Falaschi, Giovanni. "Interventi redazionali negli anni trenta." *Belfagor: Rassegna di Varia Umanità*, 40 (1985): 497–528.

Farell, William J. "The Style and the Action in *Clarissa*." *Samuel Richardson—A Collection of Critical Essays*. Ed. John Carroll. New Jersey: Prentice-Hall Inc., 1969.

Farrell, Michèle Longino. *Performing Motherhood; The Sévigné Correspondence*. Hanover and London: University Press of New England, 1991.

Fehn, Ann, Hoesterey, Ingeborg, and Tatar, Maria, eds. *Neverending Stories. Toward a Critical Narratology*. Princeton: Princeton University Press, 1992.

Felman, Shoshana. *The Literary Speech Act*. Trans. Catherine Porter. Ithaca: Cornell University Press, 1983.

Fetterley, Judith. *The Resistant Reader. A Feminist Approach to American Fiction.* Bloomington and London: Indiana University Press, 1978.

Flynn, Carol Houlihan. *Samuel Richardson. A Man of Letters.* Princeton: Princeton University Press, 1982.

Foucault, Michel. *Discipline and Punish: The Birth of the Prison.* Trans. Alan Sheridan. New York: Vintage Books, 1979.

———. *The History of Sexuality.* 3 vols. Trans. Robert Hurley. New York: Vintage Books, 1980.

Frabotta, Biancamaria and Maraini, Dacia, eds. *Donne in poesia. Antologia della poesia femminile dal dopoguerra a oggi.* Rome: Spavelli, 1976.

Goldsmith, Elizabeth, ed. *Writing the Female Voice.* Boston: Northeastern University Press, 1989.

Goreau, Angeline. *The Whole Duty of a Woman. Female Writers in Seventeenth Century England.* Garden City, New York: Doubleday & Company, Inc., 1985.

Graf, Arturo. *L'anglomania e l'influsso inglese in Italia.* Turin: Casa Editrice Ermanno Loescher, 1911.

Grey, David J, ed. *Jane Austen's Beginnings: The Juvenilia and Lady Susan.* London, Ann Arbor, Michigan: U. M. I. Research Press, 1989.

Halperin, John. "Unengaged Laughter: Jane Austen's Juvenilia." *Jane Austen's Beginnings: Juvenilia and Lady Susan.* Ed. David J. Grey. London, Ann Arbor: U. M. I. Research Press, 1989.

Herculine Barbin, Being the Recently Discovered Memoirs of a Nineteenth-Century French Hermaphrodite. Introd. Michel Foucault, trans. Richard McDougal. New York: Pantheon Books, 1980.

Hobby, Elaine. *Virtue of Necessity. English Women's Writing 1649–88.* London: Virago Press, 1988.

Hopkins, Annette B. "Jane Austen's *Love and Friendship*: A Study in Literary Relations." *South Atlantic Quarterly* 34 (1925): 34–39.

Horwitz, Barbara. "The Wicked Mother in Jane Austen's Work." *Jane Austen's Beginnings: Juvenilia and Lady Susan.* Ed. David J. Grey. London, Ann Arbor: U. M. I. Research Press, 1989.

Huf, Linda. *A Portrait of the Artist as a Young Woman.* New York: Frederick Ungar Publishing Co., 1983.

Hunt, Linda. "A Woman's Portion, Jane Austen and the Female Character." *Fetter'd or Free? British Women Novelists 1670–1815.* Eds. Mary Ann Schofield and Cecilia Macheski. Athens, Ohio: Ohio University Press, 1986.

Iser, Wolfgang. *The Act of Reading—A Theory of Aesthetic Response.* Baltimore: Johns Hopkins University Press, 1978.

Izubuchi, Keiko. "Subversive or Not? Anna Howe's Function in *Clarissa*." *Samuel Richardson: Passion and Prudence.* Ed. Valerie Grosvenor Myer. London: Vision Press, 1986.

Jameson, Fredric. *The Political Unconscious: Narrative as a Socially Symbolic Act.* Ithaca: Cornell University Press, 1981.

Jensen, Katharine. "Male Models of Female Epistolarity." *Writing the Female Voice.* Ed. Elizabeth Goldsmith. Boston: Northeastern University Press, 1989.

Jones, Ann Rosalind. "Nets and Bridles: Early Modern Conduct Books and Sixteenth-Century Women's Lyrics." *The Ideology of Conduct.* Eds. Nancy Armstrong and Leonard Tennehouse. New York and London: Methuen, 1987.

Jost, François. "Le roman épistolaire et la technique narrative au XVIII siècle." *Comparative Literature: Matter and Method*. Ed. O. Aldridge. Chicago: University of Illinois Presss, 1969.

Kany, Charles. *The Beginnings of Epistolary Novel in France, Italy, and Spain*. University of California Publications in Modern Philology, v. 21, no. 1. Berkeley: University of California, 1939.

Kaplan, Deborah. "Female Friendship and Epistolary Form: *Lady Susan* and the Development of Jane Austen's Fiction." *Criticism* 29 (Spring 1987): 163-78.

Kaufman, Linda S. *Discourses of Desire. Gender, Genre, and Epistolary Fiction*. Ithaca and London: Cornell University Press, 1986.

———. *Special Delivery: Epistolary Modes in Modern Fiction*. Chicago and London: University of Chicago Press, 1992.

Kelly, Joan. *Women, History, and Theory: The Essays of Joan Kelly*. Chicago: University of Chicago Press, 1984.

Koelb, Clayton, Noakes Susan, eds. *The Comparative Perspectives on Literature: Approaches to Theory and Practice*. Ithaca and London: Cornell University Press, 1988.

Lacan, Jacques. "Seminar on *Purloined Letter*". *The Purloined Poe: Lacan, Derrida, and Psychoanalytic Reading*. Eds. J. P. Muller and William J. Richardson. Baltimore: Johns Hopkins University Press, 1988.

Lazzaro-Weiss, Carol. *From Margins to Mainstream. Feminism and Fictional Modes in Italian Women's Writing, 1968-1990*. Philadelphia: University of Pennsylvania Press, 1993.

Lockhart, John Gibson. *Memoirs of the Life of Sir Walter Scott*. 5 vols. London: Macmillan and Co., 1900.

Lougee, Carolyn. *Le Paradis des Femmes: Women, Salons, and Social Stratification in Seventeenth Century France*. Princeton: Princeton University Press, 1976.

Maraini, Dacia. *La bionda, la bruna e l'asino*. Milan: Rizzoli, 1987.

Maranda, Pierre. "The Dialectic of Metaphor." *The Reader in the Text. Essays on Audience and Interpretation*. Eds. Susan R. Suleiman and Inge Crosman. Princeton: Princeton University Press, 1980.

Marks, Sylvia, Kasey. "*Clarissa* as Conduct Book." *South Atlantic Review* 51 (1986): 3-16.

Marsden, Christine. *The Paradox of Privacy—Epistolary Form in 'Clarissa'*. Gainsville: University of Florida Press, 1984.

Matteis, de Carlo. *Il romanzo italiano del novecento*. Florence: Scandicci, 1984.

McMasters, Julia. "Teaching *Love and Freindship*." *Jane Austen's Beginnings: The Juvenilia and Lady Susan*. Ed. David J. Grey. London, Ann Arbor: U. M. I. Research Press, 1989.

Meyer, Mitzi. "Hannah More's Tracts for the Times. Social Fiction and Female Ideology." *Fetter'd or Free? British Women Novelists 1670-1815*. Eds. Mary Ann Schofield and Cecilia Macheski. Athens, Ohio: Ohio University Press, 1986.

Migiel, Marylin, Schiesari, Juliana, eds. *Refiguring Woman: Perspectives on Gender and the Italian Renaissance*. Ithaca and London: Cornell University Press, 1991.

Miller, D.A. *The Novel and the Police*. Berkeley, Los Angeles, London: University of California Press, 1988.

Mossiker, Frances. *Madame de Sévigné: A Life and Letters*. New York: Columbia University Press, 1985.

Myer, Valerie Grosvenor, ed. *Samuel Richardson: Passion and Prudence.* London: Vision Press, 1986.

Newton, Judith Lowder. *Women, Power, and Subversion. Social Strategies in British Fiction, 1778–1860.* Athens: University of Georgia Press, 1981.

Nies, Fritz. "Un genre féminin?". *Revue d'histoire littéraire de la France* 78 (1978): 994–1003.

Ong, Walter. *Rhetoric, Romance, and Technology.* Ithaca: Cornell University Press, 1971.

Ovidius, Publius Naso. *Heroides and Amores.* Trans. Grant Showerman. Cambridge: Harvard University Press, 1971.

Palotta, Augustus. "Dacia Maraini: From Alienation to Feminism." *World Literature Today* 58 (1984): 359–63.

Pelous, Jean-Michel. "Une héroine romanesque entre le naturel et la rhétorique: la langage des passions dans les *Lettres portugaises.*" *Revue d'histoire littéraire de la France* 77 (1977): 554–63.

Perry, Ruth. *Women, Letter, and the Novel.* New York: AMS Press Inc., 1980.

Pope, Barbara Corrado. "Angels in the Devil's Workshop: Leisured and Charitable Women in Nineteenth-Century Englane and France." *Becoming Visible: Women in European History.* Eds. Renate Bridenthal and Claudia Koontz. Boston: Houghton Mifflin, 1977.

Powell, Chilton Latham. *English Domestic Relations 1488–1653.* New York: Columbia University Press, 1917.

Pucci, Susanne Rodin. "Letters from the Harem." *Writing the Female Voice.* Ed. Elizabeth Goldsmith. Boston: Northeastern University Press, 1989.

Richetti, John. *Popular Fiction before Richardson.* Oxford: Clarendon University Press, 1969.

———. "Voice and Gender in Eighteenth-Century Fiction: Haywood to Burney." *Studies in the Novel* 19 (1987): 263–72.

Rousset, Jean. *Forme et signification: essais sur les structures littéraires de Corneille à Claudel.* Paris: J. Corti, 1964.

Rudnik-Smalbraak, Marijke. *Samuel Richrdson: Minute Particulars within the Large Design.* Leiden: Leiden University Press, 1983.

Schofield, Mary Ann and Cecilia Macheski, eds. *Fetter'd or Free? British Women Novelists 1670–1815.* Athens, Ohio: Ohio University Press, 1986.

Schor, Naomi. "Fiction as Interpretation/Interpretation as Fiction." *The Reader in the Text. Essays on Audience and Interpretation.* Eds. Susan R. Suleiman and Inge Crosman. Princeton: Princeton University Press, 1980.

Singer, Frank. *The Epistolary Novel.* Philadelphia: University of Pennsylvania Press, 1933.

Smith-Rosenberg, Carroll. *Disorderly Conduct.* New York: A. A. Knopf, 1983.

Smith, Sidonie. *A Poetics of Women's Autobiography. Marginality and the Fictions of Self-Representation.* Bloomington and Indianapolis: Indiana University Press, 1987.

Spacks, Patricia Meyer. "Female Resources: Epistles, Plot, and Power." *Writing the Female Voice.* Ed. Elizabeth Goldsmith. Boston: Northeastern University Press, 1989.

———. "Plots and Possibilities: Jane Austen's Juvenilia." *Jane Austen's Beginnings, The Juvenilia and Lady Susan.* Ed. J. David Grey. London, Ann Arbor: U. M. I. Research Press, 1989.

Squarotti, Giorgio, Barberi. *La narrativa italiana del dopoguerra*. Rocca San Casciano: Capelli, 1979.

Staves, Susan. *Married Women's Separate Property in England, 1660–1883*. Cambridge: Harvard University Press, 1990.

Stockard, Jean and Johnson, Miriam M. *Sex Roles: Sex Inequality and Sex Role Development*. New Jersey: Prentice-Hall, Inc., 1980.

Straub, Kristina. *Divided Fictions—Fanny Burney and Feminine Strategy*. Lexington: Kentucky University Press, 1987.

Suleiman, Susan R. and Crosman, Inge, eds. *The Reader in the Text. Essays on Audience and Interpretation*. Princeton: Princeton University Press, 1980.

Todd, Janet. *The Sign of Angellica. Women, Writing and Fiction, 1660–1800*. New York: Columbia University Press, 1989.

———. *Women's Friendship in Literature*. New York: Columbia University Press, 1980.

Tompkins, Jane P. *Sensational Designs: The Cultural Work of American Fiction, 1790–1860*. New York: Oxford University Press, 1985.

Ty, Elenor. *Unsex'ed Revolutionaries: Five Women Novelists of the 1790s*. Toronto, Buffalo, London: University of Toronto Presss, 1993.

Verdier, Gabrielle. "Gender and Rhetoric in Some Seventeenth-Century Love Letters." *Esprit Createur* 23 (Summer 1983): 45–47.

Walker, Alice. *In Search of Our Mothers Gardens*. San Diego, New York, London: J. B. Harcourt, 1983.

Watson, Nicola. *Revolution and the Form of the British Novel 1790–1825*. Oxford: Clarendon Press, 1994.

Watt, Ian. *The Rise of the Novel*. London: Chatto and Windus, 1957.

Wlassics, Tibor. *Da Verga a Sanguineti, microcosmi critici*. Biblioteca Siciliana di cultura: Niccolò Giannotta Editore, 1976.

———. "Guido Piovene" in *Novecento. I contemporanei*. Milan: Marzorati, 1979.

Woolf, Virgina. *A Room of One's Own*. San Diego, New York, London: A Harvest/HBJ Book, 1957.

Index

Advice from a Lady of Quality to Her Children, 178 n. 35
Advice to Young Ladies from 'The London Journal' of 1855 and 1862, 30, 31–32
Aleramo, Sibilla, 150
Alcott, William, 184 n. 42
Allestree, Richard: *The Ladies Calling*, 18, 28, 39
Amossy, Ruth, 125, 126, 136
Armstrong, Nancy: *Desire and Domestic Fiction*, 12; on conduct books, 22
Aston, Jane: *The Young Woman's Guide and Instructor*, 37, 41, 182 n. 12
Austen, Jane, 141, 188 n. 41; *Lady Susan*, 105, 114, 116–23, 137, 140, 176, 179 n. 22; *Love and Friendship*, 105, 114–16, 122, 140; *Pride and Prejudice*, 142
Austin, J. L.: *How to Do Things with Words*, 190 n. 3

Ballaster, Ros: *Women's Amatory Fiction from 1684–1740*, 176, 189 n. 43, 195 n. 7
Baranczak, Stanislaw: *Breathing under Water*, 175
Baym, Nina: *Woman's Fiction*, 141–42, 149
Behn, Aphra, 141; *The Love Letters Between a Nobleman and His Sister*, 15, 38, 52, 61–63, 64, 69, 71, 76, 175
Benario, Herbert W., 58
The Black Book of Polish Censorship, 18
Black, Frank Gees: *The Epistolary Novel in the Late Eighteenth Century*, 103, 105–6, 192 n. 2, 193 n. 34, 194 n. 5
Bonatti, Maria Ines, 191 n. 1
Brooke, Frances, 104
Burney, Fanny: *Evelina*, 11, 12, 17, 19, 37, 105–13, 115, 122, 137, 143, 176; *Camille*, 46

Castiglione, Baldassar: *Il Cortigiano*, 23, 28, 180 n. 3,
Catalano, Gabriele, 194 n. 51
Cavendish, Margaret, 56
Chiari, Pietro: *Le memorie di Madama Tolot ovvero la giocatrice di lotto*, 56, 191 n. 1
Cochrane, James: *Woman as She Is and as She Should Be*, 29, 56
Cotin, Abbé, 14, 53, 88
Christie, Agatha, 126

D'Alia, Fiorella: *La donna nel romanzo del settecento*, 73
Darby, Robert, 179 n. 18
Darmon, Pierre: *Mythologie de la femme dans l'Ancienne France: XVIe–XVIIIe siècle*, 50
Davidoff, Leonore and Catherine Hall: *Family Fortunes. Men and Women of the English Middle Class 1780–1850*, 44–46, 180 n. 2, 185 n. 58
Day, Robert Adams: *Told in Letters*, 59, 60, 188 n. 30; on Behn, 188 n. 32;
Deledda, Grazia, 150
Dickinson, Emily, 158–59
Diderot, Denis, 126
Dobbin, Marjorie, 106, 192 n. 10
Dole, Charles: *Noble Womanhood*, 27, 28, 29, 42
Donzelot, Jacques: *The Policing of Families*, 22, 180 n. 2
Dostoyevsky, Fyodor, 192 n. 6
Dunton, John: *The Challenge, Sent by a Young Lady to Sir Thomas & Co., or the Female War*, 30, 31, 54, 55

Eagleton, Terry: *The Rape of Clarissa*, 13, 99, 189 n. 7, 189 n. 10, 191 n. 18
Eco, Umberto: *Lector in fabula*, 125, 126
Edgeworth, Maria, 141

206

Epstein, Julia, on Burney, 106, 107, 111, 112, 113; on Austen, 114–15, 123

Falaschi, Giovanni, 194 n. 51
Fallaci, Oriana: *Lettera a un bambino mai nato*, 19, 142, 161–74, 176, 180 n. 24
Farell, William J., 190 n. 11
Farrell, Michèle Longino: *Performing Motherhood*, 186 n. 6
Felman, Shoshana: *The Literary Speech Act*, 190 n. 13
Fenwick, Eliza, 141
Fern, Fanny: *Ruth Hall*, 19, 142, 143–49, 176
Flaubert, Gustave, 20
Flynn, Carol Houlihan: *Samuel Richardson: A Man of Letters*, 77, 97, 191 n. 18; on conduct books, 23;
Foscolo, Ugo, 192 n. 6
Foucault, Michel: *Discipline and Punish*, 16, 18, 19, 22, 26, 29, 102, 179 n. 19, 180 n. 2; *History of Sexuality*, 163
Franco, Veronica, 150
Fuller, Anne, 104

Gisborne, Thomas: *An Inquiry into the Duties of the Female Sex*, 15, 53, 57
Goldoni, Carlo, 191 n. 1
Goldsmith, Elizabeth, 12
Goreau, Angeline: *The Whole Duty of a Woman*, 183 n. 18
Grafigny, François, 15
Gramsci, Antonio: *Lettere dal carcere*, 18–19
Guilleragues, Gabriel de Lavergne, 88; *Lettres portugaises*, 15, 18, 58–61, 63, 69, 75–76, 126, 157, 175

Halperin, John, 114
Hays, Mary, 141
Haywood, Eliza, 52, 64; *Letters from a Lady of Quality to a Chevalier*, 15, 19, 69–74, 76
Havel, Václav, 175
Hearne, Mary: *The Lovers' Week*, 15, 38, 52, 61, 63–64, 71, 76, 175
Herculine Barbin, 162–63
Hobby, Elaine: *Virtue of Necessity. English Women's Writing 1649–88*, 183 n. 26

Hopkins, Annette B., 114
Horwitz, Barbara, 118
Huf, Linda: *A Portrait of the Artist as a Young Woman*, 143, 149
Hunt, Linda, 178 n. 13

Il Caffè, 26–27
Iser, Wolfgang: *The Act of Reading—A Theory of Aesthetic Response*, 126
Izubuchi, Keiko, 190 n. 15

Jameson, Fredric: *The Political Unconscious*, 183 n. 20
Jensen, Katharine, 187 n. 14
Joceline, Elizabeth: *Mother's Legacie to her Unborn Childe*, 173, 180 n. 24, 197 n. 33, 197 n. 35
Johnson, Reginald Brimley, 113
Jones, Ann Rosalind, 23
Jost, François, 104

Kamuf, Peggy, 59
Kany, Charles: *The Beginnings of Epistolary Novel in France, Italy, and Spain*, 60
Kaplan, Deborah, 120, 121
Kaufman, Linda S.: *Special Delivery*, 20
Kelly-Gadol, Joan: *Women, History, and Theory: The Essays of Joan Kelly*, 19, 180 n. 25

La Bruyère, Jean de: *Les Caractères*, 14, 53–56, 59, 60, 78
Lacan, Jacques, 19, 178 n. 9
Laclos, Choderlos de: *Les Liaisons dangereuses*, 16, 122, 123, 138, 139, 140, 176, 179 n. 16, 189 n. 9
Lady's New Year's Gift, The, 13
Landy-Houillon, Isabelle, 60, 188 n. 34
Lazzaro-Weiss, Carol: *From Margins to Mainstream*, 164
Lennox, Charlotte, 103
Leslie, Eliza: *Behavior Book*, 21, 22, 64–65
Lockhart, John Gibson: *Memoirs of the LIfe of Sir Walter Scott*, 194 n. 7
Lougee, Carolyn: *Le Paradis des Femmes*, 47–49, 186 n. 64
Louis XIV, 55
Luckock, James, 50–51

Mandeville, Bernard: *The Virgin Unmask'd*, 34–35, 38, 184 n. 37
Manzoni, Alessandro, 191 n. 1; *I Promessi Sposi*, 126–27
Maraini, Dacia: *Lettere a Marina*, 19, 142, 149–61, 176; *La bionda, la bruna, l'asino*, 149, 150, 174
Maranda, Pierre, 125
Marks, Sylvia Kasey, 189 n. 8
Marsden, Christina: *The Paradox of Privacy—Epistolary Form in 'Clarissa'*, 191 n. 19
Martial Law in Poland, 11
Matteis, Carlo de: *Il romanzo italiano del novecento*, 124
McMasters, Julia, 114
Meyer, Mitzi, 184 n. 39
Miller, D. A.: *The Novel and the Police*, 26, 28
Montagu, Lady Mary Wortley, 35, 37
Montesquieu, Charles Louis de Secondat: *Lettres persanes*, 12, 16, 26, 65–69, 71, 102, 177
More, Hannah, 44; on sentimental fiction, 37–41, 52; *Coelebs in Search of a Wife*, 39

New Letter Writer for the Use of Ladies, A, 17, 18
Nies, Fritz, 57
Noakes Susan, 20

Ong, Walter: *Rhetoric, Romance, and Technology*, 187 n. 12
Ovid: *Heroides*, 191 n. 19

Palotta, Augustus, 195 n. 24
Pancrazi, Pietro, 123
Pelous, Jean-Michel, 58
Perry, Ruth: *Women, Letter, and the Novel*, 184 n. 30
Petrarch, Francesco, 57–58
Pilkington, Laetitia, 191 n. 3
Piovene, Guido: *Lettere di una novizia*, 20, 105, 123–37, 176, 177
Poe, Edgar Allan: *The Purloined Letter*, 13, 123
Poovey, Mary: *The Proper Lady and the Woman Writer*, 183 n. 20
Pope, Barbara Corrado, 44, 185 n. 61
Powell, Chilton Latham: *English Domestic Relations 1488–1653*, 182 n. 3

Pucci, Susanne Rodin, 68

Reeve, Clara, 105
Richardson, Samuel, 29, 38, 103, 104, 105, 141; *Clarissa Harlowe*, 16, 17, 18, 20, 37, 38, 76–102, 103, 108, 109, 112, 113, 115, 120, 122, 138, 139, 140, 142, 148, 149, 177, 191 n. 1; *A Collection of the Moral and Instructive Sentiments*, 24–26, 37, 122; *Familiar Letters on Important Occasions*, 17, 25, 35–37, 77, 111; *Sir Charles Grandison*, 101
Richetti, John, 145, 192 n. 10
Rousseau, Jean-Jacques: *La Nouvelle Héloïse*, 14, 140
Rousset, Jean: *Forme et signification*, 104
Rowson, Susanna: *Charlotte Temple*, 38, 138–40, 144, 179 n. 16
Rudnik-Smalbraak, Marijke: *Samuel Richardson: Minute Particulars within the Large Design*, 190 n. 14

Schor, Naomi, 136
Scott, Sir Walter, 141, 194 n. 7
Scudéry, Madeleine de, 48, 49
Sévigné, Madam de, 15, 60, 186 n. 9
Sheridan, Frances, 104
Singer, Godfrey Frank: *The Epistolary Novel*, 75–76, 147, 195 n. 8
Smith-Rosenberg, Carroll: *Disorderly Conduct*, 184 n. 44
Southem, Brian, 116
Spacks, Patricia Meyer, 114, 179 n. 22
Squarotti, Giorgio Barberi: *La narrativa italiana del dopoguerra*, 194 n. 51
Staves, Susan: *Married Women's Separate Property in England, 1660–1883*, 45, 46–47
Stockard, Jean and Miriam M. Johnson: *Sex Roles: Sex Inequality and Sex Role Development*, 50, 186 n. 69
Straub, Kristina: *Divided Fictions—Fanny Burney and Feminine Strategy*, 111

Tasso, Torquato: *Discorso Della Virtù Femminile e Donnesca*, 28, 181 n. 3
Thornwell, Emily: *The Young Lady's Guide to Perfect Gentility in Manners, Dress, and Conversation*, 184 n. 34
Todd, Janet: *The Sign of Angellica*, 22, 28, 44, 45, 63, 74, 101, 103, 105, 186 n. 1, 191 n. 2

Ty, Elenor: *Unsex'ed Revolutionaries*, 191 n. 2

Verdier, Gabrielle, 59, 187 n. 19
Verga, Giovanni: *Storia di una capinera*, 126, 127–28, 192 n. 6
Walker, Alice: *The Color Purple*, 192 n. 6, 196 n. 26; *In Search of Our Mothers' Gardens*, 192 n. 26
Wankowicz, Melchior: *Ziele na kraterze*, 177
Watson, Nicola: *Revolution and the Form of the British Novel 1790–1825*, 14, 23, 140–41, 191 n. 2
Watt, Ian: *The Rise of the Novel*, 99, 189 n. 7
Weaver, Rev. George Sumner: *Hopes and Helps for the Young of Both Sexes*, 43

West, Jane, 44, 141, 197 n. 35
Williams, Helen Maria, 141
Winslow, Hubbard: *Woman as She Should Be*, 27
Wise, Rev. Daniel: *The Young Lady's Counsellor*, 28, 42, 196 n. 29
Wlassics, Tibor, 123
Wollstonecraft, Mary, 141, 185 n. 45
Wooley, Hannah: *The Gentlewoman's Companion*, 33–34, 35, 37, 38, 184 n. 28
Woolf, Virginia: *A Room of One's Own*, 64, 156

The Young Lady's Book of Classical Letters, 184 n. 34
The Young Lady's Friend, 40–42, 196 n. 29